The Easy
KETO DIET
Cookbook for Beginners

1800+ Days of Nutrient-Rich and Balanced Recipes for Fueling Your Body on a Ketogenic Diet | 30-Day Meal Keto Diet Plan

Maurice A. Keith

Table of Contents

INTRODUCTION

Embracing a Healthier Lifestyle

In a world filled with fast food, processed snacks, and convenience meals, it's easy to lose sight of what truly nourishes our bodies. But fear not, for this keto diet cookbook is here to help you rediscover the power of wholesome, nutritious eating. It's time to take control of your health, embrace a new way of life, and experience the transformative benefits of a ketogenic lifestyle.

At its core, the ketogenic diet focuses on fueling your body with the right kind of energy—healthy fats. By drastically reducing your carbohydrate intake and increasing your consumption of healthy fats, you initiate a metabolic shift that puts your body in a state of ketosis. In this state, your body becomes incredibly efficient at burning stored fat for energy, resulting in weight loss, improved mental clarity, and sustained energy levels throughout the day.

But the benefits of the ketogenic lifestyle go beyond shedding pounds and inches. By following a well-formulated ketogenic diet, you may experience improved blood sugar control, reduced inflammation, enhanced cognitive function, and even better heart health. It's a comprehensive approach to wellness that nourishes your body from within, providing you with the foundation to thrive and live your best life.

Within the pages of this cookbook, you'll find a treasure trove of mouthwatering recipes that will make your taste buds dance with joy. From vibrant and satisfying breakfast options to comforting and nourishing main dishes, each recipe has been carefully crafted to not only adhere to the principles of the ketogenic diet but also to excite your palate. We believe that healthy eating should never be boring or restrictive. That's why our collection features a wide range of flavors, textures, and ingredients to keep your meals exciting and delicious.

But this cookbook is not just about recipes. It's a comprehensive guide that empowers you to make informed choices, overcome challenges, and navigate the complexities of the ketogenic lifestyle. Discover practical tips for meal planning, learn how to stock your pantry with keto-friendly ingredients, and gain valuable insights into dining out while staying true to your goals. We're here to support you every step of the way and ensure that your journey to a healthier lifestyle is enjoyable, sustainable, and rewarding.

So, are you ready to embrace a healthier lifestyle? It's time to nourish your body with real, whole foods and experience the incredible benefits of the ketogenic diet. Let this cookbook be your trusted companion as you embark on this transformative journey. Together, we'll explore the endless possibilities of keto cuisine, unlock your culinary creativity, and inspire you to make positive changes that will last a lifetime. Get ready to savor the flavors, celebrate your health, and embrace the vibrant and fulfilling life you deserve. Let's embark on this exciting adventure together!

The Rising Popularity of Keto

In recent years, the ketogenic diet has taken the health and wellness world by storm. From celebrities and fitness gurus to everyday individuals seeking a healthier lifestyle, more and more people are embracing the power of keto. And it's no wonder why—the benefits are undeniable. As the popularity of the ketogenic diet continues to soar, this cookbook is here to guide you on your journey towards a healthier, more vibrant you.

The ketogenic diet is a low-carbohydrate, high-fat eating plan that encourages your body to enter a state of ketosis. Ketosis is a metabolic state in which your body switches from using glucose as its primary fuel source to utilizing stored fat for energy. By significantly reducing your carbohydrate intake and increasing your consumption of healthy fats, you can train your body to become a fat-burning machine.

The results of adopting a ketogenic lifestyle can be truly transformative. Many individuals experience substantial weight loss, improved mental clarity, increased energy levels, and enhanced athletic performance. Beyond the physical benefits, the ketogenic diet has also been shown to improve insulin sensitivity, reduce inflammation, and support overall metabolic health.

This cookbook is a celebration of the rising popularity of keto and the incredible impact it can have on your well-being. Within its pages, you'll discover a vast array of delicious and nutrient-dense recipes that will make your taste buds dance with delight. From flavorful breakfasts to satisfying lunches and indulgent dinners, each recipe has been carefully crafted to provide you with a delectable experience while keeping you firmly on track with your keto goals.

But this cookbook is more than just a collection of recipes. It's a comprehensive resource that will empower you to navigate the intricacies of the ketogenic diet with confidence and ease. You'll find practical tips for meal planning, guidance on how to make keto-friendly substitutions, and strategies for dining out without compromising your dietary goals. We believe that living a keto lifestyle should be enjoyable and sustainable, and this cookbook is designed to support you every step of the way.

So, whether you're a seasoned keto enthusiast or just starting to explore the possibilities, this cookbook is your companion on the journey towards optimal health and well-being. Embrace the rising popularity of keto and join the countless individuals who have already transformed their lives through this incredible way of eating. Let the recipes within these pages inspire you, nourish you, and ignite a passion for wholesome, flavorful cooking. It's time to embrace the power of keto and embark on a path to a healthier, happier you. Get ready to savor every bite, unlock your full potential, and revel in the wonders of the ketogenic lifestyle.

Chapter 1

Discovering the Keto Diet

Chapter 1
Discovering the Keto Diet

Unveiling the Principles

Welcome to the world of the ketogenic diet, a powerful and transformative approach to nutrition that has gained immense popularity in recent years. The ketogenic diet, or keto for short, is not just another fad diet. It's a lifestyle change that revolves around a unique set of principles aimed at optimizing your health, promoting weight loss, and enhancing overall well-being.

At its core, the ketogenic diet focuses on drastically reducing carbohydrate intake while increasing the consumption of healthy fats. By doing so, it triggers a metabolic state called ketosis, where your body shifts from using glucose as its primary fuel source to utilizing stored fat for energy. This shift has profound effects on your body's physiology, leading to numerous benefits.

The key principles of the keto diet can be summarized as follows:

Low Carbohydrate Intake: The cornerstone of the ketogenic diet is limiting your carbohydrate intake. By restricting carbs, you force your body to rely on fat as its primary fuel source, leading to weight loss and improved metabolic function.

Moderate Protein Intake: While protein is an essential macronutrient, consuming too much can potentially disrupt ketosis. The keto diet emphasizes moderate protein intake to prevent the conversion of excess protein into glucose, which can hinder ketone production.

High Healthy Fat Consumption: Healthy fats take center stage in the keto diet. Emphasizing foods like avocados, nuts and seeds, coconut oil, olive oil, and fatty fish ensures an ample supply of essential nutrients and helps keep you satiated.

Ketosis: The Holy Grail of the keto diet is achieving and maintaining a state of ketosis. Ketosis occurs when your body produces ketones, which are byproducts of fat metabolism. These

ketones provide a clean and efficient source of energy for your body and brain.

Nutrient-Dense Foods: While the keto diet restricts certain food groups, it promotes the consumption of nutrient-dense options. By focusing on whole, unprocessed foods, you provide your body with the essential vitamins, minerals, and antioxidants it needs to thrive.

Hydration and Electrolyte Balance: Staying adequately hydrated and maintaining electrolyte balance are crucial on the keto diet. As your body transitions into ketosis, it excretes more water and electrolytes, requiring replenishment to prevent imbalances and promote optimal function.

By understanding and applying these principles, you unlock the full potential of the ketogenic diet. It's important to note that individual needs and responses may vary, and consulting with healthcare professionals or registered dietitians is recommended to ensure the diet is tailored to your specific goals and health conditions.

As you embark on your journey into the world of keto, this cookbook will serve as your trusted guide, providing you with delicious and nutritious recipes that align with the principles of the ketogenic diet. Each recipe is carefully crafted to help you maintain ketosis, enjoy flavorful meals, and achieve your health and weight loss goals.

Get ready to delve into a culinary adventure that will not only tantalize your taste buds but also transform your relationship with food. Together, we will explore the incredible flavors, textures, and possibilities that the keto diet has to offer. So, let's embark on this exciting journey and discover a world of delicious keto-friendly dishes that will nourish your body and delight your senses.

A Paradigm Shift in Nutrition

In a world inundated with dietary trends and conflicting information, it's time to introduce a paradigm shift in nutrition. The ketogenic lifestyle is making waves as a groundbreaking approach that challenges conventional beliefs about dieting and healthy eating. This is not just another fleeting trend but a scientifically-backed method that has the potential to revolutionize the way we view nutrition and well-being.

The ketogenic diet, or keto for short, flips the script on traditional nutritional wisdom by shifting our primary energy source from carbohydrates to fats. By drastically reducing carbohydrate intake and increasing healthy fat consumption, we initiate a metabolic state known as ketosis. In this state, our bodies become efficient fat-burning machines, deriving energy from stored fat rather than relying on constant glucose consumption.

What makes the ketogenic lifestyle so appealing is its transformative effects on our health, well-being, and body composition. Weight loss is just the tip of the iceberg. When we enter ketosis, our bodies experience a cascade of benefits that go far beyond shedding pounds. Increased energy levels, enhanced mental clarity, stabilized blood sugar levels, improved cardiovascular health, and reduced inflammation are just some of the incredible advantages that come with adopting the ketogenic lifestyle.

At the core of the ketogenic diet lies a profound understanding of the intricate relationship between macronutrients and our bodies' metabolic processes. By fueling ourselves with healthy fats, we tap into a clean and efficient source of energy that supports optimal physical and cognitive function. The emphasis on nutrient-dense foods ensures we provide our bodies with the essential vitamins, minerals, and antioxidants needed for overall well-being.

In this cookbook, we invite you to embark on a journey that transcends traditional notions of dieting and restrictive eating. Here, you'll find a treasure trove of mouthwatering recipes carefully curated to align with the principles of the ketogenic lifestyle. From breakfast delights to satisfying main courses and indulgent desserts, each recipe is thoughtfully designed to bring you joy, nourishment, and flavor without compromising your keto goals.

As the author of this cookbook, I am not only passionate about the ketogenic lifestyle but also dedicated to sharing my knowledge and experiences with you. I have spent years researching, experimenting, and perfecting recipes to help you navigate the world of keto with confidence and pleasure. Rest assured, each recipe has been meticulously crafted and tested to ensure it meets the highest standards of taste, nutrition, and ease of preparation.

Join me on this journey of discovery, where we break free from outdated dietary dogmas and embrace the ketogenic lifestyle. Together, we will unravel the immense potential of this transformative approach to nutrition. Get ready to embark on a path of delicious, satisfying meals that will nourish your body, ignite your taste buds, and unlock the boundless benefits of the ketogenic lifestyle.

Are you ready to make a paradigm shift in your nutrition and embrace the power of the ketogenic lifestyle? Let this cookbook be your guide as we embark on a transformative journey that will redefine the way you eat, feel, and thrive. Say goodbye to conventional diets and welcome a new era of vibrant health, vitality, and culinary delight. The ketogenic lifestyle awaits, and it's time for you to take the plunge.

Nourishing Your Body with Keto

Emphasizing Whole Foods

When it comes to the ketogenic diet, the old saying holds true: you are what you eat. A key aspect of this transformative lifestyle is the emphasis on whole, nutrient-rich foods that not only support ketosis but also nourish your body from within. By prioritizing whole foods, you not only optimize your health but also expand your culinary horizons and create a vibrant, flavorful keto journey.

In a world saturated with processed and convenience foods, the ketogenic lifestyle encourages a return to the basics. Whole foods are the building blocks of a healthy and sustainable approach to nutrition. Filling your plate with a colorful array of vegetables, quality proteins, healthy fats, and a moderate amount of low-carb fruits provides your body with the essential nutrients it craves.

Vegetables take center stage in the ketogenic diet, offering a wide range of flavors, textures, and nutrients to fuel your body. Leafy greens, cruciferous vegetables, colorful bell peppers, and zucchini are just a few examples of the versatile options available to you. Packed with vitamins, minerals, and fiber, these veggies not only support ketosis but also promote optimal digestion and overall well-being.

Quality proteins play a crucial role in the ketogenic lifestyle, providing the necessary building blocks for muscle repair, hormone production, and immune function. Opt for pasture-raised meats, wild-caught fish, free-range poultry, and organic eggs to ensure you're getting the highest quality proteins without unwanted additives or hormones. Remember, the focus is on nutrient density and quality rather than quantity.

Healthy fats take center stage in the ketogenic diet, serving as your primary source of energy. Avocados, olive oil, coconut oil, nuts, and seeds are rich in heart-healthy fats that nourish your body and keep you satiated. These fats not only provide essential fatty acids but also aid in the absorption of fat-soluble vitamins, promote brain health, and support hormone balance.

While the ketogenic diet promotes whole foods, it's important to strike a balance. Avoiding processed foods, refined sugars, and artificial additives is essential to maintain the integrity of your keto journey. By eliminating these inflammatory and nutrient-poor choices, you create space for nutrient-dense whole foods to take center stage, offering a plethora of health benefits.

In this cookbook, you'll find a variety of recipes that celebrate the beauty and flavors of whole foods. From vibrant salads to hearty soups, from succulent meat dishes to satisfying vegetarian options, each recipe is carefully crafted to showcase the natural goodness of whole foods while keeping you firmly on track with your keto goals.

Embracing whole foods is not just a dietary choice; it's a commitment to your well-being. By nourishing your body with nutrient-dense ingredients, you provide the foundation for long-term health, vitality, and sustainable weight management. Get ready to savor the flavors of whole foods and embark on a keto journey that will transform the way you eat, feel, and live. Let the power of whole foods guide you to a healthier, more vibrant version of yourself.

The Power of Healthy Fats

In a world where fat has long been demonized, it's time to rewrite the narrative and embrace the power of healthy fats. The ketogenic diet breaks free from the conventional wisdom that fat is the enemy and instead celebrates the essential role that fats play in our overall health and well-being. By shifting our focus from low-fat to healthy-fat sources, we unlock a wealth of benefits that propel us forward on our keto journey.

Healthy fats are the cornerstone of the ketogenic diet, serving as the primary source of energy when carbohydrates are limited. They provide a concentrated source of calories, making us feel satiated and satisfied. But beyond their role as a fuel source, healthy fats play a critical role in supporting various bodily functions.

One of the key advantages of healthy fats is their impact on weight management. Contrary to popular belief, consuming healthy fats does not automatically lead to weight gain. In fact, incorporating healthy fats into your diet can promote weight loss and better body composition. Fats help regulate appetite, keeping you full for longer and reducing cravings. They also support fat-burning processes by encouraging your body to utilize stored fat for energy.

Healthy fats are not only beneficial for weight management but also crucial for overall health. They serve as building blocks for cell membranes, ensuring proper cell function and communication. They play a vital role in hormone production, including the synthesis of important hormones such as testosterone, estrogen, and cortisol. Additionally, fats are essential for the absorption of fat-soluble vitamins like vitamins A, D, E, and K, which are crucial for various bodily processes.

By prioritizing healthy fats, you nourish your brain and support cognitive function. The brain is composed primarily of fat, and consuming healthy fats provides the necessary building blocks for optimal brain health. Healthy fats, such as omega-3 fatty acids found in fatty fish and flaxseeds, have been linked to improved memory, focus, and mood.

In this cookbook, we celebrate the power of healthy fats by incorporating a diverse array of fat-rich ingredients into our recipes. Avocados, coconut oil, olive oil, nuts, and seeds are just a few examples of the nutrient-dense fats you'll encounter. Each recipe is thoughtfully crafted to not only provide delicious flavors but also harness the benefits of healthy fats to support your keto journey.

As you embark on this culinary adventure, remember that not all fats are created equal. While healthy fats offer numerous benefits, it's important to choose wisely. Opt for natural, unprocessed sources of fats and avoid trans fats and highly processed vegetable oils, which can contribute to inflammation and other health issues.

Join us as we celebrate the power of healthy fats and unlock their transformative potential on your keto journey. Together, let's dispel the myths surrounding fats and embrace the truth that they are an essential and invaluable part of a nourishing and vibrant lifestyle. Get ready to savor the flavors, nourish your body, and embrace the power of healthy fats as you embark on a keto journey like no other.

Chapter 2

Understanding Ketosis

Chapter 2
Understanding Ketosis

Unlocking the Metabolic State

Embark on a journey that will revolutionize the way you think about nutrition and transform your body from the inside out. Welcome to the world of ketosis, a metabolic state where your body becomes a fat-burning machine, unlocking a multitude of benefits that go far beyond weight loss.

Ketosis is a natural metabolic state that occurs when your body shifts its primary fuel source from carbohydrates to fats. By significantly reducing your carbohydrate intake and increasing your consumption of healthy fats, you prompt your body to enter a state of ketosis. In this state, your liver produces ketones from fat, which become the main source of energy for your body and brain.

The power of ketosis lies in its ability to tap into your body's stored fat reserves, allowing you to burn fat efficiently and effectively. As your body becomes fat-adapted, you may experience increased energy levels, improved mental clarity, and enhanced physical performance. Ketosis has also been shown to stabilize blood sugar levels, reduce inflammation, and support cardiovascular health.

To unlock the metabolic state of ketosis, it's important to follow a well-formulated ketogenic diet. This involves consuming a high amount of healthy fats, a moderate amount of protein, and restricting your carbohydrate intake to a minimal level. By carefully selecting your food choices and paying attention to your macronutrient ratios, you can optimize your body's ability to enter and sustain ketosis.

In this cookbook, we provide you with a wealth of delicious and nutritious recipes that will help you on your journey to unlocking the metabolic state. From savory breakfast options to satisfying main courses and mouthwatering desserts, each recipe has been carefully crafted to support ketosis while tantalizing your taste buds.

It's important to note that the transition into ketosis may come with some initial challenges as your body adjusts to this new way of fueling itself. You may experience temporary symptoms such as fatigue, brain fog, and cravings. However, with time and proper guidance, these symptoms will subside, and you will reap the rewards of a well-adapted ketogenic lifestyle.

By embracing the metabolic state of ketosis, you open the door to a world of improved health, increased vitality, and lasting well-being. This cookbook is your guide to unlocking the metabolic state and embracing the transformative power of ketosis. Join us on this extraordinary journey, as we discover the delicious flavors, abundant energy, and remarkable benefits that await you in the realm of ketosis. Get ready to ignite your body's fat-burning potential and unlock the metabolic state for a lifetime of optimal health and wellness.

The Science Behind Ketosis

At the heart of the ketogenic diet lies a fascinating scientific process called ketosis. Understanding the science behind ketosis is key to harnessing the full potential of the ketogenic diet and experiencing its numerous health benefits.

Ketosis is a natural metabolic state that occurs when your body shifts from relying on carbohydrates as its primary source of energy to utilizing fat instead. When you restrict your carbohydrate intake and consume moderate amounts of protein, your body begins to break down stored fat into molecules called ketones. These ketones are then used by your cells as an alternative fuel source.

The transition into ketosis is a remarkable feat of biochemistry. By limiting carbohydrates, you reduce the availability of glucose, which is the preferred energy source for many cells in your body. As a result, your liver starts producing ketones from fatty acids derived from stored fat. These ketones are able to cross the blood-brain barrier and provide fuel to your brain, which typically relies heavily on glucose.

One of the key advantages of ketosis is its ability to promote fat burning. In a state of ketosis, your body becomes highly efficient at burning fat for energy. This is particularly beneficial for individuals looking to lose weight or improve their body composition. By tapping into your fat stores, you can achieve sustainable and healthy weight loss while preserving muscle mass.

But the benefits of ketosis extend far beyond weight management. Many individuals report increased energy levels, improved mental clarity, and enhanced focus while in ketosis. This may be due to the fact that ketones provide a more stable and consistent energy source for the brain, as opposed to the fluctuations in energy levels that can occur with glucose metabolism.

Moreover, ketosis has been shown to have therapeutic effects on various health conditions. Research suggests that a ketogenic diet may help manage epilepsy, reduce inflammation, improve insulin sensitivity, and even support certain neurological disorders. The anti-inflammatory properties of ketosis have also been linked to potential benefits for cardiovascular health.

To achieve and maintain ketosis, it's important to follow a well-formulated ketogenic diet. This involves consuming a high amount of healthy fats, moderate protein, and minimal carbohydrates. By carefully selecting your food choices and monitoring your macronutrient ratios, you can keep your body in a state of ketosis and reap the rewards of this metabolic shift.

In this cookbook, we guide you through the science behind ketosis and provide you with a diverse array of delicious recipes that support this metabolic state. From nutrient-rich salads to flavorful main courses and decadent desserts, our recipes are designed to keep you on track with your ketogenic goals while satisfying your taste buds.

Join us on a journey into the scientific wonders of ketosis. Explore the power of this metabolic state, unlock the secrets of fat burning, and experience the profound benefits it can bring to your health and well-being. Get ready to delve into a world where biology meets nutrition, and where you can harness the extraordinary potential of ketosis to transform your body and optimize your vitality.

30 Days Keto Diet Meal Plan

DAYS	BREAKFAST	LUNCH	DINNER	SNACK/DESSERT
1	Sausage, Egg, and Cheese Breakfast Bake 14	Herby Chicken Meatballs 30	Mediterranean Beef Steaks 40	Herbed Zucchini Slices 59
2	Mocha Pre-Workout Smoothie 14	Osso Buco with Gremolata 40	Chicken and Bacon Rolls 26	Candied Georgia Pecans 59
3	Everything Bagels 15	Spicy Chicken with Bacon and Peppers 25	Kung Pao Pork 43	Ketone Gummies 58
4	Egg Tofu Scramble with Kale & Mushrooms 17	Mediterranean Filling Stuffed Portobello Mushrooms 76	Chicken Rollatini with Ricotta, Prosciutto, and Spinach 25	Roasted Spiced Nut Mix 58
5	Mini Spinach Quiche 15	Spanish Chicken 26	Pecan-Crusted Salmon 52	Oregano Sausage Balls 60
6	Sausage and Cauliflower Breakfast Casserole 17	Mascarpone Tilapia with Nutmeg 50	Loaded Cauliflower Steak 71	Bacon-Wrapped Jalapeños 60
7	BLT Breakfast Wrap 14	Eggplant and Zucchini Bites 72	Pork Rind Salmon Cakes 53	Bacon-Studded Pimento Cheese 58
8	Egg Ham Muffins 17	Shrimp Bake 47	Baked Zucchini 71	Queso Dip 62
9	Smoked Ham and Egg Muffins 14	Pesto Vegetable Skewers 71	Sushi Shrimp Rolls 47	Broccoli Cheese Dip 57
10	Quickly Blue Cheese Omelet 16	Coconut Cream Mackerel 47	Cauliflower Tikka Masala 70	Baked Crab Dip 62
11	Bacon Spaghetti Squash Fritters 15	Souvlaki Spiced Salmon Bowls 54	Cajun Cod Fillet 55	Grandma's Meringues 62
12	Something Different Breakfast Sammy 16	Grandma Bev's Ahi Poke 53	Herbed Ricotta–Stuffed Mushrooms 72	Parmesan Artichoke 60
13	Kale and Egg Bake 16	Prosciutto-Wrapped Haddock 54	Shrimp Stuffed Zucchini 48	Cubed Tofu Fries
14	Kielbasa and Roquefort Waffles 15	Bacon-Wrapped Scallops 48	Almond-Cauliflower Gnocchi 72	Baked Brie with Pecans 68
15	Keto Chai 17	Cod Cakes 47	Crunchy Fish Sticks 54	Caponata Dip 64
16	Eggs Benedict on Grilled Portobello Mushroom Caps 16	Steak and Egg Bibimbap 44	Cheesy Cauliflower Pizza Crust 70	Cocoa Custard 79

DAYS	BREAKFAST	LUNCH	DINNER	SNACK/DESSERT
17	Nutty "Oatmeal" 23	Cheese Stuffed Peppers 71	Chicken Fried Steak with Cream Gravy 39	Mixed Berry Cobbler 83
18	Keto Breakfast Pudding 20	Pancetta Sausage with Kale 39	Parmesan Artichokes 71	Peanut Butter Mousse 81
19	Tahini Banana Detox Smoothie 19	Greek Vegetable Briam 75	Low-Carb Chili 37	Pumpkin Walnut Cheesecake 85
20	Classic Coffee Cake 19	Rib Eye with Chimichurri Sauce 37	Broccoli-Cheese Fritters 74	Fluffy Coconut Mousse 82
21	Inside-Out Breakfast Burrito 18	Chili Lime Turkey Burgers 26	Green Vegetable Stir-Fry with Tofu 73	Blackberry Crisp 83
22	Not Your Average Boiled Eggs 18	Vegetable Vodka Sauce Bake 73	Lemon Thyme Roasted Chicken 28	Coffee Ice Pops 86
23	Spinach Omelet 18	Turkey Fajitas 26	Greek Vegetable Briam 75	Easy Truffles 79
24	Cross-Country Scrambler 18	Broccoli with Garlic Sauce 74	Indoor BBQ Chicken 28	Snickerdoodle Cream Cheesecake 79
25	Breakfast Almond Muffins 22	Paprika Chicken 30	Eggplant Parmesan 75	Traditional Cheesecake 81
26	Bell Peppers Stuffed with Eggs 22	Sausage and Pork Meatballs 36	Cauliflower Steak with Gremolata 76	Cinnamon Toast Crunch Nuts 81
27	Cheese Egg Muffins 22	Garlic White Zucchini Rolls 74	Baked Crustless Pizza 36	Lemonade Fat Bomb 80
28	Chorizo and Mozzarella Omelet 22	Fajita Meatball Lettuce Wraps 44	Pesto Spinach Flatbread 75	Cinnamon Roll Cheesecake 82
29	Matcha Chia N'Oatmeal 23	Italian Baked Egg and Veggies 77	Savory Sausage Cobbler 43	Chocolate Chip Brownies 85
30	Olivia's Cream Cheese Pancakes 21	Beef and Egg Rice Bowls 43	Cauliflower Rice-Stuffed Peppers 77	Strawberry Shake 83

Chapter 3

Breakfasts

Chapter 3 Breakfasts

Sausage, Egg, and Cheese Breakfast Bake

Prep time: 15 minutes | Cook time: 35 minutes | Serves 6

- 1 tablespoon unsalted butter
- ⅓ cup chopped yellow onions
- 1 pound bulk breakfast sausage
- 8 large eggs
- ⅓ cup heavy whipping cream
- 1 clove garlic, pressed
- 1 teaspoon salt
- ½ teaspoon ground black pepper
- 1 cup shredded cheddar cheese

1. Preheat the oven to 350°F. Lightly coat an 8-inch deep-dish pie dish or baking dish with coconut oil or nonstick cooking spray. 2. Heat the butter in a large skillet over medium heat. Add the onions and sauté until soft, 3 to 4 minutes. 3. Add the sausage and cook until evenly browned, 4 to 5 minutes. Drain and set aside. 4. In a large bowl, whisk the eggs, cream, garlic, salt, and pepper. 5. Spread the sausage evenly on the bottom of the prepared dish and top with the cheese. Pour the egg mixture over the cheese. 6. Bake for 35 minutes, until the eggs are set and the top is lightly golden brown. 7. Allow to cool for 3 to 5 minutes before serving. Leftovers can be covered and stored in the refrigerator for up to 4 days.

Per Serving:

calories: 394 | fat: 33g | protein: 22g | carbs: 3g | net carbs: 3g | fiber: 0g

Mocha Pre-Workout Smoothie

Prep time: 5 minutes | Cook time: 0 minutes | Serves 2

- 1 cup full-fat coconut milk
- 1 cup almond milk
- 2 scoops (25–28 grams) chocolate protein powder (use something with no or very few carbs—I use Primal Fuel)
- ½ banana
- ½ cup brewed espresso
- 1 tablespoon cocoa powder
- 4 ice cubes

1. Blend the smoothie. Put the coconut milk, almond milk, protein powder, banana, espresso, cocoa powder, and ice in a blender and blend until smooth and creamy. 2. Serve. Pour into two tall glasses and serve.

Per Serving:

calories: 372 | fat: 27g | protein: 26g | carbs: 14g | net carbs: 9g | fiber: 5g

BLT Breakfast Wrap

Prep time: 5 minutes | Cook time: 10 minutes | Serves 4

- 8 ounces (227 g) reduced-sodium bacon
- 8 tablespoons mayonnaise
- 8 large romaine lettuce leaves
- 4 Roma tomatoes, sliced
- Salt and freshly ground black pepper, to taste

1. Arrange the bacon in a single layer in the air fryer basket. (It's OK if the bacon sits a bit on the sides.) Set the air fryer to 350°F (177°C) and air fry for 10 minutes. Check for crispiness and air fry for 2 to 3 minutes longer if needed. Cook in batches, if necessary, and drain the grease in between batches. 2. Spread 1 tablespoon of mayonnaise on each of the lettuce leaves and top with the tomatoes and cooked bacon. Season to taste with salt and freshly ground black pepper. Roll the lettuce leaves as you would a burrito, securing with a toothpick if desired.

Per Serving:

calories: 343 | fat: 32g | protein: 10g | carbs: 5g | net carbs: 4g | fiber: 1g

Smoked Ham and Egg Muffins

Prep time: 5 minutes | Cook time: 25 minutes | Serves 9

- 2 cups chopped smoked ham
- ⅓ cup grated Parmesan cheese
- ¼ cup almond flour
- 9 eggs
- ⅓ cup mayonnaise, sugar-free
- ¼ teaspoon garlic powder
- ¼ cup chopped onion
- Sea salt to taste

1. Preheat your oven to 370°F. 2. Lightly grease nine muffin pans with cooking spray and set aside. Place the onion, ham, garlic powder, and salt, in a food processor, and pulse until ground. Stir in the mayonnaise, almond flour, and Parmesan cheese. Press this mixture into the muffin cups. 3. Make sure it goes all the way up the muffin sides so that there will be room for the egg. Bake for 5 minutes. Crack an egg into each muffin cup. Return to the oven and bake for 20 more minutes or until the tops are firm to the touch and eggs are cooked. Leave to cool slightly before serving.

Per Serving:

calories: 165 | fat: 11g | protein: 14g | carbs: 2g | net carbs: 1g | fiber: 1g

Kielbasa and Roquefort Waffles

Prep time: 10 minutes | Cook time: 10 minutes | Serves 2

◀ 2 tablespoons butter, melted
◀ Salt and black pepper, to taste
◀ ½ teaspoon parsley flakes
◀ ½ teaspoon chili pepper flakes
◀ 4 eggs
◀ ½ cup Roquefort cheese, crumbled
◀ 4 slices kielbasa, chopped
◀ 2 tablespoons fresh chives, chopped

1. In a mixing bowl, combine all ingredients except fresh chives. Preheat waffle iron and spray with a cooking spray. Pour in the batter and close the lid. 2. Cook for 5 minutes or until golden-brown, do the same with the rest of the batter. Decorate with fresh chives and serve while warm.

Per Serving:

calories: 655 | fat: 57g | protein: 28g | carbs: 4g | net carbs: 4g | fiber: 0g

Everything Bagels

Prep time: 15 minutes | Cook time: 14 minutes | Makes 6 bagels

◀ 1¾ cups shredded Mozzarella cheese or goat cheese Mozzarella
◀ 2 tablespoons unsalted butter or coconut oil
◀ 1 large egg, beaten
◀ 1 tablespoon apple cider
vinegar
◀ 1 cup blanched almond flour
◀ 1 tablespoon baking powder
◀ ⅛ teaspoon fine sea salt
◀ 1½ teaspoons everything bagel seasoning

1. Make the dough: Put the Mozzarella and butter in a large microwave-safe bowl and microwave for 1 to 2 minutes, until the cheese is entirely melted. Stir well. Add the egg and vinegar. Using a hand mixer on medium, combine well. Add the almond flour, baking powder, and salt and, using the mixer, combine well. 2. Lay a piece of parchment paper on the countertop and place the dough on it. Knead it for about 3 minutes. The dough should be a little sticky but pliable. (If the dough is too sticky, chill it in the refrigerator for an hour or overnight.) 3. Preheat the air fryer to 350ºF (177ºC). Spray a baking sheet or pie pan that will fit into your air fryer with avocado oil. 4. Divide the dough into 6 equal portions. Roll 1 portion into a log that is 6 inches long and about ½ inch thick. Form the log into a circle and seal the edges together, making a bagel shape. Repeat with the remaining portions of dough, making 6 bagels. 5. Place the bagels on the greased baking sheet. Spray the bagels with avocado oil and top with everything bagel seasoning, pressing the seasoning into the dough with your hands. 6. Place the bagels in the air fryer and bake for 14 minutes, or until cooked through and golden brown, flipping after 6 minutes. 7. Remove the bagels from the air fryer and allow them to cool slightly before slicing them in half and serving. Store leftovers in an airtight container in the fridge for up to 4 days or in the freezer for up to a month.

Per Serving:

calories: 290 | fat: 25g | protein: 13g | carbs: 7g | net carbs: 4g | fiber: 3g

Mini Spinach Quiche

Prep time: 5 minutes | Cook time: 15 minutes | Serves 1

◀ 2 eggs
◀ 1 tablespoon heavy cream
◀ 1 tablespoon diced green pepper
◀ 1 tablespoon diced red onion
◀ ¼ cup chopped fresh spinach
◀ ½ teaspoon salt
◀ ¼ teaspoon pepper
◀ 1 cup water

1. In medium bowl whisk together all ingredients except water. Pour into 4-inch ramekin. Generally, if the ramekin is oven-safe, it is also safe to use in pressure cooking. 2. Pour water into Instant Pot. Place steam rack into pot. Carefully place ramekin onto steam rack. Click lid closed. Press the Manual button and set time for 15 minutes. When timer beeps, quick-release the pressure. Serve warm.

Per Serving:

calories: 201 | fat: 14g | protein: 13g | carbs: 3g | net carbs: 2g | fiber: 1g

Bacon Spaghetti Squash Fritters

Prep time: 20 minutes | Cook time: 15 minutes | Serves 4

◀ ½ cooked spaghetti squash
◀ 2 tablespoons cream cheese
◀ ½ cup shredded whole-milk Mozzarella cheese
◀ 1 egg
◀ ½ teaspoon salt
◀ ¼ teaspoon pepper
◀ 1 stalk green onion, sliced
◀ 4 slices cooked bacon, crumbled
◀ 2 tablespoons coconut oil

1. Remove seeds from cooked squash and use fork to scrape strands out of shell. Place strands into cheesecloth or kitchen towel and squeeze to remove as much excess moisture as possible. 2. Place cream cheese and Mozzarella in small bowl and microwave for 45 seconds to melt together. Mix with spoon and place in large bowl. Add all ingredients except coconut oil to bowl. Mixture will be wet like batter. 3. Press the Sauté button and then press the Adjust button to set heat to Less. Add coconut oil to Instant Pot. When fully preheated, add 2 to 3 tablespoons of batter to pot to make a fritter. Let fry until firm and completely cooked through.

Per Serving:

calories: 202 | fat: 16g | protein: 9g | carbs: 2g | net carbs: 1g | fiber: 1g

Kale and Egg Bake

Prep time: 10 minutes | Cook time: 10 minutes | Serves 2

◄ ½ cup chopped kale
◄ 3 eggs, beaten
◄ 1 tablespoon organic almond milk
◄ 1 teaspoon coconut oil,
◄ melted
◄ ¼ teaspoon ground black pepper
◄ 1 cup water, for cooking

1. In the mixing bowl, mix up chopped kale, eggs, almond milk, and ground black pepper. 2. Grease the ramekins with coconut oil. 3. Pour the kale-egg mixture in the ramekins and flatten it with the help of the spatula, if needed. 4. Pour water and insert the trivet in the instant pot. 5. Put the ramekins with egg mixture on the trivet and close the lid. 6. Cook the breakfast on Manual mode (High Pressure) for 10 minutes. Make a quick pressure release.

Per Serving:

calories: 126 | fat: 9g | protein: 9g | carbs: 3g | net carbs: 3g | fiber: 0g

Eggs Benedict on Grilled Portobello Mushroom Caps

Prep time: 5 minutes | Cook time: 10 to 15 minutes | Serves 1

◄ 2 portobello mushroom caps
◄ 1 tablespoon avocado oil
◄ 2 large spinach leaves
◄ 2 slices bacon
◄ 2 eggs
◄ 1 egg yolk
◄ ¼ teaspoon freshly squeezed lemon juice
◄ 1½ tablespoons olive oil
◄ Pinch salt
◄ 1 teaspoon paprika
◄ Chopped fresh parsley, for serving
◄ Sugar-free hot sauce, for serving (optional)

1. Preheat the oven to broil or to 400°F (205°C), or heat a grill. 2. Take a damp paper towel and wipe off the mushroom caps, removing any stem. Rub them all over with the avocado oil, place on a baking sheet, and broil or roast in the oven for 10 minutes, flipping them halfway through. Alternatively, you can grill the mushroom caps for about 5 minutes on each side. 3. In a skillet while the mushrooms are baking, fry the bacon (which doesn't need any added fat) to your desired doneness. Remove from skillet and set aside. 4. Remove the mushrooms from the oven or grill, transfer to a plate, and place the spinach leaves and bacon on top. 5. To poach the eggs, fill a saucepan with water and bring to a boil, then lower the heat to a simmer. 6. Crack the eggs into a small bowl and carefully pour them into the simmering water. Turn off the heat, cover the pan, and let the eggs cook for about 5 minutes. 7. Carefully remove the eggs from the pan with a slotted spoon, straining over the pan, and place on top of the crispy bacon, spinach, and mushroom caps. 8. In a blender, combine the egg yolk, lemon juice, olive oil, and salt. Turn on the blender to

its lowest setting and let the mixture whip together. 9. When the hollandaise sauce looks creamy, turn off the blender and pour the sauce over your mushrooms topped with spinach, bacon, and eggs. 10. Sprinkle with the paprika, chopped parsley, and a dash or two of hot sauce, if desired.

Per Serving:

calories: 841 | fat: 76g | protein: 32g | carbs: 14g | net carbs: 9g | fiber: 5g

Quickly Blue Cheese Omelet

Prep time: 10 minutes | Cook time: 10 minutes | Serves 2

◄ 4 eggs
◄ Salt, to taste
◄ 1 tablespoon sesame oil
◄ ½ cup blue cheese, crumbled
◄ 1 tomato, thinly sliced

1. In a mixing bowl, beat the eggs and season with salt. 2. Set a sauté pan over medium heat and warm the oil. Add in the eggs and cook as you swirl the eggs around the pan using a spatula. Cook eggs until partially set. Top with cheese; fold the omelet in half to enclose filling. Decorate with tomato and serve while warm.

Per Serving:

calories: 321 | fat: 26g | protein: 16g | carbs: 4g | net carbs: 4g | fiber: 1g

Something Different Breakfast Sammy

Prep time: 5 minutes | Cook time: 10 minutes | Serves 1

◄ 1 medium Hass avocado, peeled and pitted (about 4 ounces/110 g of flesh)
◄ 1 lettuce leaf, torn in half
◄ 1 tablespoon mayonnaise
◄ 2 strips bacon (about 2 ounces/55 g), cooked until crispy
◄ 1 red onion ring
◄ 1 tomato slice
◄ Pinch of finely ground sea salt
◄ Pinch of ground black pepper
◄ Pinch of sesame seeds or poppy seeds (optional)

1. Cook the bacon in a medium-sized frying pan over medium heat until crispy, about 10 minutes. 2. Place the avocado halves cut side up on a plate. 3. Lay the lettuce pieces on top of one of the avocado halves, then slather the mayonnaise on the lettuce. Top the lettuce with the bacon, onion, and tomato, then sprinkle with the salt and pepper. 4. Cover the stack with the other avocado half and sprinkle with the seeds, if using. Enjoy immediately!

Per Serving:

calories: 545 | fat: 43g | protein: 19g | carbs: 20g | net carbs: 11g | fiber: 9g

Sausage and Cauliflower Breakfast Casserole

Prep time: 5 minutes | Cook time: 10 minutes | Serves 6

- ◄ 1 cup water
- ◄ ½ head cauliflower, chopped into bite-sized pieces
- ◄ 4 slices bacon
- ◄ 1 pound (454 g) breakfast sausage
- ◄ 4 tablespoons melted butter
- ◄ 10 eggs
- ◄ ⅓ cup heavy cream
- ◄ 2 teaspoons salt
- ◄ 1 teaspoon pepper
- ◄ 2 tablespoons hot sauce
- ◄ 2 stalks green onion
- ◄ 1 cup shredded sharp Cheddar cheese

1. Pour water into Instant Pot and place steamer basket in bottom. Add cauliflower. Click lid closed. 2. Press the Steam button and adjust time for 1 minute. When timer beeps, quick-release the pressure and place cauliflower to the side in medium bowl. 3. Drain water from Instant Pot, clean, and replace. Press the Sauté button. Press the Adjust button to set heat to Less. Cook bacon until crispy. Once fully cooked, set aside on paper towels. Add breakfast sausage to pot and brown (still using the Sauté function). 4. While sausage is cooking, whisk butter, eggs, heavy cream, salt, pepper, and hot sauce. 5. When sausage is fully cooked, pour egg mixture into Instant Pot. Gently stir using silicone spatula until eggs are completely cooked and fluffy. Press the Cancel button. Slice green onions. Sprinkle green onions, bacon, and cheese over mixture and let melt. Serve warm.

Per Serving:

calories: 620 | fat: 50g | protein: 30g | carbs: 5g | net carbs: 4g | fiber: 1g

Keto Chai

Prep time: 3 minutes | Cook time: 10 to 15 minutes | Serves 7

- ◄ 8 whole cloves
- ◄ 7 cardamom pods
- ◄ 2 cinnamon sticks
- ◄ 1½ teaspoons black peppercorns
- ◄ 1 (2-inch) piece fresh ginger, sliced into thin rounds
- ◄ 5 cups cold water
- ◄ 5 bags black tea
- ◄ 2 cups unsweetened (unflavored or vanilla-
- flavored) cashew milk, homemade or store-bought, or almond milk (or hemp milk for nut-free)
- ◄ 2 to 4 tablespoons Swerve confectioners'-style sweetener or equivalent amount of liquid or powdered sweetener
- ◄ 1 tablespoon coconut oil per cup of tea

1. Place the spices and ginger in a medium saucepan. Toast on low heat while lightly crushing the spices with the back of a spoon. 2. Add the water and bring to a boil. Once boiling, cover the pan, lower the heat, and simmer for 5 to 10 minutes (the longer time will create a stronger chai flavor). Remove from the heat. 3. Place the teabags in the saucepan and steep for 4 minutes. Remove the teabags and add the cashew milk and 2 tablespoons of the sweetener. Stir, taste, and add more sweetener if desired. 4. Bring the chai to a bare simmer over medium heat, then strain it into a teapot. Just before serving, place a tablespoon of coconut oil in each teacup, pour the hot tea over it, and whisk to blend the coconut oil into the tea. Store extra tea in an airtight container in the fridge for up to 1 week.

Per Serving:

calories: 35 | fat: 3g | protein: 1g | carbs: 1g | net carbs: 1g | fiber: 0g

Egg Ham Muffins

Prep time: 10 minutes | Cook time: 6 minutes | Serves 2

- ◄ 2 eggs, beaten
- ◄ 4 ounces (113 g) ham, chopped
- ◄ ½ teaspoon avocado oil
- ◄ 1 cup water, for cooking

1. Pour water in the instant pot. 2. Then brush the muffin molds with avocado oil from inside. 3. In the mixing bowl, mix up ham and beaten eggs. 4. After this, pour the mixture into the muffin molds. 5. Place the muffins in the instant pot. Close and seal the lid. Cook the meal on Manual mode (High Pressure) for 6 minutes. Then make a quick pressure release and remove the muffins.

Per Serving:

calories: 192 | fat: 16g | protein: 8g | carbs: 10g | net carbs: 8g | fiber: 2g

Egg Tofu Scramble with Kale & Mushrooms

Prep time: 10 minutes | Cook time: 25 minutes | Serves 4

- ◄ 2 tablespoons ghee
- ◄ 1 cup sliced white mushrooms
- ◄ 2 cloves garlic, minced
- ◄ 16 ounces firm tofu, pressed
- and crumbled
- ◄ Salt and black pepper to taste
- ◄ ½ cup thinly sliced kale
- ◄ 6 fresh eggs

1. Melt the ghee in a non-stick skillet over medium heat, and sauté the mushrooms for 5 minutes until they lose their liquid. Add the garlic and cook for 1 minute. 2. Crumble the tofu into the skillet, season with salt and black pepper. Cook with continuous stirring for 6 minutes. Introduce the kale in batches and cook to soften for about 7 minutes. Crack the eggs into a bowl, whisk until well combined and creamy in color, and pour all over the kale. Use a spatula to immediately stir the eggs while cooking until scrambled and no more runny, about 5 minutes. Plate, and serve with low carb crusted bread.

Per Serving:

calories: 309 | fat: 23g | protein: 21g | carbs: 6g | net carbs: 5g | fiber: 2g

Inside-Out Breakfast Burrito

Prep time: 10 minutes | Cook time: 5 minutes | Serves 2

Wrap:
- ◄ ¼ cup shredded low-moisture mozzarella cheese
- ◄ 2 large eggs
- ◄ 1 teaspoon coconut flour

Burrito:
- ◄ ½ cup cauliflower rice, cooked
- ◄ 4 ounces (113 g) breakfast sausage, cooked

- ◄ Pink Himalayan sea salt
- ◄ Freshly ground black pepper
- ◄ 2 teaspoons extra-virgin olive oil, divided

- ◄ ½ cup shredded Cheddar cheese
- ◄ 1 medium avocado, sliced

1. To make the wrap: In a medium bowl, whisk together the mozzarella, eggs, and coconut flour. Season with salt and pepper. 2. In an 8-inch skillet, heat 1 teaspoon of olive oil over medium-low heat. 3. Pour half the egg mixture into the pan and rotate the pan to spread it evenly on the skillet bottom. 4. Cook for about 1 minute on each side, flipping once. 5. Remove the egg wrap from the heat and cool. 6. Repeat steps 2 to 5 for the second wrap. 7. To make the burrito: Onto each wrap, evenly spread half the cauliflower rice, sausage, Cheddar cheese, and avocado. 8. Fold the sides in, roll up like a burrito, and enjoy!

Per Serving:

calories: 654 | fat: 55g | protein: 29g | carbs: 15g | net carbs: 6g | fiber: 9g

Not Your Average Boiled Eggs

Prep time: 10 minutes | Cook time: 10 minutes | Serves 5

Boiled Eggs:
- ◄ 10 eggs
- ◄ 1 tablespoon coconut vinegar or apple cider vinegar
- ◄ Sauce:
- ◄ 1½ cups water
- ◄ 2 tablespoons liquid aminos or tamari
- ◄ 2 tablespoons coconut aminos
- ◄ 2 tablespoons coconut

vinegar or apple cider vinegar
- ◄ 1 teaspoon minced fresh garlic or garlic powder
- ◄ 1 teaspoon minced fresh ginger or ground ginger
- ◄ 1 teaspoon sea salt
- ◄ ½ teaspoon freshly ground black pepper

Make the Boiled Eggs: 1. Place the eggs in a medium pot and add enough cold water to cover them. Add a splash of vinegar (this makes the eggs easier to peel) and bring to a boil. When the water boils, remove the pot from the heat, cover, and let sit for 10 minutes. 2. Meanwhile, fill a large bowl with water and ice. When the eggs are done, transfer them to the ice bath for another 10 minutes. 3. Peel the eggs and set them aside. Make the Sauce: 4. In a large storage bowl with a lid, whisk together the water, liquid aminos, coconut aminos, vinegar, garlic, ginger, salt, and pepper. Alternatively, you can divide the ingredients in half and add to two

large mason jars with lids. 5. Place the peeled eggs in the sauce. Cover and refrigerate. The longer the eggs soak up the sauce, the more flavorful they will be.

Per Serving:

2 eggs: calories: 144 | fat: 10g | protein: 12g | carbs: 2g | net carbs: 2g | fiber: 0g

Spinach Omelet

Prep time: 5 minutes | Cook time: 12 minutes | Serves 2

- ◄ 4 large eggs
- ◄ 1½ cups chopped fresh spinach leaves
- ◄ 2 tablespoons peeled and chopped yellow onion

- ◄ 2 tablespoons salted butter, melted
- ◄ ½ cup shredded mild Cheddar cheese
- ◄ ¼ teaspoon salt

1. In an ungreased round nonstick baking dish, whisk eggs. Stir in spinach, onion, butter, Cheddar, and salt. 2. Place dish into air fryer basket. Adjust the temperature to 320°F (160°C) and bake for 12 minutes. Omelet will be done when browned on the top and firm in the middle. 3. Slice in half and serve warm on two medium plates.

Per Serving:

calories: 380 | fat: 31g | protein: 21g | carbs: 4g | net carbs: 3g | fiber: 1g

Cross-Country Scrambler

Prep time: 5 minutes | Cook time: 28 minutes | Serves 2

- ◄ 8 strips bacon (about 8 ounces/225 g)
- ◄ 1 packed cup spiral-sliced butternut squash (about 5¼ ounces/150 g)
- ◄ ½ green bell pepper, diced

- ◄ 6 large eggs, beaten
- ◄ ½ cup (40 g) sliced green onions (green parts only)
- ◄ ¼ teaspoon ground black pepper

1. Cook the bacon in a large frying pan over medium heat until crispy, about 15 minutes. Remove the bacon from the pan, leaving the grease in the pan. When the bacon has cooled, crumble it. 2. Add the squash and bell pepper to the pan with the bacon grease. Cover and cook over medium-low heat for 8 minutes, or until the vegetables are fork-tender. 3. Add the beaten eggs, green onions, and black pepper. Mix with a large spoon until fully incorporated. 4. Cook, uncovered, for 5 minutes, stirring every minute, or until the eggs are cooked to your liking. Once complete, fold in half of the crumbled bacon. 5. Divide evenly between 2 plates, top with remaining crumbled bacon, and dig in!

Per Serving:

calories: 395 | fat: 27g | protein: 26g | carbs: 12g | net carbs: 9g | fiber: 3g

Tahini Banana Detox Smoothie

Prep time: 10 minutes | Cook time: 0 minutes | Serves 2

◄ 1½ cups unsweetened almond milk
◄ ½ cup heavy (whipping) cream
◄ 1 banana
◄ 2 scoops (25–28 grams)
◄ vanilla protein powder
◄ 2 tablespoons tahini
◄ ½ teaspoon ground cinnamon
◄ 5 ice cubes

1. Blend the smoothie. Put the almond milk, cream, banana, protein powder, tahini, cinnamon, and ice in a blender and blend until smooth and creamy. 2. Serve. Pour into two tall glasses and serve.

Per Serving:

calories: 425 | fat: 29g | protein: 25g | carbs: 16g | net carbs: 10g | fiber: 6g

Classic Coffee Cake

Prep time: 5 minutes | Cook time: 40 minutes | Serves 5 to 6

Base:
◄ 2 eggs
◄ 2 tablespoons salted grass-fed butter, softened
◄ 1 cup blanched almond flour
◄ 1 cup chopped pecans
◄ ¼ cup sour cream, at room temperature
◄ ¼ cup full-fat cream cheese, softened
◄ ½ teaspoon salt
◄ ½ teaspoon ground cinnamon
◄ ½ teaspoon ground nutmeg
◄ ¼ teaspoon baking soda

Topping:
◄ 1 cup sugar-free chocolate chips
◄ 1 cup chopped pecans
◄ ½ cup Swerve, or more to
◄ taste
◄ ½ cup heavy whipping cream

1. Pour 1 cup of filtered water into the inner pot of the Instant Pot, then insert the trivet. Using an electric mixer, combine the eggs, butter, flour, pecans, sour cream, cream cheese, salt, cinnamon, nutmeg, and baking soda. Mix thoroughly. Transfer this mixture into a well-greased, Instant Pot-friendly pan (or dish). 2. Using a sling if desired, place the pan onto the trivet, and cover loosely with aluminum foil. Close the lid, set the pressure release to Sealing, and select Manual. Set the Instant Pot to 40 minutes on High Pressure and let cook. 3. While cooking, in a large bowl, mix the chocolate chips, pecans, Swerve, and whipping cream thoroughly. Set aside. 4. Once cooked, let the pressure naturally disperse from the Instant Pot for about 10 minutes, then carefully switch the pressure release to Venting. 5. Open the Instant Pot and remove the pan. Evenly sprinkle the topping mixture over the cake. Let cool, serve, and enjoy!

Per Serving:

calories: 267 | fat: 23g | protein: 7g | carbs: 9g | net carbs: 7g | fiber: 2g

Sausage Stuffed Poblanos

Prep time: 15 minutes | Cook time: 15 minutes | Serves 4

◄ ½ pound (227 g) spicy ground pork breakfast sausage
◄ 4 large eggs
◄ 4 ounces (113 g) full-fat cream cheese, softened
◄ ¼ cup canned diced
◄ tomatoes and green chiles, drained
◄ 4 large poblano peppers
◄ 8 tablespoons shredded Pepper Jack cheese
◄ ½ cup full-fat sour cream

1. In a medium skillet over medium heat, crumble and brown the ground sausage until no pink remains. Remove sausage and drain the fat from the pan. Crack eggs into the pan, scramble, and cook until no longer runny. 2. Place cooked sausage in a large bowl and fold in cream cheese. Mix in diced tomatoes and chiles. Gently fold in eggs. 3. Cut a 4-inch to 5-inch slit in the top of each poblano, removing the seeds and white membrane with a small knife. Separate the filling into four servings and spoon carefully into each pepper. Top each with 2 tablespoons pepper jack cheese. 4. Place each pepper into the air fryer basket. 5. Adjust the temperature to 350ºF (177ºC) and set the timer for 15 minutes. 6. Peppers will be soft and cheese will be browned when ready. Serve immediately with sour cream on top.

Per Serving:

calories: 429 | fat: 36g | protein: 21g | carbs: 5g | net carbs: 4g | fiber: 1g

Salmon Bacon Rolls with Dipping Sauce

Prep time: 10 minutes | Cook time: 10 minutes | Makes 16 rolls

◄ 8 strips bacon (about 8 oz/225 g)
◄ 8 ounces (225 g) smoked salmon, cut into 16 squares
◄ Dipping Sauce:
◄ ½ cup (105 g) mayonnaise
◄ 2 tablespoons sugar-free barbecue sauce
◄ Special Equipmnt:
◄ Toothpicks

1. Cook the bacon in a large frying pan over medium heat until much of the fat is rendered and the bacon is lightly browned but not crispy, 8 to 10 minutes. (You want the bacon to remain pliable so that you can bend it.) 2. Cut the cooked bacon in half lengthwise to create 16 narrow strips. Place a square of salmon on one end of a bacon strip. Roll the salmon in the bacon, secure with a toothpick, and place on a clean plate. Repeat with the remaining bacon and salmon, making a total of 16 rolls. 3. Make the dipping sauce: Place the mayonnaise and barbecue sauce in a small bowl and stir to combine. Serve alongside the salmon rolls.

Per Serving:

calories: 324 | fat: 29g | protein: 14g | carbs: 3g | net carbs: 2g | fiber: 1g

Bacon, Cheese, and Avocado Melt

Prep time: 5 minutes | Cook time: 3 to 5 minutes | Serves 2

◀ 1 avocado
◀ 4 slices cooked bacon, chopped
◀ 2 tablespoons salsa
◀ 1 tablespoon heavy cream
◀ ¼ cup shredded Cheddar cheese

1. Preheat the air fryer to 400°F (204°C). 2. Slice the avocado in half lengthwise and remove the stone. To ensure the avocado halves do not roll in the basket, slice a thin piece of skin off the base. 3. In a small bowl, combine the bacon, salsa, and cream. Divide the mixture between the avocado halves and top with the cheese. 4. Place the avocado halves in the air fryer basket and air fry for 3 to 5 minutes until the cheese has melted and begins to brown. Serve warm.

Per Serving:

calories: 357 | fat: 30g | protein: 14g | carbs: 11g | net carbs: 4g | fiber: 7g

Keto Quiche

Prep time: 10 minutes | Cook time: 1 hour | Makes 1 (6-inch) quiche

Crust:
◀ 1¼ cups blanched almond flour
◀ 1¼ cups grated Parmesan or
Filling:
◀ ½ cup chicken or beef broth (or vegetable broth for vegetarian)
◀ 1 cup shredded Swiss cheese (about 4 ounces / 113 g)
◀ 4 ounces (113 g) cream cheese (½ cup)
◀ 1 tablespoon unsalted butter,

Gouda cheese
◀ ¼ teaspoon fine sea salt
◀ 1 large egg, beaten

melted
◀ 4 large eggs, beaten
◀ ⅓ cup minced leeks or sliced green onions
◀ ¾ teaspoon fine sea salt
◀ ⅛ teaspoon cayenne pepper
◀ Chopped green onions, for garnish

1. Preheat the air fryer to 325°F (163°C). Grease a pie pan. Spray two large pieces of parchment paper with avocado oil and set them on the countertop. 2. Make the crust: In a medium-sized bowl, combine the flour, cheese, and salt and mix well. Add the egg and mix until the dough is well combined and stiff. 3. Place the dough in the center of one of the greased pieces of parchment. Top with the other piece of parchment. Using a rolling pin, roll out the dough into a circle about 1/16 inch thick. 4. Press the pie crust into the prepared pie pan. Place it in the air fryer and bake for 12 minutes, or until it starts to lightly brown. 5. While the crust bakes, make the filling: In a large bowl, combine the broth, Swiss cheese, cream cheese, and butter. Stir in the eggs, leeks, salt, and cayenne pepper. When the crust is ready, pour the mixture into the crust. 6. Place the quiche in the air fryer and bake for 15 minutes. Turn the heat down to 300°F (149°C) and bake for an additional 30 minutes, or until a knife inserted 1 inch from the edge comes out clean. You may have to cover the edges of the crust with foil to prevent burning. 7. Allow the quiche to cool for 10 minutes before garnishing it with

chopped green onions and cutting it into wedges. 8. Store leftovers in an airtight container in the refrigerator for up to 4 days or in the freezer for up to a month. Reheat in a preheated 350°F (177°C) air fryer for a few minutes, until warmed through.

Per Serving:

calories: 580 | fat: 43g | protein: 31g | carbs: 20g | net carbs: 15g fiber: 5g

Almond Pancakes

Prep time: 10 minutes | Cook time: 15 minutes per batch | Serves 6

◀ 4 eggs, beaten
◀ 2 cups almond flour
◀ ½ cup butter, melted
◀ 2 tablespoons granulated erythritol
◀ 1 tablespoon avocado oil
◀ 1 teaspoon baking powder
◀ 1 teaspoon vanilla extract
◀ Pinch of salt
◀ ¾ cup water, divided

1. In a blender, combine all the ingredients, except for the ½ cup of the water. Pulse until fully combined and smooth. Let the batter rest for 5 minutes before cooking. 2. Fill each cup with 2 tablespoons of the batter, about two-thirds of the way full. Cover the cups with aluminum foil. 3. Pour the remaining ½ cup of the water and insert the trivet in the Instant Pot. Place the cups on the trivet. 4. Set the lid in place. Select the Manual mode and set the cooking time for 15 minutes on High Pressure. When the timer goes off, do a quick pressure release. Carefully open the lid. 5. Repeat with the remaining batter, until all the batter is used. Add more water to the pot before cooking each batch, if needed. 6. Serve warm.

Per Serving:

3 bites: calories: 423 | fat: 39g | protein: 12g | carbs: 8g | net carbs 4g | fiber: 4g

Keto Breakfast Pudding

Prep time: 5 minutes | Cook time: 0 minutes | Serves 3

◀ 1½ cups (350 ml) full-fat coconut milk
◀ 1 cup (110 g) frozen raspberries
◀ ¼ cup (60 ml) MCT oil or melted coconut oil, or ¼ cup (40 g) unflavored MCT oil powder
◀ ¼ cup (40 g) collagen peptides or protein powder
◀ 2 tablespoons chia seeds
◀ 1 tablespoon apple cider vinegar
◀ 1 teaspoon vanilla extract
◀ 1 tablespoon erythritol, or 4 drops liquid stevia
◀ Toppings (optional):
◀ Unsweetened shredded coconut
◀ Hulled hemp seeds
◀ Fresh berries of choice

1. Place all the pudding ingredients in a blender or food processor and blend until smooth. Serve in bowls with your favorite toppings if desired.

Per Serving:

calories: 403 | fat: 34g | protein: 15g | carbs: 9g | net carbs: 6g fiber: 3g

Creamy Keto Coffee

Prep time: 2 minutes | Cook time: 0 minutes | Serves 1

- 1 cup brewed coffee
- ¼ to ⅓ cup full-fat coconut, nut, or dairy milk
- 1 tablespoon cacao butter
- 1 scoop grass-fed collagen peptides
- 1 scoop MCT powder
- 2 or 3 drops stevia extract (optional)
- Pinch of sea salt
- Ground cinnamon, for garnish

1. Place all the ingredients in a blender and blend until smooth. 2. Garnish with ground cinnamon.

Per Serving:

calories: 320 | fat: 30g | protein: 11g | carbs: 3g | net carbs: 2g | fiber: 1g

Breakfast Cobbler

Prep time: 20 minutes | Cook time: 30 minutes | Serves 4

Filling:
- 10 ounces (283 g) bulk pork sausage, crumbled
- ¼ cup minced onions
- 2 cloves garlic, minced
- ½ teaspoon fine sea salt
- ½ teaspoon ground black pepper

Biscuits:
- 3 large egg whites
- ¾ cup blanched almond flour
- 1 teaspoon baking powder
- ¼ teaspoon fine sea salt

- 1 (8 ounces / 227 g) package cream cheese (or Kite Hill brand cream cheese style spread for dairy-free), softened
- ¾ cup beef or chicken broth

- 2½ tablespoons very cold unsalted butter, cut into ¼-inch pieces
- Fresh thyme leaves, for garnish

1. Preheat the air fryer to 400ºF (204ºC). 2. Place the sausage, onions, and garlic in a pie pan. Using your hands, break up the sausage into small pieces and spread it evenly throughout the pie pan. Season with the salt and pepper. Place the pan in the air fryer and bake for 5 minutes. 3. While the sausage cooks, place the cream cheese and broth in a food processor or blender and purée until smooth. 4. Remove the pork from the air fryer and use a fork or metal spatula to crumble it more. Pour the cream cheese mixture into the sausage and stir to combine. Set aside. 5. Make the biscuits: Place the egg whites in a medium-sized mixing bowl or the bowl of a stand mixer and whip with a hand mixer or stand mixer until stiff peaks form. 6. In a separate medium-sized bowl, whisk together the almond flour, baking powder, and salt, then cut in the butter. When you are done, the mixture should still have chunks of butter. Gently fold the flour mixture into the egg whites with a rubber spatula. 7. Use a large spoon or ice cream scoop to scoop the dough into 4 equal-sized biscuits, making sure the butter is evenly distributed. Place the biscuits on top of the sausage and cook in the air fryer for 5 minutes, then turn the heat down to 325ºF (163ºC) and bake for another 17 to 20 minutes, until the biscuits are golden brown. Serve garnished with fresh thyme leaves. 8. Store leftovers in an airtight

container in the refrigerator for up to 3 days. Reheat in a preheated 350ºF (177ºC) air fryer for 5 minutes, or until warmed through.

Per Serving:

calories: 586 | fat: 53g | protein: 20g | carbs: 8g | net carbs: 6g | fiber: 2g

Olivia's Cream Cheese Pancakes

Prep time: 15 minutes | Cook time: 15 minutes | Serves 3

- 2 medium eggs
- 2 ounces cream cheese
- ½ teaspoon vanilla extract
- ¼ cup blanched almond flour
- 1 teaspoon Swerve

- confectioners'-style sweetener
- ¼ teaspoon baking powder
- Salted butter, for serving
- Sugar-free syrup, for serving

1 Combine the eggs, cream cheese, vanilla, almond flour, sweetener, and baking powder in a blender and blend on medium-high speed until smooth. Use a fork to pop the large bubbles on the top of the batter. 2 Coat a medium-sized skillet with coconut oil spray or ghee and place over medium heat. Once hot, pour one-third of the batter into the pan. Flip the pancake when the sides are firm and bubbles appear evenly throughout, 1 to 3 minutes, then cook for another 1 to 3 minutes on the second side. 3 Repeat with the remaining batter to make a total of 3 pancakes. 4 Serve topped with butter and sugar-free syrup.

Per Serving:

calories: 487 | fat: 40g | protein: 21g | carbs: 12g | net carbs: 6g | fiber: 6g

Almond Flour Pancakes

Prep time: 5 minutes | Cook time: 10 minutes | Serves 6

- 2 cups (8 ounces / 227 g) blanched almond flour
- ¼ cup erythritol
- 1 tablespoon baking powder
- ¼ teaspoon sea salt
- 4 large eggs

- ⅔ cup unsweetened almond milk
- ¼ cup avocado oil, plus more for frying
- 2 teaspoons vanilla extract

1. In a blender, combine all ingredients and blend until smooth. Let the batter rest for 5 to 10 minutes. 2. Preheat a large, very lightly oiled skillet over medium-low heat. (Keep oil very minimal for perfectly round pancakes.) Working in batches, pour circles of batter onto the pan, 2 tablespoons (⅛ cup) at a time for 3-inch pancakes. Cook 1½ to 2 minutes, until bubbles start to form on the edges. Flip and cook another minute or two, until browned on the other side. 3. Repeat with the remaining batter.

Per Serving:

calories: 355 | fat: 31g | protein: 12g | carbs: 12g | net carbs: 5g | fiber: 7g

Cheese Egg Muffins

Prep time: 5 minutes | Cook time: 10 minutes | Serves 6

- ◄ 4 eggs
- ◄ 2 tablespoons heavy cream
- ◄ ¼ teaspoon salt
- ◄ ⅛ teaspoon pepper
- ◄ ⅓ cup shredded Cheddar cheese
- ◄ 1 cup water

1. In a large bowl, whisk eggs and heavy cream. Add salt and pepper. 2. Pour mixture into 6 silicone cupcake baking molds. Sprinkle cheese into each cup. 3. Pour water into Instant Pot and place steam rack in bottom of pot. Carefully set filled silicone molds steadily on steam rack. If all do not fit, separate into two batches. 4. Click lid closed. Press the Manual button and adjust time for 10 minutes. When timer beeps, allow a quick release and remove lid. Egg bites will look puffy at first, but will become smaller once they begin to cool. Serve warm.

Per Serving:

calories: 90 | fat: 6g | protein: 6g | carbs: 1g | net carbs: 1g | fiber: 0g

Bell Peppers Stuffed with Eggs

Prep time: 5 minutes | Cook time: 14 minutes | Serves 2

- ◄ 2 eggs, beaten
- ◄ 1 tablespoon coconut cream
- ◄ ¼ teaspoon dried oregano
- ◄ ¼ teaspoon salt
- ◄ 1 large bell pepper, cut into halves and deseeded
- ◄ 1 cup water

1. In a bowl, stir together the eggs, coconut cream, oregano and salt. 2. Pour the egg mixture in the pepper halves. 3. Pour the water and insert the trivet in the Instant Pot. Put the stuffed pepper halves on the trivet. 4. Set the lid in place. Select the Manual mode and set the cooking time for 14 minutes on High Pressure. When the timer goes off, do a quick pressure release. Carefully open the lid. 5. Serve warm.

Per Serving:

calories: 99 | fat: 6g | protein: 6g | carbs: 5g | net carbs: 4g | fiber: 1g

Chorizo and Mozzarella Omelet

Prep time: 5 minutes | Cook time: 10 minutes | Serves 1

- ◄ 2 eggs
- ◄ 6 basil leaves
- ◄ 2 ounces mozzarella cheese
- ◄ 1 tablespoon butter
- ◄ 1 tablespoon water
- ◄ 4 thin slices chorizo
- ◄ 1 tomato, sliced
- ◄ Salt and black pepper, to taste

1. Whisk the eggs along with the water and some salt and pepper. Melt the butter in a skillet and cook the eggs for 30 seconds. Spread the chorizo slices over. Arrange the tomato and mozzarella over the chorizo. Cook for about 3 minutes. Cover the skillet and cook for 3 minutes until omelet is set. 2. When ready, remove the pan from heat; run a spatula around the edges of the omelet and flip it onto a warm plate, folded side down. Serve garnished with basil leaves and green salad.

Per Serving:

calories: 632 | fat: 49g | protein: 39g | carbs: 9g | net carbs: 7g | fiber: 2g

Breakfast Almond Muffins

Prep time: 5 minutes | Cook time: 20 minutes | Serves 4

- ◄ 2 drops liquid stevia
- ◄ 2 cups almond flour
- ◄ 2 teaspoons baking powder
- ◄ ½ teaspoon salt
- ◄ 8 oz cream cheese, softened
- ◄ ¼ cup melted butter
- ◄ 1 egg
- ◄ 1 cup unsweetened almond milk

1. Preheat oven to 400ºF and grease a 12-cup muffin tray with cooking spray. Mix the flour, baking powder, and salt in a large bowl. 2. In a separate bowl, beat the cream cheese, stevia, and butter using a hand mixer and whisk in the egg and milk. Fold in the flour, and spoon the batter into the muffin cups two-thirds way up. 3. Bake for 20 minutes until puffy at the top and golden brown, remove to a wire rack to cool slightly for 5 minutes before serving. Serve with tea.

Per Serving:

calories: 546 | fat: 50g | protein: 13g | carbs: 11g | net carbs: 6g | fiber: 5g

Bacon & Cheese Zucchini Balls

Prep time: 15 minutes | Cook time: 10 minutes | Serves 6

- ◄ 4 cups zoodles
- ◄ ½ pound bacon, chopped
- ◄ 6 ounces cottage cheese, curds
- ◄ 6 ounces cream cheese
- ◄ 1 cup fontina cheese
- ◄ ½ cup dill pickles, chopped, squeezed
- ◄ 2 cloves garlic, crushed
- ◄ 1 cup grated Parmesan cheese
- ◄ ½ teaspoon caraway seeds
- ◄ ¼ teaspoon dried dill weed
- ◄ ½ teaspoon onion powder
- ◄ Salt and black pepper, to taste
- ◄ 1 cup crushed pork rinds
- ◄ Cooking oil

1.Thoroughly mix zoodles, cottage cheese, dill pickles, ½ cup of Parmesan cheese, garlic, cream cheese, bacon, and fontina cheese until well combined. Shape the mixture into balls. Refrigerate for 3 hours. 2. In a mixing bowl, mix the remaining ½ cup of Parmesan cheese, crushed pork rinds, dill, black pepper, onion powder, caraway seeds, and salt. Roll cheese ball in Parmesan mixture to coat. 3. Set a skillet over medium heat and warm 1-inch of oil. Fry cheeseballs until browned on all sides. Set on a paper towel to soak up any excess oil.

Per Serving:

calories: 702 | fat: 53g | protein: 47g | carbs: 10g | net carbs: 7g | fiber: 3g

Matcha Chia N'Oatmeal

Prep time: 5 minutes | Cook time: 0 minutes | Serves 3

- ◀ 1 cup full-fat coconut milk
- ◀ 1 cup water
- ◀ 2 teaspoons matcha powder
- ◀ 2 scoops collagen peptides
- ◀ 5 drops stevia extract
- ◀ ¼ cup whole chia seeds
- ◀ 1 tablespoon ground chia seeds (optional)
- ◀ Shredded coconut or coconut flakes, for garnish

1. Put all the ingredients except the whole and ground chia seeds and the shredded coconut in a blender and blend until smooth. Taste and add more stevia if desired. 2. Pour the mixture into a large glass mason jar, add the whole chia seeds, cover, and shake well to combine. Refrigerate for 8 hours or overnight to allow the chia seeds to gel. 3. After it sets, whisk the mixture vigorously to break up the gelled seeds so that they're evenly distributed and the mixture is smooth and thick. 4. Add the ground chia seeds (if using), cover, and shake to combine. Place in the refrigerator to set for up to 1 hour, until thickened a bit more. If you prefer a thinner consistency, you can omit the ground chia seeds. 5. Garnish with shredded coconut before serving.

Per Serving:

calories: 291 | fat: 23g | protein: 12g | carbs: 12g | net carbs: 3g | fiber: 9g

Meritage Eggs

Prep time: 5 minutes | Cook time: 8 minutes | Serves 2

- ◀ 2 teaspoons unsalted butter (or coconut oil for dairy-free), for greasing the ramekins
- ◀ 4 large eggs
- ◀ 2 teaspoons chopped fresh thyme
- ◀ ½ teaspoon fine sea salt
- ◀ ¼ teaspoon ground black pepper
- ◀ 2 tablespoons heavy cream (or unsweetened, unflavored almond milk for dairy-free)
- ◀ 3 tablespoons finely grated Parmesan cheese (or Kite Hill brand chive cream cheese style spread, softened, for dairy-free)
- ◀ Fresh thyme leaves, for garnish (optional)

1. Preheat the air fryer to 400ºF (204ºC). Grease two (4 ounces / 113 g) ramekins with the butter. 2. Crack 2 eggs into each ramekin and divide the thyme, salt, and pepper between the ramekins. Pour 1 tablespoon of the heavy cream into each ramekin. Sprinkle each ramekin with 1½ tablespoons of the Parmesan cheese. 3. Place the ramekins in the air fryer and bake for 8 minutes for soft-cooked yolks (longer if you desire a harder yolk). 4. Garnish with a sprinkle of ground black pepper and thyme leaves, if desired. Best served fresh.

Per Serving:

calories: 326 | fat: 27g | protein: 18g | carbs: 1g | net carbs: 1g | fiber: 0g

Smoky Sausage Patties

Prep time: 30 minutes | Cook time: 9 minutes | Serves 8

- ◀ 1 pound (454 g) ground pork
- ◀ 1 tablespoon coconut aminos
- ◀ 2 teaspoons liquid smoke
- ◀ 1 teaspoon dried sage
- ◀ 1 teaspoon sea salt
- ◀ ½ teaspoon fennel seeds
- ◀ ½ teaspoon dried thyme
- ◀ ½ teaspoon freshly ground black pepper
- ◀ ¼ teaspoon cayenne pepper

1. In a large bowl, combine the pork, coconut aminos, liquid smoke, sage, salt, fennel seeds, thyme, black pepper, and cayenne pepper. Work the meat with your hands until the seasonings are fully incorporated. 2. Shape the mixture into 8 equal-size patties. Using your thumb, make a dent in the center of each patty. Place the patties on a plate and cover with plastic wrap. Refrigerate the patties for at least 30 minutes. 3. Working in batches if necessary, place the patties in a single layer in the air fryer, being careful not to overcrowd them. 4. Set the air fryer to 400ºF (204ºC) and air fry for 5 minutes. Flip and cook for about 4 minutes more.

Per Serving:

calories: 177 | fat: 13g | protein: 13g | carbs: 2g | net carbs: 1g | fiber: 1g

Nutty "Oatmeal"

Prep time: 5 minutes | Cook time: 4 minutes | Serves 4

- ◀ 2 tablespoons coconut oil
- ◀ 1 cup full-fat coconut milk
- ◀ 1 cup heavy whipping cream
- ◀ ½ cup macadamia nuts
- ◀ ½ cup chopped pecans
- ◀ ⅓ cup Swerve, or more to taste
- ◀ ¼ cup unsweetened coconut flakes
- ◀ 2 tablespoons chopped hazelnuts
- ◀ 2 tablespoons chia seeds
- ◀ ½ teaspoon ground cinnamon

1. Before you get started, soak the chia seeds for about 5 to 10 minutes (can be up to 20, if desired) in 1 cup of filtered water. After soaking, set the Instant Pot to Sauté and add the coconut oil. Once melted, pour in the milk, whipping cream, and 1 cup of filtered water. Then add the macadamia nuts, pecans, Swerve, coconut flakes, hazelnuts, chia seeds, and cinnamon. Mix thoroughly inside the Instant Pot. 2. Close the lid, set the pressure release to Sealing, and hit Cancel to stop the current program. Select Manual, set the Instant Pot to 4 minutes on High Pressure, and let cook. 3. Once cooked, carefully switch the pressure release to Venting. 4. Open the Instant Pot, serve, and enjoy!

Per Serving:

calories: 506 | fat: 53g | protein: 6g | carbs: 11g | net carbs: 5g | fiber: 6g

Chapter **4**

Poultry

Chapter 4 Poultry

Spicy Chicken with Bacon and Peppers

Prep time: 5 minutes | Cook time: 13 minutes | Serves 6

- ◄ 2 slices bacon, chopped
- ◄ 1½ pounds (680 g) ground chicken
- ◄ 2 garlic cloves, minced
- ◄ ½ cup green onions, chopped
- ◄ 1 green bell pepper, seeded and chopped
- ◄ 1 red bell pepper, seeded and chopped
- ◄ 1 serrano pepper, chopped
- ◄ 1 tomato, chopped
- ◄ 1 cup water
- ◄ ⅓ cup chicken broth
- ◄ 1 teaspoon paprika
- ◄ 1 teaspoon onion powder
- ◄ ¼ teaspoon ground allspice
- ◄ 2 bay leaves
- ◄ Sea salt and ground black pepper, to taste

1. Press the Sauté button to heat your Instant Pot. 2. Add the bacon and cook for about 3 minutes until crisp. Reserve the bacon in a bowl. 3. Add the ground chicken to the bacon grease of the pot and brown for 2 to 3 minutes, crumbling it with a spatula. Reserve it in the bowl of bacon. 4. Add the garlic, green onions, and peppers and sauté for 3 minutes until tender. Add the remaining ingredients to the Instant Pot, along with the cooked bacon and chicken. Stir to mix well. 5. Lock the lid. Select the Poultry mode and set the cooking time for 5 minutes at High Pressure. 6. When the timer beeps, perform a natural pressure release for 10 minutes, then release any remaining pressure. Carefully remove the lid. Serve warm.

Per Serving:

calories: 236 | fat: 14g | protein: 25g | carbs: 3g | net carbs: 2g | fiber: 1g

Chicken Rollatini with Ricotta, Prosciutto, and Spinach

Prep time: 15 minutes | Cook time: 35 minutes | Serves 4

- ◄ 4 (3-ounce) boneless skinless chicken breasts, pounded to about ⅓ inch thick
- ◄ 4 ounces ricotta cheese
- ◄ 4 slices prosciutto (4 ounces)
- ◄ 1 cup fresh spinach
- ◄ ½ cup almond flour
- ◄ ½ cup grated Parmesan cheese
- ◄ 2 eggs, beaten
- ◄ ¼ cup good-quality olive oil

1. Preheat the oven. Set the oven temperature to 400°F. 2. Prepare the chicken. Pat the chicken breasts dry with paper towels. Spread ¼ of the ricotta in the middle of each breast. Place the prosciutto over the ricotta and ¼ cup of the spinach on the prosciutto. Fold the long edges of the chicken breast over the filling, then roll the chicken breast up to enclose the filling. Place the rolls seam-side down on your work surface. 3. Bread the chicken. On a plate, stir together the almond flour and Parmesan and set it next to the beaten eggs. Carefully dip a chicken roll in the egg, then roll it in the almond-flour mixture until it is completely covered. Set the rolls seam-side down on your work surface. Repeat with the other rolls. 4. Brown the rolls. In a medium skillet over medium heat, warm the olive oil. Place the rolls seam-side down in the skillet and brown them on all sides, turning them carefully, about 10 minutes in total. Transfer the rolls, seam-side down, to a 9-by-9-inch baking dish. 5. Bake. Bake the chicken rolls for 25 minutes, or until they're cooked through. 6. Serve. Place one chicken roll on each of four plates and serve them immediately.

Per Serving:

calories: 438 | fat: 30g | protein: 40g | carbs: 2g | net carbs: 2g | fiber: 0g

Cilantro Chicken Breasts with Mayo-Avocado Sauce

Prep time: 10 minutes | Cook time: 16 minutes | Serves 4

For the Sauce
- ◄ 1 avocado, pitted
- ◄ ½ cup mayonnaise
- ◄ Salt to taste

For the Chicken
- ◄ 3 tablespoons ghee
- ◄ 4 chicken breasts
- ◄ Pink salt and black pepper to taste
- ◄ 1 cup chopped cilantro leaves
- ◄ ½ cup chicken broth

1. Spoon the avocado, mayonnaise, and salt into a small food processor and puree until a smooth sauce is derived. Pour sauce into a jar and refrigerate while you make the chicken. 2. Melt ghee in a large skillet, season chicken with salt and black pepper and fry for 4 minutes on each side to golden brown. Remove chicken to a plate. 3. Pour the broth in the same skillet and add the cilantro. Bring to simmer covered for 3 minutes and add the chicken. Cover and cook on low heat for 5 minutes until the liquid has reduced and chicken is fragrant. Dish chicken only into serving plates and spoon the mayoavocado sauce over.

Per Serving:

calories: 561 | fat: 41g | protein: 36g | carbs: 7g | net carbs: 6g | fiber: 4g

Spanish Chicken

Prep time: 20 minutes | Cook time: 50 minutes | Serves 4

- ½ cup mushrooms, chopped
- 1 pound (454 g) chorizo sausages, chopped
- 2 tablespoons avocado oil
- 4 cherry peppers, chopped
- 1 red bell pepper, seeded, chopped
- 1 onion, peeled and sliced
- 2 tablespoons garlic, minced
- 2 cups tomatoes, chopped
- 4 chicken thighs
- Salt and black pepper, to taste
- ½ cup chicken stock
- 1 teaspoon turmeric
- 1 tablespoon vinegar
- 2 teaspoons dried oregano
- Fresh parsley, chopped, for serving

1. Set a pan over medium heat and warm half of the avocado oil, stir in the chorizo sausages, and cook for 5-6 minutes until browned; remove to a bowl. Heat the rest of the oil, place in the chicken thighs, and apply pepper and salt for seasoning. Cook each side for 3 minutes and set aside on a bowl. 2. In the same pan, add the onion, bell pepper, cherry peppers, and mushrooms, and cook for 4 minutes. Stir in the garlic and cook for 2 minutes. Pour in the stock, turmeric, salt, tomatoes, pepper, vinegar, and oregano. Stir in the chorizo sausages and chicken, place everything to the oven at 400°F, and bake for 30 minutes. Ladle into serving bowls and garnish with chopped parsley to serve.

Per Serving:

calories: 507 | fat: 39g | protein: 29g | carbs: 10g | net carbs: 6g | fiber: 4g

Chili Lime Turkey Burgers

Prep time: 10 minutes | Cook time: 3 minutes | Serves 4

Burgers:
- 2 pounds (907 g) ground turkey
- 1½ ounces (43 g) diced red onion
- 2 cloves garlic, minced
- 1½ teaspoons minced

Dipping Sauce:
- ½ cup sour cream
- 4 teaspoons sriracha
- 1 tablespoon chopped

- cilantro
- 1½ teaspoons salt
- 1 teaspoon Mexican chili powder
- Juice and zest of 1 lime
- ½ cup water

- cilantro, plus more for garnish
- 1 teaspoon lime juice

1. Make the burgers: In a large bowl, add the turkey, onion, garlic, cilantro, salt, chili powder, and lime juice and zest. Use a wooden spoon to mix until the ingredients are well distributed. 2. Divide the meat into four 8-ounce / 227-g balls. Use a kitchen scale to measure for accuracy. Pat the meat into thick patties, about 1 inch thick. 3. Add the water and trivet to the Instant Pot. Place the turkey patties on top of the trivet, overlapping if necessary. 4. Close the lid and seal the vent. Cook on High Pressure for 3 minutes. Quick release the steam. 5. Remove the patties from the pot. 6. Make the dipping sauce: In a small bowl, whisk together the sour cream, sriracha, cilantro, and lime juice. 7. Top each patty with 2 tablespoons of the sauce and garnish with fresh cilantro.

Per Serving:

calories: 417 | fat: 25g | protein: 44g | carbs: 5g | net carbs: 4g | fiber: 1g

Turkey Fajitas

Prep time: 20 minutes | Cook time: 12 minutes | Serves 4

- 2 pound turkey breasts, skinless, boneless, sliced
- 1 teaspoon garlic powder
- 1 teaspoon chili powder
- 2 teaspoons cumin
- 2 tablespoons lime juice
- Salt and black pepper, to taste
- 1 teaspoon sweet paprika
- 2 tablespoons coconut oil
- 1 teaspoon ground coriander
- 1 green bell pepper, seeded, sliced
- 1 red bell pepper, seeded, sliced
- 1 onion, sliced
- 1 tablespoon fresh cilantro, chopped
- 1 avocado, sliced
- 2 limes, cut into wedges

1. In a bowl, combine lime juice, cumin, garlic powder, coriander, paprika, salt, chili powder, and black pepper. Toss in the turkey pieces to coat well. Set a pan over medium heat and warm oil, place in the turkey, cook each side for 3 minutes and set to a plate. 2. Add the remaining oil to the pan and stir in the bell peppers and onion, and cook for 6 minutes. Take the turkey back to the pan. Add a topping of fresh cilantro, lime wedges, and avocado and serve.

Per Serving:

calories: 522 | fat: 31g | protein: 49g | carbs: 16g | net carbs: 9g | fiber: 7g

Chicken and Bacon Rolls

Prep time: 10 minutes | Cook time: 35 minutes | Serves 4

- 1 tablespoon fresh chives, chopped
- 8 ounces blue cheese
- 2 pounds chicken breasts, skinless, boneless, halved
- 12 bacon slices
- 2 tomatoes, chopped
- Salt and ground black pepper, to taste

1. Set a pan over medium heat, place in the bacon, cook until halfway done, remove to a plate. 2. In a bowl, stir together blue cheese, chives, tomatoes, pepper and salt. 3. Use a meat tenderizer to flatten the chicken breasts, season and lay blue cheese mixture on top. 4 Roll them up, and wrap each in a bacon slice. 5 Place the wrapped chicken breasts in a greased baking dish, and roast in the oven at 370°F for 30 minutes. 6 Serve on top of wilted kale.

Per Serving:

calories: 632 | fat: 38g | protein: 67g | carbs: 6g | net carbs: 5g | fiber: 1g

Garlic Dill Wings

Prep time: 5 minutes | Cook time: 25 minutes | Serves 4

- 2 pounds (907 g) bone-in chicken wings, separated at joints
- ½ teaspoon salt
- ½ teaspoon ground black pepper
- ½ teaspoon onion powder
- ½ teaspoon garlic powder
- 1 teaspoon dried dill

1. In a large bowl, toss wings with salt, pepper, onion powder, garlic powder, and dill until evenly coated. Place wings into ungreased air fryer basket in a single layer, working in batches if needed. 2. Adjust the temperature to 400°F (204°C) and air fry for 25 minutes, shaking the basket every 7 minutes during cooking. Wings should have an internal temperature of at least 165°F (74°C) and be golden brown when done. Serve warm.

Per Serving:

calories: 485 | fat: 33g | protein: 41g | carbs: 2g | net carbs: 2g | fiber: 0g

Bacon and Chicken Cottage Pie

Prep time: 20 minutes | Cook time: 40 minutes | Serves 4

- ½ cup onion, chopped
- 4 bacon slices
- 3 tablespoons butter
- 1 carrot, chopped
- 3 garlic cloves, minced
- Salt and ground black pepper, to taste
- ¾ cup crème fraîche
- ½ cup chicken stock
- 12 ounces chicken breasts, cubed
- 2 tablespoons Dijon mustard
- ¾ cup cheddar cheese, shredded
- For the dough
- ¾ cup almond flour
- 3 tablespoons cream cheese
- 1½ cup mozzarella cheese, shredded
- 1 egg
- 1 teaspoon onion powder
- 1 teaspoon garlic powder
- 1 teaspoon Italian seasoning
- Salt and ground black pepper, to taste

1. Set a pan over medium heat and warm butter and sauté the onion, garlic, black pepper, bacon, and carrot, for 5 minutes. Add in the chicken, and cook for 3 minutes. Stir in the crème fraîche, salt, mustard, black pepper, and stock, cook for 7 minutes. Add in the cheddar and set aside. 2. In a bowl, combine the mozzarella cheese with the cream cheese, and heat in a microwave for 1 minute. Stir in the garlic powder, salt, flour, black pepper, Italian seasoning, onion powder, and egg. Knead the dough well, split into 4 pieces, and flatten each into a circle. Set the chicken mixture into 4 ramekins, top each with a dough circle, place in an oven at 370° F for 25 minutes.

Per Serving:

calories: 871 | fat: 68g | protein: 49g | carbs: 14g | net carbs: 9g | fiber: 4g

Uncle Marty's Chicken

Prep time: 10 minutes | Cook time: 20 minutes | Serves 4

- 1½ pounds (680 g) boneless skinless chicken breasts, halved lengthwise
- Salt, to taste
- Freshly ground black pepper, to taste
- 2 eggs
- 3 tablespoons heavy (whipping) cream
- 2 cups almond flour
- 1 tablespoon dried oregano
- 1 tablespoon garlic powder
- ¼ cup olive oil

1. Cover the chicken in plastic wrap and use a meat tenderizer or heavy skillet to flatten each piece—pound it pretty vigorously so it is as thin as possible. Season with salt and pepper. 2. In a shallow dish, whisk together the eggs and cream. 3. In another shallow dish, season the almond flour with lots of salt and pepper and stir in the oregano and garlic powder. 4. Place a large skillet over medium-high heat and add the olive oil. 5. Dip each piece of chicken first in the egg wash and then in the almond flour. Coat both sides of the chicken with the flour and carefully transfer the chicken to the hot oil. Cook for about 5 minutes per side or until the almond flour starts to turn golden brown. 6. Remove from the skillet and place on a paper towel-lined platter (you can also transfer the pieces to a baking sheet and keep them warm in a 250°F (121°C) oven until ready to serve). Refrigerate leftovers in an airtight container for up to 1 week. Reheat in a skillet over medium heat until warmed through.

Per Serving:

calories: 456 | fat: 28g | protein: 45g | carbs: 6g | net carbs: 4g | fiber: 2g

Mushroom Chicken Alfredo

Prep time: 15 minutes | Cook time: 10 minutes | Serves 4

- ½ cup sliced cremini mushrooms
- ¼ cup chopped leek
- 1 tablespoon sesame oil
- 1 teaspoon chili flakes
- 1 cup heavy cream
- 1 pound (454 g) chicken fillet, chopped
- 1 teaspoon Italian seasoning
- 1 tablespoon cream cheese

1. Brush the instant pot boil with sesame oil from inside. 2. Put the chicken in the instant pot in one layer. 3. Then top it with mushrooms and leek. 4. Sprinkle the ingredients with chili flakes, heavy cream, Italian seasoning, and cream cheese. 5. Close and seal the lid. 6. Cook the meal on Manual mode (High Pressure) for 10 minutes. 7. When the time is finished, allow the natural pressure release for 10 minutes.

Per Serving:

calories: 367 | fat: 24g | protein: 34g | carbs: 2g | net carbs: 2g | fiber: 0g

Bruschetta and Cheese Stuffed Chicken

Prep time: 10 minutes | Cook time: 10 minutes | Serves 4

- ◄ 6 ounces (170 g) diced Roma tomatoes
- ◄ 2 tablespoons avocado oil
- ◄ 1 tablespoon thinly sliced fresh basil, plus more for garnish
- ◄ 1½ teaspoons balsamic vinegar
- ◄ Pinch of salt
- ◄ Pinch of black pepper
- ◄ 4 boneless, skinless chicken breasts (about 2 pounds / 907 g)
- ◄ 12 ounces (340 g) goat cheese, divided
- ◄ 2 teaspoons Italian seasoning, divided
- ◄ 1 cup water

1. Prepare the bruschetta by mixing the tomatoes, avocado oil, basil, vinegar, salt, and pepper in a small bowl. Let it marinate until the chicken is done. 2. Pat the chicken dry with a paper towel. Butterfly the breast open but do not cut all the way through. Stuff each breast with 3 ounces (85 g) of the goat cheese. Use toothpicks to close the edges. 3. Sprinkle ½ teaspoon of the Italian seasoning on top of each breast. 4. Pour the water into the pot. Place the trivet inside. Lay a piece of aluminum foil on top of the trivet and place the chicken breasts on top. It is okay if they overlap. 5. Close the lid and seal the vent. Cook on High Pressure for 10 minutes. Quick release the steam. 6. Remove the toothpicks and top each breast with one-fourth of the bruschetta.

Per Serving:

calories: 581 | fat: 34g | protein: 64g | carbs: 5g | net carbs: 4g | fiber: 1g

Buffalo Chicken Wings

Prep time: 10 minutes | Cook time: 20 to 25 minutes | Serves 4

- ◄ 2 tablespoons baking powder
- ◄ 1 teaspoon smoked paprika
- ◄ Sea salt and freshly ground black pepper, to taste
- ◄ 2 pounds (907 g) chicken wings or chicken drumettes
- ◄ Avocado oil spray
- ◄ ⅓ cup avocado oil
- ◄ ½ cup Buffalo hot sauce, such as Frank's RedHot
- ◄ ¼ cup (4 tablespoons) unsalted butter
- ◄ 2 tablespoons apple cider vinegar
- ◄ 1 teaspoon minced garlic

1. In a large bowl, stir together the baking powder, smoked paprika, and salt and pepper to taste. Add the chicken wings and toss to coat. 2. Set the air fryer to 400°F (204°C). Spray the wings with oil. 3. Place the wings in the basket in a single layer, working in batches, and air fry for 20 to 25 minutes. Check with an instant-read thermometer and remove when they reach 155°F (68°C). Let rest until they reach 165°F (74°C). 4. While the wings are cooking, whisk together the avocado oil, hot sauce, butter, vinegar, and garlic in a small saucepan over medium-low heat until warm. 5. When the wings are done cooking, toss them with the Buffalo sauce. Serve warm.

Per Serving:

calories: 616 | fat: 52g | protein: 28g | carbs: 3g | net carbs: 3g | fiber: 0g

Lemon Thyme Roasted Chicken

Prep time: 10 minutes | Cook time: 60 minutes | Serves 6

- ◄ 1 (4-pound / 1.8-kg) chicken
- ◄ 2 teaspoons dried thyme
- ◄ 1 teaspoon garlic powder
- ◄ ½ teaspoon onion powder
- ◄ 2 teaspoons dried parsley
- ◄ 1 teaspoon baking powder
- ◄ 1 medium lemon
- ◄ 2 tablespoons salted butter, melted

1. Rub chicken with thyme, garlic powder, onion powder, parsley and baking powder. 2. Slice lemon and place four slices on top of chicken, breast side up, and secure with toothpicks. Place remaining slices inside of the chicken. 3. Place entire chicken into the air fryer basket, breast side down. 4. Adjust the temperature to 350°F (177°C) and air fry for 60 minutes. 5. After 30 minutes, flip chicken so breast side is up. 6. When done, internal temperature should be 165°F (74°C) and the skin golden and crispy. To serve, pour melted butter over entire chicken.

Per Serving:

calories: 495 | fat: 32g | protein: 43g | carbs: 2g | net carbs: 2g | fiber: 1g

Indoor BBQ Chicken

Prep time: 10 minutes | Cook time: 45 minutes | Serves 4

- ◄ 1 tablespoon sriracha sauce
- ◄ 2 teaspoons chili powder
- ◄ 2 teaspoons garlic powder
- ◄ 2 teaspoons onion powder
- ◄ 1 teaspoon salt
- ◄ 1 teaspoon black pepper
- ◄ 1 tablespoon apple cider vinegar
- ◄ 1 tablespoon paprika
- ◄ 1 (1-gram) packet 0g net carb sweetener
- ◄ ½ teaspoon xanthan gum
- ◄ 1 cup crushed tomatoes
- ◄ 4 medium chicken thighs with skin

1. Preheat oven to 375°F. Line a baking sheet with parchment paper or greased foil. 2. In a small saucepan over medium-high heat, make the barbecue sauce by mixing all the ingredients except the chicken and bring to boil. Let simmer 5 minutes, stirring regularly. 3. Using a basting brush, apply about half the barbecue sauce to both sides of thighs. Place chicken on baking sheet. 4. Cook 20 minutes. Flip chicken and reapply remaining sauce. Cook another 20 minutes until chicken is thoroughly cooked. 5. Serve warm or cold.

Per Serving:

calories: 225 | fat: 12g | protein: 22g | carbs: 7g | net carbs: 5g | fiber: 2g

Turkey & Mushroom Bake

Prep time: 15 minutes | Cook time: 40 minutes | Serves 8

- ◄ 4 cups mushrooms, sliced
- ◄ 1 egg, whisked
- ◄ 3 cups green cabbage, shredded
- ◄ 3 cups turkey meat, cooked and chopped
- ◄ ½ cup chicken stock
- ◄ ½ cup cream cheese
- ◄ 1 teaspoon poultry seasoning
- ◄ 2 cups cheddar cheese, grated
- ◄ ½ cup Parmesan cheese, grated
- ◄ Salt and ground black pepper, to taste
- ◄ ¼ teaspoon garlic powder

1. Set a pan over medium-low heat. Stir in chicken broth, egg, Parmesan cheese, black pepper, garlic powder, poultry seasoning, cheddar cheese, cream cheese, and salt, and simmer. Place in the cabbage and turkey meat, and set away from the heat. 2Add the mushrooms, pepper, turkey mixture and salt in a baking dish and spread. Place aluminum foil to cover, set in an oven at 390°F, and bake for 35 minutes. Allow cooling and enjoy.

Per Serving:

calories: 473 | fat: 30g | protein: 39g | carbs: 10g | net carbs: 9g | fiber: 3g

Baked Spaghetti Squash Carbonara with Chicken

Prep time: 15 minutes | Cook time: 40 minutes | Serves 6

- ◄ 1 small spaghetti squash
- ◄ ½ cup extra-virgin olive oil, divided
- ◄ 6 ounces (170 g) thick-cut bacon (preferably nitrate-free), cut into ½-inch-thick strips
- ◄ 1 pound (454 g) boneless, skinless chicken thighs, cut into ½-inch cubes
- ◄ 4 garlic cloves, minced
- ◄ 3 large egg yolks
- ◄ ½ cup heavy cream
- ◄ 1 cup freshly grated Parmesan cheese, divided
- ◄ ¼ teaspoon freshly ground black pepper
- ◄ ¼ cup fresh Italian parsley, chopped

1. Preheat the oven to 400°F (205°C). With a very sharp knife, cut the spaghetti squash in half lengthwise. Scoop out all the seeds, and coat the cut sides of the squash with 1 tablespoon of oil per side. 2. Place squash halves cut-side down in a 9-by-13-inch glass baking dish and roast until just barely tender, 20 to 25 minutes. Remove from the oven and flip the halves to cut-side up and allow to cool for 10 minutes. 3. Meanwhile, prepare the filling. Cook the bacon in a large skillet over medium heat and fry until crispy and fat has been rendered, 4 to 5 minutes. 4. Using a slotted spoon, transfer the cooked bacon to a large bowl and cover to keep warm, reserving the rendered fat. 5. Add the remaining 2 tablespoons of olive oil to the fat in the skillet and heat over medium heat. Sauté the cubed chicken until golden and cooked through, stirring frequently, 5 to 6 minutes. Add the minced garlic and sauté for another 30 seconds.

6. Transfer the cooked chicken, garlic, and all the cooking fat to the bowl with the cooked bacon, and cover. 7. In a small bowl, beat together the egg yolks, heavy cream, ¼ cup of Parmesan, and pepper. Set aside. 8. When the cooked squash is just cool enough to handle, but still very warm (you can use potholders to handle the squash), use a fork to gently scrape the cooked flesh in rows to form long pasta-like strings and place in a large bowl. Reserve the baking dish and keep the oven on. Add the remaining ¼ cup of olive oil to the squash and toss to coat well. 9. Tossing with tongs, slowly pour the egg-and-cream mixture onto the warm squash, tossing until the eggs thicken and the cheese melts. Add the cooked bacon, chicken, and reserved fats, and toss to coat well. 10. Transfer the squash mixture and sauce to the glass baking dish, top with the remaining ¾ cup of Parmesan cheese, and cover with aluminum foil. Bake for 10 minutes. Remove the foil and bake for an additional 5 minutes, or until bubbly and cheese is golden and melted. Serve warm, garnished with chopped parsley.

Per Serving:

calories: 565 | fat: 47g | protein: 26g | carbs: 10g | net carbs: 9g | fiber: 1g

Turkey Meatloaf Florentine Muffins

Prep time: 10 minutes | Cook time: 25 minutes | Serves 6

- ◄ ½ pound (227 g) frozen spinach, thawed
- ◄ 2 pounds (907 g) ground turkey
- ◄ ½ cup (2 ounces / 57 g) blanched almond flour
- ◄ 2 large eggs
- ◄ 4 cloves garlic, minced
- ◄ 2 teaspoons sea salt
- ◄ ½ teaspoon black pepper
- ◄ 2¼ cups (9 ounces / 255 g) shredded Mozzarella cheese, divided into 1½ cups (6 ounces / 170 g) and ¾ cup (3 ounces / 85 g)
- ◄ ⅓ cup no-sugar-added marinara sauce

1. Preheat the oven to 375°F (190°C). Lightly grease 12 cups of a muffin tin and place on top of a sheet pan for easier cleanup. 2. Drain the spinach and squeeze it tightly in a kitchen towel to remove as much water as possible. 3. In a large bowl, mix together the spinach, turkey, almond flour, eggs, garlic, sea salt, and black pepper. Mix until just combined, but do not overwork the meat. 4. Fill each muffin cup with 2 tablespoons of the turkey mixture. Create a well with the back of a measuring spoon or your hands. Pack each well with 2 tablespoons Mozzarella (1½ cups or 6 ounces / 170 g total). Top with 2 more tablespoons turkey mixture, lightly pressing down along the sides to seal the filling inside. 5. Spread 1 teaspoon marinara sauce over each meatloaf muffin. Sprinkle each with another 1 tablespoon Mozzarella (¾ cup or 3 ounces / 85 g total). 6. Bake for 20 to 25 minutes, until the internal temperature reaches at least 160°F (71°C). Let rest for 5 minutes before serving (temperature will rise another 5 degrees while resting).

Per Serving:

calories: 380 | fat: 16g | protein: 52g | carbs: 6g | net carbs: 4g | fiber: 2g

Baked Chicken with Acorn Squash and Goat's Cheese

Prep time: 15 minutes | Cook time: 45 minutes | Serves 6

◄ 6 chicken breasts, butterflied
◄ 1 pound (454 g) acorn squash, cubed
◄ Salt and black pepper, to taste
◄ 1 cup goat's cheese, shredded
◄ 1 tablespoon dried parsley
◄ 3 tablespoons olive oil

1. Arrange the chicken breasts and squash in a baking dish. Season with salt, black pepper, and parsley. Drizzle with olive oil and pour a cup of water. Cover with aluminium foil and bake in the oven for 30 minutes at 420ºF. Discard the foil, scatter goat's cheese, and bake for 15-20 minutes. Remove to a serving plate and enjoy.

Per Serving:

calories: 266 | fat: 18g | protein: 21g | carbs: 5g | net carbs: 5g | fiber: 0g

Paprika Chicken Wings

Prep time: 10 minutes | Cook time: 13 minutes | Serves 4

◄ 1 pound (454 g) boneless chicken wings
◄ 1 teaspoon ground paprika
◄ 1 teaspoon avocado oil
◄ ¼ teaspoon minced garlic
◄ ¾ cup beef broth

1. Pour the avocado oil in the instant pot. 2. Rub the chicken wings with ground paprika and minced garlic and put them in the instant pot. 3. Cook the chicken on Sauté mode for 4 minutes from each side. 4. Then add beef broth and close the lid. 5. Sauté the meal for 5 minutes more.

Per Serving:

calories: 226 | fat: 9g | protein: 34g | carbs: 1g | net carbs: 1g | fiber: 0g

Paprika Chicken

Prep time: 10 minutes | Cook time: 25 minutes | Serves 4

◄ 4 (4-ounce) chicken breasts, skin-on
◄ Sea salt
◄ Freshly ground black pepper
◄ 1 tablespoon olive oil
◄ ½ cup chopped sweet onion
◄ ½ cup heavy (whipping) cream
◄ 2 teaspoons smoked paprika
◄ ½ cup sour cream
◄ 2 tablespoons chopped fresh parsley

1. Lightly season the chicken with salt and pepper. 2. Place a large skillet over medium-high heat and add the olive oil. 3. Sear the chicken on both sides until almost cooked through, about 15 minutes in total. Remove the chicken to a plate. 4. Add the onion to the skillet and sauté until tender, about 4 minutes. 5. Stir in the cream and paprika and bring the liquid to a simmer. 6. Return the chicken and any accumulated juices to the skillet and simmer the chicken for 5 minutes until completely cooked. 7. Stir in the sour cream and remove the skillet from the heat. 8. Serve topped with the parsley.

Per Serving:

calories: 389 | fat: 30g | protein: 25g | carbs: 4g | net carbs: 4g | fiber: 0g

Herby Chicken Meatballs

Prep time: 10 minutes | Cook time: 16 minutes | Serves 3

◄ 1 pound ground chicken
◄ Salt and black pepper, to taste
◄ 2 tablespoons ranch dressing
◄ ½ cup almond flour
◄ ¼ cup mozzarella cheese, grated
◄ 1 tablespoon dry Italian seasoning
◄ ¼ cup hot sauce + more for serving
◄ 1 egg

1. In a bowl, combine chicken meat, pepper, ranch dressing, Italian seasoning, flour, hot sauce, mozzarella cheese, salt, and the egg. Form 9 meatballs, arrange them on a lined baking tray and cook for 16 minutes at 480ºF. Place the chicken meatballs in a bowl and serve with the hot sauce.

Per Serving:

calories: 390 | fat: 26g | protein: 36g | carbs: 3g | net carbs: 2g | fiber: 1g

Chicken with Anchovy Tapenade

Prep time: 10 minutes | Cook time: 10 minutes | Serves 2

◄ 1 chicken breast, cut into 4 pieces
For the tapenade
◄ 1 cup black olives, pitted
◄ 1 ounce anchovy fillets, rinsed
◄ 1 garlic clove, crushed
◄ Salt and ground black
◄ 2 tablespoons coconut oil
◄ 3 garlic cloves, crushed

pepper, to taste
◄ 2 tablespoons olive oil
◄ ¼ cup fresh basil, chopped
◄ 1 tablespoon lemon juice

1.Using a food processor, combine the olives, salt, olive oil, basil, lemon juice, anchovy, and black pepper, blend well. Set a pan over medium heat and warm coconut oil, stir in the garlic, and sauté for 2 minutes. 2. Place in the chicken pieces and cook each side for 4 minutes. Split the chicken among plates and apply a topping of the anchovy tapenade.

Per Serving:

calories: 611 | fat: 52g | protein: 22g | carbs: 16g | net carbs: 12g | fiber: 4g

Balsamic Turkey Thighs

Prep time: 5 minutes | Cook time: 1 hour | Serves 8

- ◄ ¼ cup (60 ml) balsamic vinegar
- ◄ ¼ cup (60 ml) refined avocado oil or refined olive oil
- ◄ 1 tablespoon Dijon mustard
- ◄ 2 teaspoons finely ground gray sea salt
- ◄ 1 teaspoon Italian seasoning
- ◄ 2½ pounds (1.2 kg) bone-in, skin-on turkey thighs

1. Place the vinegar, oil, mustard, salt, and seasoning in a large casserole dish or resealable plastic bag. Mix thoroughly. Add the turkey thighs and cover. Marinate in the refrigerator for 1 hour or up to 24 hours. 2. When ready to cook, preheat the oven to 350°F (177°C). Lay the turkey thighs on an unlined rimmed baking sheet or cast-iron pan. Bake for 55 to 60 minutes, until the internal temperature reaches 165°F (74°C) and the juices run clear. 3. Turn the oven broiler to high. (If your oven does not offer that option, simply"broil" is fine.) Broil for 3 to 5 minutes, until browned. Allow to rest for 5 minutes before slicing and serving.

Per Serving:

calories: 333 | fat: 25g | protein: 27g | carbs: 0g | net carbs: 0g | fiber: 0g

White Wine Seared Chicken Breasts

Prep time: 10 minutes | Cook time: 30 minutes | Serves 4

- ◄ 4 medium boneless, skinless chicken breasts (8 ounces / 227 g each)
- ◄ 1 teaspoon sea salt
- ◄ ¼ teaspoon black pepper
- ◄ 4 tablespoons (½ stick) butter, cut into 1- tablespoon pats
- ◄ 2 cloves garlic, minced
- ◄ 1 medium shallot, finely chopped
- ◄ ½ cup white cooking wine
- ◄ ½ cup chicken broth
- ◄ ½ tablespoon chopped fresh parsley
- ◄ ½ tablespoon fresh thyme, chopped

1. Season the chicken on both sides with sea salt and black pepper. 2. In a large skillet or sauté pan, melt 1 tablespoon of the butter over medium-high heat. Add the chicken and sauté for 5 to 8 minutes per side, until cooked through and browned. 3. Remove the chicken from the pan and cover with foil. 4. Add another 1 tablespoon butter to the pan. Add the garlic and shallot, and sauté for about 1 minute, until fragrant. 5. Add the wine and broth to the pan and use a wooden spoon to scrape any browned bits from the bottom. Bring to a gentle boil, then lower the heat and simmer for about 7 to 8 minutes, until the liquid volume is reduced by half. 6. Reduce the heat to low. Stir in the remaining 2 tablespoons butter, parsley, and thyme, just until the butter melts. 7. Serve the sauce over the chicken.

Per Serving:

calories: 288 | fat: 14g | protein: 29g | carbs: 2g | net carbs: 2g | fiber: 0g

Chicken Breasts with Cheddar & Pepperoni

Prep time: 10 minutes | Cook time: 35 minutes | Serves 4

- ◄ 12 ounces canned tomato sauce
- ◄ 1 tablespoon olive oil
- ◄ 4 chicken breast halves, skinless and boneless
- ◄ Salt and ground black
- pepper, to taste
- ◄ 1 teaspoon dried oregano
- ◄ 4 ounces cheddar cheese, sliced
- ◄ 1 teaspoon garlic powder
- ◄ 2 ounces pepperoni, sliced

1. Preheat your oven to 390°F. In a bowl, combine chicken with oregano, salt, garlic, and pepper. 2. Heat a pan with the olive oil over medium heat, add in the chicken, cook each side for 2 minutes, and remove to a baking dish. Top with the cheddar cheese slices spread the sauce, then cover with pepperoni slices. Bake for 30 minutes. Serve warm garnished with fresh oregano if desired.

Per Serving:

calories: 348 | fat: 24g | protein: 29g | carbs: 4g | net carbs: 4g | fiber: 0g

Creamy Stuffed Chicken with Parma Ham

Prep time: 10 minutes | Cook time: 25 minutes | Serves 4

- ◄ 4 chicken breasts
- ◄ 2 tablespoons olive oil
- ◄ 3 cloves garlic, minced
- ◄ 3 shallots, finely chopped
- ◄ 4 tablespoons dried mixed
- herbs
- ◄ 8 slices Parma ham
- ◄ 8 ounces cream cheese
- ◄ 2 lemons, zested Salt to taste

1. Preheat the oven to 350°F. 2. Heat the oil in a small skillet and sauté the garlic and shallots with a pinch of salt and lemon zest for 3 minutes; let it cool. After, stir the cream cheese and mixed herbs into the shallot mixture. 3. Score a pocket in each chicken breast, fill the holes with the cream cheese mixture and cover with the cut-out chicken. Wrap each breast with two Parma ham and secure the ends with a toothpick. Lay the chicken parcels on a greased baking sheet and cook in the oven for 20 minutes. Remove to rest for 4 minutes before serving with green salad and roasted tomatoes.

Per Serving:

calories: 557 | fat: 35g | protein: 50g | carbs: 9g | net carbs: 7g | fiber: 1g

Chicken Paella with Chorizo

Prep time: 15 minutes | Cook time: 45 minutes | Serves 6

- 18 chicken drumsticks
- 12 ounces chorizo, chopped
- 1 white onion, chopped
- 4 ounces jarred piquillo peppers, finely diced
- 2 tablespoons olive oil
- ½ cup chopped parsley
- 1 teaspoon smoked paprika
- 2 tablespoons tomato puree
- ½ cup white wine
- 1 cup chicken broth
- 2 cups cauli rice
- 1 cup chopped green beans
- 1 lemon, cut in wedges
- Salt and pepper, to taste

1. Preheat the oven to 350ºF. 2. Heat the olive oil in a cast iron pan over medium heat, meanwhile season the chicken with salt and black pepper, and fry in the hot oil on both sides for 10 minutes to lightly brown. After, remove onto a plate with a perforated spoon. 3. Then, add the chorizo and onion to the hot oil, and sauté for 4. minutes. Include the tomato puree, piquillo peppers, and paprika, and let simmer for 2 minutes. Add the broth, and bring the ingredients to boil for 6 minutes until slightly reduced. 4Stir in the cauli rice, white wine, green beans, half of the parsley, and lay the chicken on top. Transfer the pan to the oven and continue cooking for 20 to 25 minutes. Let the paella sit to cool for 10 minutes before serving garnished with the remaining parsley and lemon wedges.

Per Serving:

calories: 736 | fat: 46g | protein: 56g | carbs: 15g | net carbs: 11g | fiber: 4g

Chicken Goujons with Tomato Sauce

Prep time: 15 minutes | Cook time: 40 minutes | Serves 8

- 1½ pounds chicken breasts, skinless, boneless, cubed
- Salt and ground black pepper, to taste
- 1 egg
- 1 cup almond flour
- ¼ cup Parmesan cheese, grated
- ½ teaspoon garlic powder
- 1½ teaspoons dried parsley
- ½ teaspoon dried basil
- 4 tablespoons avocado oil
- 4 cups spaghetti squash, cooked
- 6 ounces gruyere cheese, shredded
- 1½ cups tomato sauce
- Fresh basil, chopped, for serving

1. In a bowl, combine the almond flour with 1 teaspoon parsley, Parmesan cheese, black pepper, garlic powder, and salt. In a separate bowl, combine the egg with black pepper and salt. Dip the chicken in the egg, and then in almond flour mixture. 2. Set a pan over medium heat and warm 3 tablespoons avocado oil, add in the chicken, cook until golden, and remove to paper towels. In a bowl, combine the spaghetti squash with salt, dried basil, rest of the parsley, 1 tablespoon avocado oil, and black pepper. 3. Sprinkle

this into a baking dish, top with the chicken pieces, followed by the tomato sauce. Scatter shredded gruyere cheese on top, and bake for 30 minutes at 360ºF. Remove, and sprinkle with fresh basil before serving.

Per Serving:

calories: 461 | fat: 29g | protein: 34g | carbs: 16g | net carbs: 12g fiber: 4g

Fluffy Chicken

Prep time: 5 minutes | Cook time: 0 minutes | Serves 8

- ½ cup chicken broth
- 1 (1-ounce) package ranch powder seasoning mix
- 2 pounds boneless, skinless chicken breasts
- 8 ounces full-fat cream
- cheese, softened
- 8 slices no-sugar-added bacon, cooked and crumbled
- ½ cup shredded Cheddar cheese

1. Add chicken broth to slow cooker and stir in ranch powder seasoning packet. 2. Add chicken and cover. Cook 2 hours 45 minutes on high or 5 hours 15 minutes on low. 3. Remove lid Drain excess broth, leaving around ½ cup for moisture depending on preference. 4. Shred chicken. 5. In a small microwave-safe bowl microwave cream cheese 20–30 seconds. Combine with crumbled bacon and Cheddar cheese. 6. Add cream cheese mixture to shredded chicken. Cover and heat 10 minutes on high temperature until cheeses melt. Serve warm.

Per Serving:

calories: 362 | fat: 21g | protein: 36g | carbs: 3g | net carbs: 3g fiber: 0g

Cheese Stuffed Chicken

Prep time: 15 minutes | Cook time: 20 minutes | Serves 4

- 12 ounces (340 g) chicken fillet
- 4 ounces (113 g) provolone cheese, sliced
- 1 tablespoon cream cheese
- ½ teaspoon dried cilantro
- ½ teaspoon smoked paprika
- 1 cup water, for cooking

1. Beat the chicken fillet well and rub it with dried cilantro and smoked paprika. 2. Then spread it with cream cheese and top with Provolone cheese. 3. Roll the chicken fillet into the roll and wrap in the foil. 4. Pour water and insert the rack in the instant pot. 5. Place the chicken roll on the rack. Close and seal the lid. 6. Cook it on Manual mode (High Pressure) for 20 minutes. 7. Make a quick pressure release and slice the chicken roll into the servings.

Per Serving:

calories: 271 | fat: 15g | protein: 32g | carbs: 1g | net carbs: 1g fiber: 0g

Blackened Cajun Chicken Tenders

Prep time: 10 minutes | Cook time: 17 minutes | Serves 4

- 2 teaspoons paprika
- 1 teaspoon chili powder
- ½ teaspoon garlic powder
- ½ teaspoon dried thyme
- ¼ teaspoon onion powder

- ⅛ teaspoon ground cayenne pepper
- 2 tablespoons coconut oil
- 1 pound (454 g) boneless, skinless chicken tenders
- ¼ cup full-fat ranch dressing

1. In a small bowl, combine all seasonings. 2. Drizzle oil over chicken tenders and then generously coat each tender in the spice mixture. Place tenders into the air fryer basket. 3. Adjust the temperature to 375ºF (191ºC) and air fry for 17 minutes. 4. Tenders will be 165ºF (74ºC) internally when fully cooked. Serve with ranch dressing for dipping.

Per Serving:

calories: 287 | fat: 18g | protein: 27g | carbs: 3g | net carbs: 2g | fiber: 1g

Blackened Chicken

Prep time: 10 minutes | Cook time: 20 minutes | Serves 4

- 1 large egg, beaten
- ¾ cup Blackened seasoning
- 2 whole boneless, skinless chicken breasts (about 1 pound / 454

- g each), halved
- 1 to 2 tablespoons oil

1. Place the beaten egg in one shallow bowl and the Blackened seasoning in another shallow bowl. 2. One at a time, dip the chicken pieces in the beaten egg and the Blackened seasoning, coating thoroughly. 3. Preheat the air fryer to 360ºF (182ºC). Line the air fryer basket with parchment paper. 4. Place the chicken pieces on the parchment and spritz with oil. 5. Cook for 10 minutes. Flip the chicken, spritz it with oil, and cook for 10 minutes more until the internal temperature reaches 165ºF (74ºC) and the chicken is no longer pink inside. Let sit for 5 minutes before serving.

Per Serving:

calories: 270 | fat: 6g | protein: 48g | carbs: 2g | net carbs: 2g | fiber: 0g

Duck Shish Kebab

Prep time: 10 minutes | Cook time: 20 minutes | Serves 2

- 2 boneless, skin-on duck breasts, cut into 1-inch cubes
- 1 teaspoon Chinese five-spice powder
- ¼ teaspoon pink Himalayan sea salt
- ¼ teaspoon freshly ground black pepper

- 1 red bell pepper, cored, seeded, and cut into 1-inch chunks
- ½ small red onion, cut into 1-inch slices and then quartered 1 teaspoon extra-virgin olive oil

1. If using bamboo skewers, soak them in water for 30 minutes. Preheat the oven to 350ºF (180ºC). Line a baking sheet with parchment paper. 2. In a large bowl, sprinkle the duck cubes with the five-spice powder, salt, and pepper. Toss the duck to evenly distribute the seasonings. 3. Using metal or bamboo skewers, alternate pieces of bell pepper, duck, and onion, then repeat. Keep the fat side of the duck cubes facing outward in the same direction. 4. In a large sauté pan or skillet, heat the olive oil over medium-high heat. 5. Place the skewers in the skillet and cook for about 1 minute on each side, except the fat side. Cook the fat side for 2 to 3 minutes. The skewers should be browned on all sides. 6. Transfer the skewers to the baking sheet and bake for 15 to 20 minutes, until the duck is cooked through and the vegetables are tender. Serve.

Per Serving:

calories: 297 | fat: 21g | protein: 22g | carbs: 5g | net carbs: 3g | fiber: 2g

Chicken Gumbo

- 2 sausages, sliced
- 3 chicken breasts, cubed
- 1 cup celery, chopped
- 2 tablespoons dried oregano
- 2 bell peppers, seeded and chopped
- 1 onion, peeled and chopped
- 2 cups tomatoes, chopped
- 4 cups chicken broth
- 3 tablespoons dried thyme
- 2 tablespoons garlic powder
- 2 tablespoons dry mustard
- 1 teaspoon cayenne powder
- 1 tablespoon chili powder
- Salt and black pepper, to taste
- 6 tablespoons cajun seasoning
- 3 tablespoons olive oil

1. In a pot over medium heat warm olive oil. Add the sausages, chicken, pepper, onion, dry mustard, chili, tomatoes, thyme, bell peppers, salt, oregano, garlic powder, cayenne, and cajun seasoning. 2. Cook for 10 minutes. Add the remaining ingredients and bring to a boil. Reduce the heat and simmer for 20 minutes covered. Serve hot divided between bowls.

Per Serving:

calories: 376 | fat: 17g | protein: 36g | carbs: 20g | net carbs: 16g | fiber: 6g

Chicken, Eggplant and Gruyere Gratin

- 3 tablespoons butter
- 1 eggplant, chopped
- 2 tablespoons gruyere cheese, grated
- Salt and black pepper, to taste
- 2 garlic cloves, minced
- 6 chicken thighs

1.Set a pan over medium heat and warm 1 tablespoon butter, place in the chicken thighs, season with pepper and salt, cook each side for 3 minutes and lay them in a baking dish. In the same pan melt the rest of the butter and cook the garlic for 1 minute. 2. Stir in the eggplant, pepper, and salt, and cook for 10 minutes. Ladle this mixture over the chicken, spread with the cheese, set in the oven at 350ºF, and bake for 30 minutes. Turn on the oven's broiler, and broil everything for 2 minutes. Split among serving plates and enjoy.

Per Serving:

calories: 500 | fat: 35g | protein: 34g | carbs: 9g | net carbs: 8g | fiber: 2g

Chapter 5

Beef, Pork, and Lamb

Chapter 5 Beef, Pork, and Lamb

Cardamom Beef Stew Meat with Broccoli

Prep time: 10 minutes | Cook time: 50 minutes | Serves 2

- 9 ounces (255 g) beef stew meat, chopped
- 1 teaspoon ground cardamom
- ½ teaspoon salt
- 1 cup chopped broccoli
- 1 cup water

1. Preheat the instant pot on the Sauté mode. 2. When the title "Hot" is displayed, add chopped beef stew meat and cook it for 4 minutes (for 2 minutes from each side). 3. Then add the ground cardamom, salt, and broccoli. 4. Add water and close the instant pot lid. 5. Sauté the stew for 45 minutes to get the tender taste. 6. Enjoy!

Per Serving:

calories: 256 | fat: 8g | protein: 40g | carbs: 4g | net carbs: 2g | fiber: 2g

Sausage and Pork Meatballs

Prep time: 15 minutes | Cook time: 8 to 12 minutes | Serves 8

- 1 large egg
- 1 teaspoon gelatin
- 1 pound (454 g) ground pork
- ½ pound (227 g) Italian sausage, casings removed, crumbled
- ⅓ cup Parmesan cheese
- ¼ cup finely diced onion
- 1 tablespoon tomato paste
- 1 teaspoon minced garlic
- 1 teaspoon dried oregano
- ¼ teaspoon red pepper flakes
- Sea salt and freshly ground black pepper, to taste
- Keto-friendly marinara sauce, for serving

1. Beat the egg in a small bowl and sprinkle with the gelatin. Allow to sit for 5 minutes. 2. In a large bowl, combine the ground pork, sausage, Parmesan, onion, tomato paste, garlic, oregano, and red pepper flakes. Season with salt and black pepper. 3. Stir the gelatin mixture, then add it to the other ingredients and, using clean hands, mix to ensure that everything is well combined. Form into 1½-inch round meatballs. 4. Set the air fryer to 400°F (204°C). Place the meatballs in the air fryer basket in a single layer, cooking in batches as needed. Air fry for 5 minutes. Flip and cook for 3 to 7 minutes more, or until an instant-read thermometer reads 160°F (71°C).

Per Serving:

calories: 285 | fat: 20g | protein: 22g | carbs: 3g | net carbs: 2g | fiber: 1g

Cilantro Lime Shredded Pork

Prep time: 5 minutes | Cook time: 30 minutes | Serves 4

- 1 tablespoon chili adobo sauce
- 1 tablespoon chili powder
- 2 teaspoons salt
- 1 teaspoon garlic powder
- 1 teaspoon cumin
- ½ teaspoon pepper
- 1 (2½ to 3 pounds / 1.1 to 1.4 kg) cubed pork butt
- 1 tablespoon coconut oil
- 2 cups beef broth
- 1 lime, cut into wedges
- ¼ cup chopped cilantro

1. In a small bowl, mix adobo sauce, chili powder, salt, garlic powder, cumin, and pepper. 2. Press the Sauté button on Instant Pot and add coconut oil to pot. Rub spice mixture onto cubed pork butt. Place pork into pot and sear for 3 to 5 minutes per side. Add broth. 3. Press the Cancel button. Lock Lid. Press the Manual button and adjust time to 30 minutes. 4. When timer beeps, let pressure naturally release until the float valve drops, and unlock lid. 5. Shred pork with fork. Pork should easily fall apart. For extra-crispy pork, place single layer in skillet on stove over medium heat. Cook for 10 to 15 minutes or until water has cooked out and pork becomes brown and crisp. Serve warm with fresh lime wedges and cilantro garnish.

Per Serving:

calories: 570 | fat: 36g | protein: 55g | carbs: 3g | net carbs: 2g | fiber: 1g

Baked Crustless Pizza

Prep time: 5 minutes | Cook time: 20 minutes | Serves 2

- 8 ounces (227 g) chopped Italian sausage
- 15 slices pepperoni
- 10 large black olives, sliced
- ½ cup grated Mozzarella cheese

1. Preheat the oven to 350°F (180°C). 2. In a skillet over medium heat, cook the sausage. Drain the grease and spread the sausage on the bottom of an 8-by-8-inch baking dish or pie pan. 3. Layer the pepperoni slices, black olives, and cheese over the sausage. 4. Bake, covered, for 10 to 15 minutes or until the cheese is melted and hot throughout.

Per Serving:

½ skillet: calories: 480 | fat: 40g | protein: 27g | carbs: 3g | net carbs: 2g | fiber: 1g

Rib Eye with Chimichurri Sauce

Prep time: 15 minutes | Cook time: 15 minutes | Serves 4

For The Chimichurri:
- ½ cup good-quality olive oil
- ½ cup finely chopped fresh parsley
- 2 tablespoons red wine vinegar
- 2 tablespoons finely chopped fresh cilantro

For The Steak:
- 4 (5-ounce) rib eye steaks
- 1 tablespoon good-quality olive oil

- 1½ tablespoons minced garlic
- 1 tablespoon finely chopped chile pepper
- ½ teaspoon sea salt
- ¼ teaspoon freshly ground black pepper

- Sea salt, for seasoning
- Freshly ground black pepper, for seasoning

Make The Chimichurri: 1. In a medium bowl, stir together the olive oil, parsley, vinegar, cilantro, garlic, chile, salt, and pepper. Let it stand for 15 minutes to mellow the flavors. Make The Steak: 1. Prepare the steaks. Let the steaks come to room temperature and lightly oil them with the olive oil and season them with salt and pepper. 2. Grill the steaks. Preheat the grill to high heat. Grill the steaks for 6 to 7 minutes per side for medium (140°F internal temperature) or until they're done the way you like them. 3. Rest and serve. Let the steaks rest for 10 minutes and then serve them topped with generous spoonfuls of the chimichurri sauce.

Per Serving:

calories: 503 | fat: 42g | protein: 29g | carbs: 1g | net carbs: 1g | fiber: 0g

Crispy Baked Pork Chops with Mushroom Gravy

Prep time: 10 minutes | Cook time: 25 minutes | Serves 4

- 4 tablespoons extra-virgin olive oil, divided
- ½ cup almond flour
- 2 teaspoons dried sage, divided
- 1½ teaspoons salt, divided
- ½ teaspoon freshly ground black pepper, divided
- 1 large egg
- ¼ cup flax meal
- ¼ cup walnuts, very finely chopped

- 4 (4-ounce / 113-g) boneless pork chops
- 1 tablespoon unsalted butter
- 4 ounces (113 g) chopped mushrooms
- 2 cloves garlic, minced
- 1 teaspoon dried thyme
- 8 ounces (227 g) cream cheese, room temperature
- ½ cup heavy cream
- ¼ cup chicken stock

1. Preheat the oven to 400ºF (205ºC). Line a baking sheet with aluminum foil and coat with 1 tablespoon of olive oil. 2. In a small, shallow bowl, combine the almond flour, 1 teaspoon of sage, ½ teaspoon of salt, and ¼ teaspoon of pepper. In a second small bowl, whisk the egg. In a third small bowl, stir together the flax meal and walnuts. 3. One at a time, dredge each pork chop first in the flour mixture, then in the egg, then in the flax-and-walnut mixture to fully coat all sides. Place on the prepared baking sheet and drizzle the pork chops evenly with 1 tablespoon of olive oil. 4. Bake until cooked through and golden brown, 18 to 25 minutes, depending on the thickness of the pork. 5. While the pork is baking, prepare the gravy. Heat the remaining 2 tablespoons of olive oil and the butter in a medium saucepan over medium heat. Add the mushrooms and sauté until very tender, 4 to 6 minutes. Add the garlic, remaining 1 teaspoon of sage and 1 teaspoon of salt, thyme, and remaining ¼ teaspoon of pepper, and sauté for an additional 30 seconds. 6. Add the cream cheese to the mushrooms, reduce heat to low, and stir until melted and creamy, 2 to 3 minutes. Whisk in the cream and stock until smooth. Cook over low heat, whisking frequently, until the mixture is thick and creamy, another 3 to 4 minutes. 7. Serve each pork chop covered with a quarter of the mushroom gravy.

Per Serving:

calories: 799 | fat: 69g | protein: 36g | carbs: 11g | net carbs: 7g | fiber: 4g

Low-Carb Chili

Prep time: 15 minutes | Cook time: 3 hours | Serves 6

- 2 tablespoons olive oil
- 1 large onion, diced
- 3 garlic cloves, minced
- 1 medium red bell pepper, chopped
- 1 medium yellow bell pepper, chopped
- 2 pounds (907 g) ground beef
- 1 (6-ounce / 170-g) can tomato paste
- 4 cups water
- 1 tablespoon chili powder
- 1½ teaspoons red pepper flakes

- 1 teaspoon ground cumin
- 1 teaspoon paprika
- ¾ teaspoon dry mustard
- ¾ teaspoon ground coriander
- ½ teaspoon dried oregano
- ½ teaspoon ground allspice
- 2 cups beef broth
- 1½ teaspoons ground cayenne pepper (more or less depending on your heat preference)
- ½ cup apple cider vinegar
- Sliced scallion, green parts only, for garnish

1. In a large saucepan over medium heat, heat the olive oil. 2. Add the onion, garlic, and red and yellow bell peppers. Sauté for about 5 minutes until the vegetables cook down. 3. Add the beef. Cook for 5 to 7 minutes, stirring with a wooden spoon and breaking up the beef until mostly browned. 4. Add the tomato paste and water. Give it a good stir. 5. Stir in the chili powder, red pepper flakes, cumin, paprika, mustard, coriander, oregano, and allspice. Bring the chili to a low boil, reduce the heat to simmer, cover the pan, and cook for at least 2 hours. Periodically check the chili and stir in some broth when it starts getting thick. 6. About 20 minutes before serving, stir in the cayenne and vinegar. Spoon into bowls and top with scallion.

Per Serving:

calories: 551 | fat: 43g | protein: 28g | carbs: 13g | net carbs: 10g | fiber: 3g

Italian Sausage Stew

Prep time: 15 minutes | Cook time: 22 minutes | Serves 6

- ◁ 1 pound Italian sausage, sliced
- ◁ 1 red bell pepper, seeded and chopped
- ◁ 2 onions, chopped
- ◁ Salt and black pepper, to taste
- ◁ 1 cup fresh parsley, chopped
- ◁ 6 green onions, chopped
- ◁ ¼ cup avocado oil
- ◁ 1 cup beef stock
- ◁ 4 garlic cloves
- ◁ 24 ounces canned diced tomatoes
- ◁ 16 ounces okra, trimmed and sliced
- ◁ 6 ounces tomato sauce
- ◁ 2 tablespoons coconut aminos
- ◁ 1 tablespoon hot sauce

1. Set a pot over medium heat and warm oil, place in the sausages, and cook for 2 minutes. Stir in the onions, green onions, garlic, black pepper, bell pepper, and salt, and cook for 5 minutes. 2. Add in the hot sauce, stock, tomatoes, coconut aminos, okra, and tomato sauce, bring to a simmer and cook for 15 minutes. Adjust the seasoning with salt and black pepper. Share into serving bowls and sprinkle with fresh parsley to serve.

Per Serving:

calories: 435 | fat: 28g | protein: 23g | carbs: 20g | net carbs: 16g | fiber: 4g

Bacon Mac 'n' Cheese

Prep time: 10 minutes | Cook time: 50 minutes | Serves 4

- ◁ 1 large head cauliflower (about 1⅔ pounds/750 g), cored and broken into ½-inch (1¼-cm) pieces
- ◁ ⅓ cup (22 g) finely chopped fresh parsley
- ◁ 6 strips bacon (about 6 ounces/170 g), cooked until crisp, then crumbled (reserve the grease)
- ◁ 2 cups (475 ml) unsweetened nondairy milk
- ◁ 2 tablespoons unflavored gelatin
- ◁ 1 tablespoon fresh lemon juice
- ◁ 1 teaspoon onion powder
- ◁ 1 teaspoon finely ground gray sea salt
- ◁ ¼ teaspoon garlic powder
- ◁ ⅓ cup (22 g) nutritional yeast
- ◁ 2 large eggs, beaten
- ◁ 2 teaspoons prepared yellow mustard
- ◁ 2 ounces (60 g) pork dust or ground pork rinds

1. Preheat the oven to 350°F (177°C) and grease a shallow 1½-quart (1.4-L) casserole dish with coconut oil. Set aside. 2. Place the cauliflower, parsley, and bacon in a large bowl and toss to combine. 3. Place the reserved bacon grease, milk, gelatin, lemon juice, onion powder, salt, and garlic powder in a medium-sized saucepan. Bring to a boil over medium heat, whisking occasionally. Once boiling, continue to boil for 5 minutes. 4. Whisk in the nutritional yeast, eggs, and mustard and gently cook for 3 minutes, whisking constantly. 5. Remove the saucepan from the heat and pour the "cheese" sauce over the cauliflower mixture. (If you've overcooked the sauce or didn't whisk it well enough, you may end up with small pieces of cooked egg; for an ultra-smooth sauce, pour the sauce through a fine-mesh strainer.) Toss with a spatula until all the cauliflower pieces are coated in the cheese sauce. 6. Transfer the coated cauliflower to the prepared casserole dish and smooth it out with the back of a spatula. Sprinkle the pork dust evenly over the top. Bake for 40 to 45 minutes, until the cauliflower is fork-tender, checking with a sharp knife on the edge of the casserole. 7. Allow to sit for 15 minutes before serving.

Per Serving:

calories: 440 | fat: 27g | protein: 35g | carbs: 15g | net carbs: 8g | fiber: 7g

Onion Pork Kebabs

Prep time: 22 minutes | Cook time: 18 minutes | Serves 3

- ◁ 2 tablespoons tomato purée
- ◁ ½ fresh serrano, minced
- ◁ ⅓ teaspoon paprika
- ◁ 1 pound (454 g) pork, ground
- ◁ ½ cup green onions, finely chopped
- ◁ 3 cloves garlic, peeled and finely minced
- ◁ 1 teaspoon ground black pepper, or more to taste
- ◁ 1 teaspoon salt, or more to taste

1. Thoroughly combine all ingredients in a mixing dish. Then form your mixture into sausage shapes. 2. Cook for 18 minutes at 355°F (179°C). Mound salad on a serving platter, top with air-fried kebabs and serve warm. Bon appétit!

Per Serving:

calories: 355 | fat: 23g | protein: 29g | carbs: 6g | net carbs: 4g | fiber: 2g

Winter Veal and Sauerkraut

Prep time: 10 minutes | Cook time: 1 hour | Serves 4

- ◁ 1 pound veal, cut into cubes
- ◁ 18 ounces sauerkraut, rinsed and drained
- ◁ Salt and black pepper, to taste
- ◁ ½ cup ham, chopped
- ◁ 1 onion, chopped
- ◁ 2 garlic cloves, minced
- ◁ 1 tablespoon butter
- ◁ ½ cup Parmesan cheese, grated
- ◁ ½ cup sour cream

1. Heat a pot with the butter over medium heat, add in the onion, and cook for 3 minutes. Stir in garlic, and cook for 1 minute. Place in the veal and ham, and cook until slightly browned. Place in the sauerkraut, and cook until the meat becomes tender, about 30 minutes. Stir in sour cream, pepper, and salt. Top with Parmesan cheese and bake for 20 minutes at 350°F.

Per Serving:

calories: 410 | fat: 25g | protein: 32g | carbs: 10g | net carbs: 6g | fiber: 4g

Breaded Pork Chops

Prep time: 5 minutes | Cook time: 20 minutes | Serves 2

- 2 (8-ounce / 227-g) boneless pork loin chops
- ¼ cup pork panko crumbs
- 1 teaspoon extra-virgin olive oil
- 1 teaspoon grated Parmesan cheese
- ¼ teaspoon pink Himalayan sea salt
- ¼ teaspoon onion powder
- ¼ teaspoon paprika
- ¼ teaspoon garlic powder
- ⅛ teaspoon freshly ground black pepper
- ⅛ teaspoon dried parsley
- ⅛ teaspoon dried basil
- ⅛ teaspoon dried oregano
- Pinch of cayenne pepper

1. Preheat the oven to 425°F (220°C). Place a baking rack on a small baking sheet. 2. Pat the chops dry with a paper towel. 3. In a food processor, combine the pork crumbs, olive oil, Parmesan, salt, onion powder, paprika, garlic powder, pepper, parsley, basil, oregano, and cayenne and run on high until the mixture forms a uniform, fine powder. Transfer the mixture to a resealable 1-gallon plastic bag. 4. Add the chops to the bag, one at a time, shaking to coat them in the breading. 5. Transfer the chops to the rack and bake for 20 minutes, until an instant-read thermometer registers 160°F (71°C) or the juices run clear when the meat is pierced.

Per Serving:

calories: 435 | fat: 23g | protein: 57g | carbs: 0g | net carbs: 0g | fiber: 0g

Chicken Fried Steak with Cream Gravy

Prep time: 5 minutes | Cook time: 10 minutes | Serves 4

- 4 small thin cube steaks (about 1 pound / 454 g)
- ½ teaspoon salt
- ½ teaspoon freshly ground black pepper

Cream Gravy:
- ½ cup heavy cream
- 2 ounces (57 g) cream cheese
- ¼ cup bacon grease
- 2 to 3 tablespoons water
- ¼ teaspoon garlic powder
- 1 egg, lightly beaten
- 1 cup crushed pork rinds (about 3 ounces / 85 g)

- 2 to 3 dashes Worcestershire sauce
- Salt and freshly ground black pepper, to taste

1. Preheat the air fryer to 400°F (204°C). 2. Working one at a time, place the steak between two sheets of parchment paper and use a meat mallet to pound to an even thickness. 3. In a small bowl, combine the salt, pepper, and garlic power. Season both sides of each steak with the mixture. 4. Place the egg in a small shallow dish and the pork rinds in another small shallow dish. Dip each steak first in the egg wash, followed by the pork rinds, pressing lightly to form an even coating. Working in batches if necessary, arrange the steaks in a single layer in the air fryer basket. Air fry for 10 minutes until crispy and cooked through. 5. To make the cream gravy: In

a heavy-bottomed pot, warm the cream, cream cheese, and bacon grease over medium heat, whisking until smooth. Lower the heat if the mixture begins to boil. Continue whisking as you slowly add the water, 1 tablespoon at a time, until the sauce reaches the desired consistency. Season with the Worcestershire sauce and salt and pepper to taste. Serve over the chicken fried steaks.

Per Serving:

calories: 527 | fat: 46g | protein: 28g | carbs: 1g | net carbs: 1g | fiber: 0g

Pancetta Sausage with Kale

Prep time: 15 minutes | Cook time: 20 minutes | Serves 8

- 2 cups kale
- 8 cups chicken broth
- A drizzle of olive oil
- 1 cup heavy cream
- 6 pancetta slices, chopped
- 1 pound (454 g) radishes, chopped
- 2 garlic cloves, minced
- Salt and black pepper, to taste
- A pinch of red pepper flakes
- 1 onion, chopped
- 1½ pounds hot pork sausage, chopped

1. Set a pot over medium heat. Add in a drizzle of olive oil and warm. Stir in garlic, onion, pancetta, and sausage; cook for 5 minutes. Pour in broth, radishes, and kale, and simmer for 10 minutes. 2. Stir in salt, red pepper flakes, black pepper, and heavy cream, and cook for about 5 minutes. Serve.

Per Serving:

calories: 432 | fat: 36g | protein: 21g | carbs: 8g | net carbs: 6g | fiber: 2g

Deconstructed Egg Rolls

Prep time: 10 minutes | Cook time: 15 minutes | Serves 6

- 1 pound (454 g) ground pork
- 1 tablespoon untoasted, cold-pressed sesame oil
- 6 cups finely shredded cabbage
- 2 teaspoons minced garlic
- 1 tablespoon minced fresh ginger
- 1 tablespoon coconut aminos or wheat-free tamari
- 1 teaspoon fish sauce (optional)
- ¼ cup chopped green onions, for garnish

1. Place the pork and oil in a large cast-iron skillet over medium-high heat and cook, crumbling the meat with a wooden spoon, until cooked through, about 10 minutes. (Do not drain the drippings from the pan.) 2. Add the cabbage, garlic, ginger, coconut aminos, and fish sauce, if using, to the skillet. Sauté until the cabbage is soft, 3 to 5 minutes. 3. Divide among six plates or bowls and serve garnished with the green onions.

Per Serving:

calories: 250 | fat: 19g | protein: 14g | carbs: 6g | net carbs: 3g | fiber: 3g

Beef Sausage Meat Loaf

Prep time: 10 minutes | Cook time: 1 hour 15 minutes | Serves 6

- ◀ 1½ pounds Italian sausage meat
- ◀ 1 pound grass-fed ground beef
- ◀ ½ cup almond flour
- ◀ ¼ cup heavy (whipping) cream
- ◀ 1 egg, lightly beaten
- ◀ ½ onion, finely chopped
- ◀ ½ red bell pepper, chopped
- ◀ 2 teaspoons minced garlic
- ◀ 1 teaspoon dried oregano
- ◀ ¼ teaspoon sea salt
- ◀ ⅛ teaspoon freshly ground black pepper

1. Preheat the oven. Set the oven temperature to 400°F. 2. Make the meat loaf. In a large bowl, mix together the sausage, ground beef, almond flour, cream, egg, onion, red bell pepper, garlic, oregano, salt, and pepper until everything is well combined. Press the mixture into a 9-inch loaf pan. 3. Bake. Bake for 1 hour to 1 hour and 15 minutes, or until the meat loaf is cooked through. Drain off and throw out any grease and let the meat loaf stand for 10 minutes. 4. Serve. Cut the meat loaf into six slices, divide them between six plates, and serve it immediately.

Per Serving:

calories: 394 | fat: 34g | protein: 19g | carbs: 1g | net carbs: 1g | fiber: 0g

Osso Buco with Gremolata

Prep time: 35 minutes | Cook time: 1 hour 2 minutes | Serves 6

- ◀ 4 bone-in beef shanks
- ◀ Sea salt, to taste
- ◀ 2 tablespoons avocado oil
- ◀ 1 small turnip, diced
- ◀ 1 medium onion, diced
- ◀ 1 medium stalk celery, diced
- ◀ 4 cloves garlic, smashed

For the Gremolata:

- ◀ ½ cup loosely packed parsley leaves
- ◀ 1 tablespoon unsweetened tomato purée
- ◀ ½ cup dry white wine
- ◀ 1 cup chicken broth
- ◀ 1 sprig fresh rosemary
- ◀ 2 sprigs fresh thyme
- ◀ 3 Roma tomatoes, diced
- ◀ 1 clove garlic, crushed
- ◀ Grated zest of 2 lemons

1. On a clean work surface, season the shanks all over with salt. 2. Set the Instant Pot to Sauté and add the oil. When the oil shimmers, add 2 shanks and sear for 4 minutes per side. Remove the shanks to a bowl and repeat with the remaining shanks. Set aside. 3. Add the turnip, onion, and celery to the pot and cook for 5 minutes or until softened. 4. Add the garlic and unsweetened tomato purée and cook 1 minute more, stirring frequently. 5. Deglaze the pot with the wine, scraping the bottom with a wooden spoon to loosen any browned bits. Bring to a boil. 6. Add the broth, rosemary, thyme, and shanks, then add the tomatoes on top of the shanks. 7. Secure the lid. Press the Manual button and set cooking time for 40 minutes on High Pressure. 8. Meanwhile, for the gremolata: In a small food processor, combine the parsley, garlic, and lemon zest and pulse until the parsley is finely chopped. Refrigerate until ready to use.

9. When timer beeps, allow the pressure to release naturally for 20 minutes, then release any remaining pressure. Open the lid. 10. To serve, transfer the shanks to large, shallow serving bowl. Ladle the braising sauce over the top and sprinkle with the gremolata.

Per Serving:

calories: 605 | fat: 30g | protein: 69g | carbs: 8g | net carbs: 6g | fiber: 2g

Mediterranean Beef Steaks

Prep time: 20 minutes | Cook time: 20 minutes | Serves 4

- ◀ 2 tablespoons coconut aminos
- ◀ 3 heaping tablespoons fresh chives
- ◀ 2 tablespoons olive oil
- ◀ 3 tablespoons dry white wine
- ◀ 4 small-sized beef steaks
- ◀ 2 teaspoons smoked cayenne pepper
- ◀ ½ teaspoon dried basil
- ◀ ½ teaspoon dried rosemary
- ◀ 1 teaspoon freshly ground black pepper
- ◀ 1 teaspoon sea salt, or more to taste

1. Firstly, coat the steaks with the cayenne pepper, black pepper, salt, basil, and rosemary. 2. Drizzle the steaks with olive oil, white wine, and coconut aminos. 3. Finally, roast in the air fryer for 20 minutes at 340°F (171°C). Serve garnished with fresh chives. Bon appétit!

Per Serving:

calories: 276 | fat: 17g | protein: 26g | carbs: 2g | net carbs: 1g | fiber: 1g

Spinach and Provolone Steak Rolls

Prep time: 10 minutes | Cook time: 12 minutes | Makes 8 rolls

- ◀ 1 (1 pound / 454 g) flank steak, butterflied
- ◀ 8 (1 ounce / 28 g, ¼-inch-thick) deli slices provolone cheese
- ◀ 1 cup fresh spinach leaves
- ◀ ½ teaspoon salt
- ◀ ¼ teaspoon ground black pepper

1. Place steak on a large plate. Place provolone slices to cover steak, leaving 1-inch at the edges. Lay spinach leaves over cheese. Gently roll steak and tie with kitchen twine or secure with toothpicks. Carefully slice into eight pieces. Sprinkle each with salt and pepper. 2. Place rolls into ungreased air fryer basket, cut side up. Adjust the temperature to 400°F (204°C) and air fry for 12 minutes. Steak rolls will be browned and cheese will be melted when done and have an internal temperature of at least 150°F (66°C) for medium steak and 180°F (82°C) for well-done steak. Serve warm.

Per Serving:

calories: 199 | fat: 12g | protein: 23g | carbs: 1g | net carbs: 0g | fiber: 1g

Juicy No-Fail Burger

Prep time: 10 minutes | Cook time: 15 minutes | Serves 4

- 1 pound grass-fed ground beef
- 1 egg, lightly beaten
- ½ onion, finely chopped
- 1 teaspoon minced garlic
- 1 teaspoon Worcestershire
- sauce
- 1 teaspoon dried parsley
- ¼ teaspoon sea salt
- ⅛ teaspoon freshly ground black pepper
- 1 tablespoon olive oil

1. Make the burgers. In a medium bowl, combine the ground beef, egg, onion, garlic, Worcestershire sauce, parsley, salt, and pepper until everything is well mixed. Form the mixture into four equal patties, each about ¾ inch thick. Lightly oil the patties with olive oil. 2. Grill the burgers. Preheat the grill to medium heat. Grill the burgers, turning them once, until they're just cooked through (160°F internal temperature), about 8 minutes per side. 3. Serve. Let the burgers rest for 5 minutes, then serve them immediately.

Per Serving:

calories: 379 | fat: 33g | protein: 19g | carbs: 1g | net carbs: 1g | fiber: 0g

Korean Beef and Pickled Vegetable Bowls

Prep time: 15 minutes | Cook time: 10 minutes | Serves 6

- 1 tablespoon vegetable oil
- 5 garlic cloves, thinly sliced
- 1 tablespoon julienned fresh ginger
- 2 dried red chiles
- 1 cup sliced onions
- 1 pound (454 g) 80% lean ground beef
- 1 tablespoon gochujang, adjusted to taste
- 1 cup fresh basil leaves, divided
- 1 tablespoon coconut aminos
- 1 teaspoon Swerve
- 2 tablespoons freshly squeezed lime juice
- 1 teaspoon salt
- 1 teaspoon freshly ground pepper
- ¼ cup water
- 1 teaspoon sesame oil
- For the Pickled Vegetables:
- 1 cucumber, peeled, coarsely grated
- 1 turnip, coarsely grated
- ¼ cup white vinegar
- ½ teaspoon salt
- ½ teaspoon Swerve

1. Select Sauté mode of the Instant Pot. When the pot is hot, add the oil and heat until it is shimmering. 2. Add the garlic, ginger, and chiles and sauté for 1 minute. 3. Add the onions and sauté for 1 minute. 4. Add the ground beef and cooking for 4 minutes.. 5. Add the gochujang, ½ cup of basil, coconut aminos, sweetener, lime juice, salt, pepper, water, and sesame oil, and stir to combine. 6. Lock the lid. Select Manual mode. Set the time for 4 minutes on High Pressure. 7. When cooking is complete, let the pressure release naturally for 5 minutes, then release any remaining pressure. Unlock the lid and stir in the remaining ½ cup of basil. 8. Meanwhile, put the cucumber and turnip in a medium bowl and mix with the vinegar, salt, and sweetener. To serve, portion the basil beef into individual bowls and serve with the pickled salad.

Per Serving:

calories: 298 | fat: 20g | protein: 22g | carbs: 8g | net carbs: 7g | fiber: 1g

Chipotle-Spiced Meatball Subs

Prep time: 15 minutes | Cook time: 35 minutes | Serves 15

Meatballs:
- 1⅔ pounds (750 g) ground pork
- 1 pound (455 g) ground chicken
- ½ cup (160 g) grated white onions

Sauce:
- 2½ cups (600 ml) crushed tomatoes
- ½ cup (120 ml) refined avocado oil or melted chicken fat
- ⅔ cup (80 ml) chicken bone broth
- 1 tablespoon dried oregano leaves

For Serving:
- 1 large head green cabbage
- Finely chopped fresh

- 1½ teaspoons dried oregano leaves
- 1¼ teaspoons ground cumin
- 1 teaspoon finely ground gray sea salt

- 1¼ teaspoons chipotle powder
- 1 teaspoon garlic powder
- ½ teaspoon onion powder
- ½ teaspoon smoked paprika
- ½ teaspoon finely ground gray sea salt
- ¼ teaspoon ground black pepper

cilantro (optional)

1. Preheat the oven to 350°F (177°C) and line a rimmed baking sheet with parchment paper or a silicone baking mat. 2. Place the ingredients for the meatballs in a large bowl. Mix with your hands until combined. 3. Wet your hands and pinch a 1½-tablespoon piece from the bowl, then roll it between your palms to form a ball. Place on the prepared baking sheet and repeat with the remaining meat mixture, making a total of 30 meatballs. Keeping your palms wet will help you shape the meatballs quicker. 4. Bake the meatballs for 25 to 30 minutes, until the internal temperature reaches 165°F (74°C). 5. Meanwhile, place the ingredients for the sauce in a large saucepan. Stir to combine, then cover, placing the lid slightly askew to allow steam to escape. Bring to a boil over medium-high heat, then reduce the heat to low and simmer for 20 minutes. 6. While the meatballs and sauce are cooking, remove 30 medium-sized leaves from the head of cabbage and lightly steam for 1 to 2 minutes. 7. Remove the meatballs from the oven and transfer to the saucepan with the sauce. Turn them to coat, cover, and cook on low for 5 minutes. 8. To serve, stack 2 cabbage leaves on top of one another, top with 2 meatballs, a dollop of extra sauce, and a sprinkle of cilantro, if using.

Per Serving:

calories: 253 | fat: 17g | protein: 18g | carbs: 8g | net carbs: 5g | fiber: 3g

Baked Pork Meatballs in Pasta Sauce

Prep time: 10 minutes | Cook time: 35 minutes | Serves 6

- 2 pounds (907 g) ground pork
- 1 tablespoon olive oil
- 1 cup pork rinds, crushed
- 3 cloves garlic, minced
- ½ cup coconut milk
- 2 eggs, beaten
- ½ cup grated Parmesan cheese
- ½ cup grated asiago cheese
- Salt and black pepper to taste
- ¼ cup chopped parsley
- 2 jars sugar-free marinara sauce
- ½ teaspoon Italian seasoning
- 1 cup Italian blend kinds of cheeses
- Chopped basil to garnish

1. Preheat the oven to 400ºF, line a cast iron pan with foil and oil it with cooking spray. Set aside. 2. Combine the coconut milk and pork rinds in a bowl. Mix in the ground pork, garlic, Asiago cheese, Parmesan cheese, eggs, salt, and pepper, just until combined. Form balls of the mixture and place them in the prepared pan. Bake in the oven for 20 minutes at a reduced temperature of 370ºF. 3. Transfer the meatballs to a plate. Pour half of the marinara sauce in the baking pan. Place the meatballs back in the pan and pour the remaining marinara sauce all over them. Sprinkle with the Italian blend cheeses, drizzle with the olive oil, and then sprinkle with Italian seasoning. 4. Cover the pan with foil and put it back in the oven to bake for 10 minutes. After, remove the foil, and cook for 5 minutes. Once ready, take out the pan and garnish with basil. Serve on a bed of squash spaghetti.

Per Serving:

calories: 575 | fat: 43g | protein: 39g | carbs: 8g | net carbs: 5g | fiber: 3g

Pork Cubes with Fennel

Prep time: 8 minutes | Cook time: 30 minutes | Serves 2

- 1 teaspoon lemon juice
- 10 ounces (283 g) pork loin, chopped
- ½ cup water
- 1 ounce (28 g) fennel, chopped
- 1 teaspoon salt
- ½ teaspoon peppercorns

1. Sprinkle the chopped pork loin with the lemon juice. 2. Then strew the meat with the salt. 3. Place the meat in the meat mold. 4. Insert the meat mold in the instant pot. 5. Add water, fennel, and peppercorns. 6. Close the lid and lock it. 7. Set the Meat/Stew mode and put a timer on 30 minutes. 8. Serve the pork cubes with hot gravy.

Per Serving:

calories: 349 | fat: 20g | protein: 39g | carbs: 2g | net carbs: 1g | fiber: 1g

Easy Smoked Ham Hocks with Smoky Whole-Grain Mustard

Prep time: 5 minutes | Cook time: 10 minutes | Serves 4

- Smoky Whole-Grain Mustard:
- ¼ cup prepared yellow mustard
- ¼ cup brown mustard seeds
- 2 tablespoons Swerve confectioners'-style sweetener or equivalent amount of liquid or powdered sweetener
- ¼ cup coconut vinegar or apple cider vinegar
- 2 teaspoons chili powder
- ½ teaspoon freshly ground black pepper
- 2 tablespoons coconut oil, melted
- ½ teaspoon liquid smoke
- 4 (3 ounces / 85 g) smoked ham hock steaks
- 2 cups sauerkraut, warmed, for serving
- Cornichons or other pickles of choice, for serving

1. To make the mustard: In a small bowl, stir together the prepared mustard, mustard seeds, sweetener, vinegar, chili powder, and pepper. Stir in the melted coconut oil and liquid smoke; mix well to combine. Refrigerate overnight to allow the flavors to blend before using. 2. Preheat the oven to 425ºF (220ºC). Place the smoked ham hocks on a rimmed baking sheet and bake for 10 minutes, or until the skin gets crispy. 3. Place each ham hock on a plate with ½ cup sauerkraut and 2 to 4 tablespoons of the smoky mustard. 4. Store extras in an airtight container in the fridge for up to 3 days. To reheat, place in a skillet over medium heat and sauté for 3 minutes per side, or until warmed to your liking.

Per Serving:

calories: 195 | fat: 15g | protein: 9g | carbs: 6g | net carbs: 4g | fiber: 2g

Pork Adobo

Prep time: 10 minutes | Cook time: 30 minutes | Serves 6

- 1 pound (454 g) pork belly, chopped
- 1 bay leaf
- 1 teaspoon salt
- 2 tablespoons apple cider
- vinegar
- 1 teaspoon cayenne pepper
- 1 garlic clove, peeled
- 2 cups water

1. Put all ingredients in the instant pot. 2. Close and seal the lid. 3. Cook Adobo pork for 30 minutes on Manual mode (High Pressure). 4. When the cooking time is finished, make a quick pressure release and transfer the pork belly in the bowls. 5. Add 1 ladle of the pork gravy.

Per Serving:

calories: 352 | fat: 20g | protein: 35g | carbs: 0g | net carbs: 0g | fiber: 0g

Beef and Egg Rice Bowls

Prep time: 5 minutes | Cook time: 15 minutes | Serves 4

- ◄ 2 cups cauli rice
- ◄ 3 cups frozen mixed vegetables
- ◄ 3 tablespoons ghee
- ◄ 1 pound skirt steak
- ◄ Salt and black pepper to taste
- ◄ 4 eggs
- ◄ Hot sauce for topping

1. Mix the cauli rice and mixed vegetables in a bowl, sprinkle with a little water, and steam in the microwave for 1 minute until tender. Share into 4 serving bowls. 2. Melt the ghee in a skillet, season the beef with salt and black pepper, and brown for 5 minutes on each side. Use a perforated spoon to ladle the meat onto the vegetables. 3. Wipe out the skillet and return to medium heat, crack in an egg, season with salt and pepper and cook until the egg white has set, but the yolk is still runny 3 minutes. 4. Remove egg onto the vegetable bowl and fry the remaining 3 eggs. Add to the other bowls. Drizzle the beef bowls with hot sauce and serve.

Per Serving:

calories: 491 | fat: 32g | protein: 31g | carbs: 22g | net carbs: 15g | fiber: 7g

Kung Pao Pork

Prep time: 15 minutes | Cook time: 10 minutes | Serves 4

Stir-Fried Pork:
- ◄ 2 tablespoons refined avocado oil or hazelnut oil
- ◄ 1 pound (455 g) pork stir-fry pieces
- ◄ 4 small cloves garlic, minced
- ◄ 1 (1-inch/2.5-cm) piece fresh ginger root
- ◄ 2 to 4 dried chilis

Salad Dressing:
- ◄ 2 tablespoons unsweetened smooth almond butter
- ◄ 2 tablespoons refined avocado oil or hazelnut oil
- ◄ 1 tablespoon plus 1 teaspoon

For Serving:
- ◄ 1 cucumber, spiral sliced
- ◄ ½ bunch fresh cilantro

- ◄ 2 tablespoons coconut aminos
- ◄ 2 teaspoons apple cider vinegar
- ◄ 2 drops liquid stevia
- ◄ ¼ cup (40 g) roasted cashews, roughly chopped

  apple cider vinegar
- ◄ 1 tablespoon toasted sesame oil
- ◄ 1 tablespoon coconut aminos

  (about 1 ounce/28 g), chopped

1. If you want to marinate the pork before cooking, place all the ingredients for the stir-fry, except the cashews, in a large casserole dish. Toss to coat, then refrigerate for at least 1 hour and up to 12 hours. 2. To prepare the stir-fry: Place a medium-sized frying pan over medium heat. If you didn't marinate the pork, pour the oil into the hot pan and wait until the oil is hot, about 1 minute, then add the remaining stir-fry ingredients. If you did marinate the pork, add the marinated stir-fry ingredients, including the marinating juices,

to the hot pan. Cook for 10 minutes, stirring frequently, or until the pork is cooked through. Remove from the heat and stir in the chopped cashews. 3. Meanwhile, make the salad dressing: Place the ingredients for the dressing in a small bowl and whisk to combine. 4. Place the spiral-sliced cucumber and cilantro on a serving platter and toss quickly. Place the stir-fried pork on the platter, next to the salad, and drizzle the salad and pork with the dressing.

Per Serving:

calories: 453 | fat: 32g | protein: 28g | carbs: 12g | net carbs: 10g | fiber: 2g

Savory Sausage Cobbler

Prep time: 15 minutes | Cook time: 34 minutes | Serves 4

Filling:
- ◄ 1 pound (454 g) ground Italian sausage
- ◄ 1 cup sliced mushrooms

Biscuits:
- ◄ 3 large egg whites
- ◄ ¾ cup blanched almond flour
- ◄ 1 teaspoon baking powder
- ◄ ¼ teaspoon fine sea salt

- ◄ 1 teaspoon fine sea salt
- ◄ 2 cups marinara sauce

- ◄ 2½ tablespoons very cold unsalted butter, cut into ¼-inch pieces
- ◄ Fresh basil leaves, for garnish

1. Preheat the air fryer to 400°F (204°C). 2. Place the sausage in a pie pan (or a pan that fits into your air fryer). Use your hands to break up the sausage and spread it evenly on the bottom of the pan. Place the pan in the air fryer and air fry for 5 minutes. 3. Remove the pan from the air fryer and use a fork or metal spatula to crumble the sausage more. Season the mushrooms with the salt and add them to the pie pan. Stir to combine the mushrooms and sausage, then return the pan to the air fryer and air fry for 4 minutes, or until the mushrooms are soft and the sausage is cooked through. 4. Remove the pan from the air fryer. Add the marinara sauce and stir well. Set aside. 5. Make the biscuits: Place the egg whites in a large mixing bowl or the bowl of a stand mixer. Using a hand mixer or stand mixer, whip the egg whites until stiff peaks form. 6. In a medium-sized bowl, whisk together the almond flour, baking powder, and salt, then cut in the butter. Gently fold the flour mixture into the egg whites with a rubber spatula. 7. Using a large spoon or ice cream scoop, spoon one-quarter of the dough on top of the sausage mixture, making sure the butter stays in separate clumps. Repeat with the remaining dough, spacing the biscuits about 1 inch apart. 8. Place the pan in the air fryer and cook for 5 minutes, then lower the heat to 325°F (163°C) and bake for another 15 to 20 minutes, until the biscuits are golden brown. Serve garnished with fresh basil leaves. 9. Store leftovers in an airtight container in the refrigerator for up to 3 days. Reheat in a preheated 350°F (177°C) air fryer for 5 minutes, or until warmed through.

Per Serving:

calories: 572 | fat: 49g | protein: 23g | carbs: 11g | net carbs: 7g | fiber: 4g

Garlic Balsamic London Broil

Prep time: 30 minutes | Cook time: 8 to 10 minutes | Serves 8

- 2 pounds (907 g) London broil
- 3 large garlic cloves, minced
- 3 tablespoons balsamic vinegar
- 3 tablespoons whole-grain
- mustard
- 2 tablespoons olive oil
- Sea salt and ground black pepper, to taste
- ½ teaspoon dried hot red pepper flakes

1. Score both sides of the cleaned London broil. 2. Thoroughly combine the remaining ingredients; massage this mixture into the meat to coat it on all sides. Let it marinate for at least 3 hours. 3. Set the air fryer to 400ºF (204ºC); Then cook the London broil for 15 minutes. Flip it over and cook another 10 to 12 minutes. Bon appétit!

Per Serving:

calories: 285 | fat: 13g | protein: 37g | carbs: 2g | net carbs: 2g | fiber: 0g

Steak and Egg Bibimbap

Prep time: 10 minutes | Cook time: 15 minutes | Serves 2

For the Steak
- 1 tablespoon ghee or butter
- 8 ounces skirt steak
- Pink Himalayan salt

- Freshly ground black pepper
- 1 tablespoon soy sauce (or coconut aminos)

For the Egg and Cauliflower Rice
- 2 tablespoons ghee or butter, divided
- 2 large eggs
- 1 large cucumber, peeled and cut into matchsticks

- 1 tablespoon soy sauce
- 1 cup cauliflower rice
- Pink Himalayan salt
- Freshly ground black pepper

To Make the Steak 1. Over high heat, heat a large skillet. 2. Using a paper towel, pat the steak dry. Season both sides with pink Himalayan salt and pepper. 3. Add the ghee or butter to the skillet. When it melts, put the steak in the skillet. 4. Sear the steak for about 3 minutes on each side for medium-rare. 5. Transfer the steak to a cutting board and let it rest for at least 5 minutes. 6. Slice the skirt steak across the grain and divide it between two bowls. To Make the Egg and Cauliflower Rice 1. In a second large skillet over medium-high heat, heat 1 tablespoon of ghee. When the ghee is very hot, crack the eggs into it. When the whites have cooked through, after 2 to 3 minutes, carefully transfer the eggs to a plate. 2. In a small bowl, marinate the cucumber matchsticks in the soy sauce. 3. Clean out the skillet from the eggs, and add the remaining 1 tablespoon of ghee or butter to the pan over medium-high heat. Add the cauliflower rice, season with pink Himalayan salt and pepper, and stir, cooking for 5 minutes. Turn the heat up to high at the end of the cooking to get a nice crisp on the "rice." 4. Divide the rice between two bowls. 5. Top the rice in each bowl with an

egg, the steak, and the marinated cucumber matchsticks and serve.

Per Serving:

calories: 590 | fat: 45g | protein: 39g | carbs: 8g | net carbs: 5g | fiber: g

Pork Meatballs with Thyme

Prep time: 15 minutes | Cook time: 16 minutes | Serves 8

- 2 cups ground pork
- 1 teaspoon dried thyme
- ½ teaspoon chili flakes
- ½ teaspoon garlic powder

- 1 tablespoon coconut oil
- ¼ teaspoon ground ginger
- 3 tablespoons almond flour
- ¼ cup water

1. In the mixing bowl, mix up ground pork, dried thyme, chili flakes, garlic powder, ground ginger, and almond flour. 2. Make the meatballs. 3. Melt the coconut oil in the instant pot on Sauté mode. 4. Arrange the meatballs in the instant pot in one layer and cook them for 3 minutes from each side. 5. Then add water and cook the meatballs for 10 minutes.

Per Serving:

calories: 264 | fat: 19g | protein: 20g | carbs: 1g | net carbs: 1g | fiber: 0g

Fajita Meatball Lettuce Wraps

Prep time: 10 minutes | Cook time: 10 minutes | Serves 4

- 1 pound (454 g) ground beef (85% lean)
- ½ cup salsa, plus more for serving if desired
- ¼ cup chopped onions
- ¼ cup diced green or red

For Serving (Optional):
- 8 leaves Boston lettuce
- Pico de gallo or salsa

- bell peppers
- 1 large egg, beaten
- 1 teaspoon fine sea salt
- ½ teaspoon chili powder
- ½ teaspoon ground cumin
- 1 clove garlic, minced

- Lime slices

1. Spray the air fryer basket with avocado oil. Preheat the air fryer to 350ºF (177ºC). 2. In a large bowl, mix together all the ingredients until well combined. 3. Shape the meat mixture into eight 1-inch balls. Place the meatballs in the air fryer basket, leaving a little space between them. Air fry for 10 minutes, or until cooked through and no longer pink inside and the internal temperature reaches 145ºF (63ºC). 4. Serve each meatball on a lettuce leaf, topped with pico de gallo or salsa, if desired. Serve with lime slices if desired. 5. Store leftovers in an airtight container in the fridge for 3 days or in the freezer for up to a month. Reheat in a preheated 350ºF (177ºC) air fryer for 4 minutes, or until heated through.

Per Serving:

calories: 277 | fat: 18g | protein: 21g | carbs: 6g | net carbs: 4g | fiber: 2g

Beef Provençal

Prep time: 10 minutes | Cook time: 35 minutes | Serves 4

◄ 12 ounces beef steak racks
◄ 2 fennel bulbs, sliced
◄ Salt and black pepper, to taste
◄ 3 tablespoons olive oil

◄ ½ cup apple cider vinegar
◄ 1 teaspoon herbs de Provence
◄ 1 tablespoon swerve

1. In a bowl, mix the fennel with 2 tablespoons of oil, swerve, and vinegar, toss to coat well, and set to a baking dish. Season with herbs de Provence, pepper and salt, and cook in the oven at 400ºF for 15 minutes. 2. Sprinkle black pepper and salt to the beef, place into an oiled pan over medium heat, and cook for a couple of minutes. Place the beef to the baking dish with the fennel, and bake for 20 minutes. Split everything among plates and enjoy.

Per Serving:

calories: 251 | fat: 15g | protein: 19g | carbs: 8g | net carbs: 4g | fiber: 4g

Stuffed Meatballs with Mozzarella

Prep time: 10 minutes | Cook time: 20 minutes | Serves 6

◄ 1 pound (454 g) ground pork
◄ 1 teaspoon chili flakes
◄ ½ teaspoon salt
◄ ⅓ cup shredded Mozzarella cheese

◄ 1 tablespoon butter
◄ ¼ cup chicken broth
◄ ½ teaspoon garlic powder

1. Mix up ground pork, chili flakes, salt, and garlic powder. 2. Then make the meatballs with the help of the fingertips. 3. Make the mini balls from the cheese. 4. Fill the meatballs with the mini cheese balls. 5. Toss the butter in the instant pot. 6. Heat it up on Sauté mode and add the prepared meatballs. 7. Cook the on Sauté mode for 3 minutes from each side. 8. Then add chicken broth and close the lid. 9. Cook the meal on Meat/Stew mode for 10 minutes.

Per Serving:

calories: 132 | fat: 5g | protein: 20g | carbs: 0g | net carbs: 0g | fiber: 0g

Beef Bourguignon

Prep time: 10 minutes | Cook time: 1 hour | Serves 4

◄ 3 tablespoons coconut oil
◄ 1 tablespoon dried parsley flakes
◄ 1 cup red wine
◄ 1 teaspoon dried thyme
◄ Salt and black pepper, to taste
◄ 1 bay leaf

◄ ⅓ cup coconut flour
◄ 2 pounds beef, cubed
◄ 12 small white onions
◄ 4 pancetta slices, chopped
◄ 2 garlic cloves, minced
◄ ½ pound mushrooms, chopped

1. In a bowl, combine the wine with bay leaf, olive oil, thyme, pepper, parsley, salt, and the beef cubes; set aside for 3 hours. Drain the meat, and reserve the marinade. Toss the flour over the meat to coat. 2. Heat a pan over medium heat, stir in the pancetta, and cook until slightly browned. Place in the onions and garlic, and cook for 3 minutes. Stir-fry in the meat and mushrooms for 4-5 minutes. 3. Pour in the marinade and 1 cup of water; cover and cook for 50 minutes. Season to taste and serve.

Per Serving:

calories: 728 | fat: 47g | protein: 53g | carbs: 21g | net carbs: 14g | fiber: 7g

Chapter 6
Fish and Seafood

Chapter 6　Fish and Seafood

Shrimp Bake

Prep time: 15 minutes | Cook time: 5 minutes | Serves 4

- 14 ounces (397 g) shrimp, peeled
- 1 egg, beaten
- ½ cup coconut milk
- 1 cup Cheddar cheese, shredded
- ½ teaspoon coconut oil
- 1 teaspoon ground coriander

1. In the mixing bowl, mix shrimps with egg, coconut milk, Cheddar cheese, coconut oil, and ground coriander. 2. Then put the mixture in the baking ramekins and put in the air fryer. 3. Cook the shrimps at 400°F (204°C) for 5 minutes.

Per Serving:

calories: 289 | fat: 19g | protein: 29g | carbs: 2g | net carbs: 1g | fiber: 1g

Cod Cakes

Prep time: 5 minutes | Cook time: 20 minutes | Serves 2

- 2 tablespoons plus 1 teaspoon extra-virgin olive oil, divided
- ¼ medium onion, chopped
- 1 garlic clove, minced
- 1 cup cauliflower rice, fresh or thawed frozen
- 1 pound (454 g) cod fillets
- ½ cup almond flour
- 1 large egg
- 2 tablespoons chopped fresh parsley
- 2 tablespoons ground flaxseed
- 1 tablespoon freshly squeezed lemon juice
- 1 teaspoon dried dill
- ½ teaspoon ground cumin
- ½ teaspoon pink Himalayan sea salt
- ¼ teaspoon freshly ground black pepper
- Tartar sauce

1. In a medium sauté pan or skillet, heat 1 tablespoon of olive oil over medium heat. Add the onion and garlic and cook for about 7 minutes, until tender. 2. Add the cauliflower rice and continue to stir for 5 to 7 minutes, until warmed through and tender. Transfer to a large bowl. 3. In the same skillet, heat 1 teaspoon of olive oil over medium-high heat. Cook the cod for 4 to 5 minutes on each side, until cooked through. Let the cod cool for a couple of minutes. 4. Add the almond flour, egg, parsley, flaxseed, lemon juice, dill, cumin, salt, and pepper to the bowl with the cauliflower rice. Using your hands, mix until the ingredients are well combined. 5. Add the fish to the bowl and mix well. I like to use a fluffing motion to keep the fish in chunks, rather than smashing it all. 6. In the skillet, heat the remaining 1 tablespoon of olive oil over medium heat. 7. Using a ½ cup measuring cup, form the fish cakes by packing the mixture into the cup, then slipping the cake out of the cup onto a plate. You should be able to shape 4 cakes. 8. Place the fish cakes in the hot oil and cook for about 5 minutes per side, flipping once, until golden brown on both sides. 9. Place the cod cakes on serving plates, and serve with tartar sauce.

Per Serving:

calories: 531 | fat: 34g | protein: 45g | carbs: 12g | net carbs: 6g | fiber: 6g

Sushi Shrimp Rolls

Prep time: 5 minutes | Cook time: 0 minutes | Serves 5

- 2 cups cooked and chopped shrimp
- 1 tablespoon sriracha sauce
- ¼ cucumber, julienned
- 5 hand roll nori sheets
- ¼ cup mayonnaise

1. Combine shrimp, mayonnaise, cucumber and sriracha sauce in a bowl. Lay out a single nori sheet on a flat surface and spread about 1/5 of the shrimp mixture. Roll the nori sheet as desired. Repeat with the other ingredients. Serve with sugar-free soy sauce.

Per Serving:

calories: 180 | fat: 12g | protein: 16g | carbs: 2g | net carbs: 1g | fiber: 1g

Coconut Cream Mackerel

Prep time: 10 minutes | Cook time: 6 minutes | Serves 4

- 2 pounds (907 g) mackerel fillet
- 1 cup coconut cream
- 1 teaspoon ground coriander
- 1 teaspoon cumin seeds
- 1 garlic clove, peeled, chopped

1. Chop the mackerel roughly and sprinkle it with coconut cream, ground coriander, cumin seeds, and garlic. 2. Then put the fish in the air fryer and cook at 400°F (204°C) for 6 minutes.

Per Serving:

calories: 430 | fat: 31g | protein: 29g | carbs: 6g | net carbs: 5g | fiber: 1g

Salmon Oscar

Prep time: 5 minutes | Cook time: 20 minutes | Serves 2

- ◄ ¼ cup (½ stick) butter
- ◄ 1 tablespoon finely minced onion
- ◄ 1½ teaspoons white wine vinegar
- ◄ 1 teaspoon freshly squeezed lemon juice
- ◄ ½ teaspoon dried tarragon
- ◄ ¼ teaspoon dried parsley
- ◄ 1 large egg yolk
- ◄ 2 tablespoons heavy
- ◄ (whipping) cream
- ◄ 1 tablespoon extra-virgin olive oil
- ◄ 2 (8-ounce / 227-g) salmon fillets
- ◄ Pink Himalayan sea salt
- ◄ Freshly ground black pepper
- ◄ 1 (6- to 8-ounce / 170- to 227-g) container lump crab meat

1. In a small saucepan, melt the butter over medium heat. 2. Add the onion and cook for 3 to 5 minutes, until it begins to turn translucent. Add the vinegar, lemon juice, tarragon, and parsley. Stir to combine. 3. In a small bowl, whisk together the egg yolk and cream. 4. Once the mixture in the saucepan starts to simmer, remove it from the heat and slowly add the egg mixture, whisking while you pour. Continue to whisk for 2 to 3 minutes, until the sauce thickens. Cover and set aside. 5. Season the salmon fillets with salt and pepper. 6. In a medium sauté pan or skillet, heat the olive oil over medium-high heat. Place the fillets skin-side up in the skillet. Cook for 4 to 5 minutes, then turn and cook for an additional 4 to 5 minutes on the other side, until the flesh flakes easily with a fork. 7. Transfer the salmon to a serving plate, then place the crab in the skillet and quickly heat it, stirring gently. 8. Top the salmon fillets with the crab, then drizzle on the sauce. Serve at once.

Per Serving:

calories: 741 | fat: 53g | protein: 62g | carbs: 1g | net carbs: 1g | fiber: 0g

Shrimp Stuffed Zucchini

Prep time: 15 minutes | Cook time: 25 minutes | Serves 4

- ◄ 4 medium zucchinis
- ◄ 1 pound small shrimp, peeled, deveined
- ◄ 1 tablespoon minced onion
- ◄ 2 teaspoons butter
- ◄ ¼ cup chopped tomatoes
- ◄ Salt and black pepper to taste
- ◄ 1 cup pork rinds, crushed
- ◄ 1 tablespoon chopped basil leaves
- ◄ 2 tablespoons melted butter

1. Preheat the oven to 350ºF and trim off the top and bottom ends of the zucchinis. Lay them flat on a chopping board, and cut a ¼ -inch off the top to create a boat for the stuffing. Scoop out the seeds with a spoon and set the zucchinis aside. 2. Melt the firm butter in a small skillet and sauté the onion and tomato for 6 minutes. Transfer the mixture to a bowl and add the shrimp, half of the pork rinds, basil leaves, salt, and black pepper. 3. Combine the ingredients and stuff the zucchini boats with the mixture. Sprinkle the top of the boats with the remaining pork rinds and drizzle the melted

butter over them. 4. Place on a baking sheet and bake for 15 to 20 minutes. The shrimp should no longer be pink by this time. Remove the zucchinis after and serve with a tomato and mozzarella salad.

Per Serving:

calories: 300 | fat: 16g | protein: 26g | carbs: 10g | net carbs: 6g | fiber: 4g

Bacon-Wrapped Scallops

Prep time: 5 minutes | Cook time: 10 minutes | Serves 4

- ◄ 8 (1-ounce / 28-g) sea scallops, cleaned and patted dry
- ◄ 8 slices sugar-free bacon
- ◄ ¼ teaspoon salt
- ◄ ¼ teaspoon ground black pepper

1. Wrap each scallop in 1 slice bacon and secure with a toothpick. Sprinkle with salt and pepper. 2. Place scallops into ungreased air fryer basket. Adjust the temperature to 360ºF (182ºC) and air fry for 10 minutes. Scallops will be opaque and firm, and have an internal temperature of 135ºF (57ºC) when done. Serve warm.

Per Serving:

calories: 267 | fat: 18g | protein: 22g | carbs: 1g | net carbs: 1g | fiber: 0g

Salmon with Tarragon-Dijon Sauce

Prep time: 5 minutes | Cook time: 15 minutes | Serves 4

- ◄ 1¼ pounds (567 g) salmon fillet (skin on or removed), cut into 4 equal pieces
- ◄ ¼ cup avocado oil mayonnaise
- ◄ ¼ cup Dijon or stone-ground mustard
- ◄ Zest and juice of ½ lemon
- ◄ 2 tablespoons chopped fresh tarragon or 1 to 2 teaspoons dried tarragon
- ◄ ½ teaspoon salt
- ◄ ¼ teaspoon freshly ground black pepper
- ◄ 4 tablespoons extra-virgin olive oil, for serving

1. Preheat the oven to 425ºF(220ºC). Line a baking sheet with parchment paper. 2. Place the salmon pieces, skin-side down, on a baking sheet. 3. In a small bowl, whisk together the mayonnaise, mustard, lemon zest and juice, tarragon, salt, and pepper. Top the salmon evenly with the sauce mixture. 4. Bake until slightly browned on top and slightly translucent in the center, 10 to 12 minutes, depending on the thickness of the salmon. Remove from the oven and leave on the baking sheet for 10 minutes. Drizzle each fillet with 1 tablespoon olive oil before serving.

Per Serving:

calories: 490 | fat: 39g | protein: 27g | carbs: 3g | net carbs: 2g | fiber: 1g

Creamy Hoki with Almond Bread Crust

Prep time: 10 minutes | Cook time: 35 minutes | Serves 4

- 1 cup flaked smoked hoki, bones removed
- 1 cup cubed hoki fillets, cubed
- 4 eggs
- 1 cup water
- 3 tablespoons almond flour
- 1 onion, sliced
- 2 cups sour cream
- 1 tablespoon chopped parsley
- 1 cup pork rinds, crushed
- 1 cup grated cheddar cheese
- Salt and black pepper to taste
- 2 tablespoons butter

1. Preheat the oven to 360ºF and lightly grease a baking dish with cooking spray. 2. Then, boil the eggs in water in a pot over medium heat to be well done for 10 minutes, run the eggs under cold water and peel the shells. After, place on a cutting board and chop them. 3. Melt the butter in a saucepan over medium heat and sauté the onion for 4 minutes. Turn the heat off and stir in the almond flour to form a roux. Turn the heat back on and cook the roux to be golden brown and stir in the cream until the mixture is smooth. Season with salt and black pepper, and stir in the parsley. 4. Spread the smoked and cubed fish in the baking dish, sprinkle the eggs on top, and spoon the sauce over. In a bowl, mix the pork rinds with the cheddar cheese, and sprinkle it over the sauce. 5. Bake the casserole in the oven for 20 minutes until the top is golden and the sauce and cheese are bubbly. Remove the bake after and serve with a steamed green vegetable mix.

Per Serving:

calories: 411 | fat: 31g | protein: 27g | carbs: 6g | net carbs: 4g | fiber: 2g

Italian Tuna Roast

Prep time: 15 minutes | Cook time: 21 to 24 minutes | Serves 8

- Cooking spray
- 1 tablespoon Italian seasoning
- ⅛ teaspoon ground black pepper
- 1 tablespoon extra-light
- olive oil
- 1 teaspoon lemon juice
- 1 tuna loin (approximately 2 pounds / 907 g, 3 to 4 inches thick)

1. Spray baking dish with cooking spray and place in air fryer basket. Preheat the air fryer to 390ºF (199ºC). 2. Mix together the Italian seasoning, pepper, oil, and lemon juice. 3. Using a dull table knife or butter knife, pierce top of tuna about every half inch: Insert knife into top of tuna roast and pierce almost all the way to the bottom. 4. Spoon oil mixture into each of the holes and use the knife to push seasonings into the tuna as deeply as possible. 5. Spread any remaining oil mixture on all outer surfaces of tuna. 6. Place tuna roast in baking dish and roast at 390ºF (199ºC) for 20 minutes. Check temperature with a meat thermometer. Cook for an additional 1 to 4 minutes or until temperature reaches 145ºF (63ºC). 7. Remove basket from the air fryer and let tuna sit in the basket for 10 minutes.

Per Serving:

calories: 206 | fat: 6g | protein: 35g | carbs: 1g | net carbs: 1g | fiber: 0g

Chunky Fish Soup with Tomatoes

Prep time: 10 minutes | Cook time: 8 minutes | Serves 4

- 2 teaspoons olive oil
- 1 yellow onion, chopped
- 1 bell pepper, sliced
- 1 celery, diced
- 2 garlic cloves, minced
- 3 cups fish stock
- 2 ripe tomatoes, crushed
- ¾ pound (340 g) haddock
- fillets
- 1 cup shrimp
- 1 tablespoon sweet Hungarian paprika
- 1 teaspoon hot Hungarian paprika
- ½ teaspoon caraway seeds

1. Set the Instant Pot to Sauté. Add and heat the oil. Once hot, add the onions and sauté until soft and fragrant. 2. Add the pepper, celery, and garlic and continue to sauté until soft. 3. Stir in the remaining ingredients. 4. Lock the lid. Select the Manual mode and set the cooking time for 5 minutes at High Pressure. 5. When the timer beeps, perform a quick pressure release. Carefully remove the lid. 6. Divide into serving bowls and serve hot.

Per Serving:

calories: 177 | fat: 5g | protein: 26g | carbs: 8g | net carbs: 6g | fiber: 2g

Tuna Salad Wrap

Prep time: 5 minutes | Cook time: 0 minutes | Serves 2

- 2 (5 ounce / 142 g) cans tuna packed in olive oil, drained
- 3 tablespoons mayonnaise
- 1 tablespoon chopped red onion
- 2 teaspoons dill relish
- ¼ teaspoon pink Himalayan sea salt
- ¼ teaspoon freshly ground black pepper
- Pinch of dried or fresh dill
- 2 low-carb tortillas
- 2 romaine lettuce leaves
- ¼ cup grated Cheddar cheese

1. In a medium bowl, combine the tuna, mayonnaise, onion, relish, salt, pepper, and dill. 2. Place a lettuce leaf on each tortilla, then split the tuna mixture evenly between the wraps, spreading it evenly over the lettuce. 3. Sprinkle the Cheddar on top of each, then fold the tortillas and serve.

Per Serving:

calories: 549 | fat: 33g | protein: 42g | carbs: 21g | net carbs: 5g | fiber: 16g

Cayenne Flounder Cutlets

Prep time: 15 minutes | Cook time: 10 minutes | Serves 2

- 1 egg
- 1 cup Pecorino Romano cheese, grated
- Sea salt and white pepper, to taste
- ½ teaspoon cayenne pepper
- 1 teaspoon dried parsley flakes
- 2 flounder fillets

1. To make a breading station, whisk the egg until frothy. 2. In another bowl, mix Pecorino Romano cheese, and spices. 3. Dip the fish in the egg mixture and turn to coat evenly; then, dredge in the cracker crumb mixture, turning a couple of times to coat evenly. 4. Cook in the preheated air fryer at 390ºF (199ºC) for 5 minutes; turn them over and cook another 5 minutes. Enjoy!

Per Serving:

calories: 438 | fat: 29g | protein: 41g | carbs: 3g | net carbs: 3g | fiber: 0g

Tuna Steak

Prep time: 10 minutes | Cook time: 12 minutes | Serves 4

- 1 pound (454 g) tuna steaks, boneless and cubed
- 1 tablespoon mustard
- 1 tablespoon avocado oil
- 1 tablespoon apple cider vinegar

1. Mix avocado oil with mustard and apple cider vinegar. 2. Then brush tuna steaks with mustard mixture and put in the air fryer basket. 3. Cook the fish at 360ºF (182ºC) for 6 minutes per side.

Per Serving:

calories: 180 | fat: 9g | protein: 25g | carbs: 1g | net carbs: 1g | fiber: 0g

Poke Salad Bowls

Prep time: 15 minutes | Cook time: 0 minutes | Makes 2 bowls

- ¼ cup gluten-free soy sauce
- 2 tablespoons sesame oil
- 1 teaspoon chili garlic sauce
- 2 cups salad greens
- ¼ pound (113 g) ahi tuna, diced
- ¼ pound (113 g) snow crab leg meat, chopped
- ½ large cucumber, diced
- 1 large carrot, julienned or peeled into ribbons
- ½ avocado, sliced
- Sliced scallion, green parts only, for garnish
- Sesame seeds, for garnish
- 3 tablespoons pickled ginger, for garnish (optional)

1. In a large bowl, whisk together the soy sauce, sesame oil, and chili garlic sauce. 2. Add the salad greens and toss to combine. Transfer the greens to two bowls. 3. To the bowl you just tossed the salad in, add the tuna, crab meat, cucumber, and carrot and toss again. Top the greens with the seafood and veggie mixture. 4. Add the sliced avocado and garnish with scallion, sesame seeds, and pickled ginger (if using). Serve immediately.

Per Serving:

calories: 578 | fat: 30g | protein: 59g | carbs: 18g | net carbs: 12g | fiber: 6g

Mascarpone Tilapia with Nutmeg

Prep time: 10 minutes | Cook time: 20 minutes | Serves 2

- 10 ounces (283 g) tilapia
- ½ cup mascarpone
- 1 garlic clove, diced
- 1 teaspoon ground nutmeg
- 1 tablespoon olive oil
- ½ teaspoon salt

1. Pour olive oil in the instant pot. 2. Add diced garlic and sauté it for 4 minutes. 3. Add tilapia and sprinkle it with ground nutmeg. Sauté the fish for 3 minutes per side. 4. Add mascarpone and close the lid. 5. Sauté tilapia for 10 minutes.

Per Serving:

calories: 293 | fat: 17g | protein: 33g | carbs: 3g | net carbs: 2g | fiber: 1g

Pan-Seared Halibut with Citrus Butter Sauce

Prep time: 10 minutes | Cook time: 15 minutes | Serves 4

- 4 (5-ounce) halibut fillets, each about 1 inch thick
- Sea salt
- Freshly ground black pepper
- ¼ cup butter
- 2 teaspoons minced garlic
- 1 shallot, minced
- 3 tablespoons dry white
- wine
- 1 tablespoon freshly squeezed lemon juice
- 1 tablespoon freshly squeezed orange juice
- 2 teaspoons chopped fresh parsley
- 2 tablespoons olive oil

1. Pat the fish dry with paper towels and then lightly season the fillets with salt and pepper. Set aside on a paper towel–lined plate. 2. Place a small saucepan over medium heat and melt the butter. 3. Sauté the garlic and shallot until tender, about 3 minutes. 4. Whisk in the white wine, lemon juice, and orange juice and bring the sauce to a simmer, cooking until it thickens slightly, about 2 minutes. 5. Remove the sauce from the heat and stir in the parsley; set aside. 6. Place a large skillet over medium-high heat and add the olive oil. 7. Panfry the fish until lightly browned and just cooked through, turning them over once, about 10 minutes in total. 8. Serve the fish immediately with a spoonful of sauce for each.

Per Serving:

calories: 319 | fat: 26g | protein: 22g | carbs: 2g | net carbs: 2g | fiber: 0g

Crispy Fish Nuggets

Prep time: 15 minutes | Cook time: 9 minutes | Serves 4

- ◄ 1 pound (454 g) tilapia fillet
- ◄ ½ cup almond flour
- ◄ 3 eggs, beaten
- ◄ ¼ cup avocado oil
- ◄ 1 teaspoon salt

1. Cut the fish into the small pieces (nuggets) and sprinkle withs alt. 2. Then dip the fish nuggets in the eggs and coat in the almond flour. 3. Heat up avocado oil for 3 minutes on Sauté mode. 4. Put the prepared fish nuggets in the hot oil and cook them on Sauté mode for 3 minutes from each side or until they are golden brown.

Per Serving:

calories: 179 | fat: 8g | protein: 26g | carbs: 2g | net carbs: 1g | fiber: 1g

Rosemary Baked Haddock

Prep time: 7 minutes | Cook time: 10 minutes | Serves 2

- ◄ 2 eggs, beaten
- ◄ 12 ounces (340 g) haddock fillet, chopped
- ◄ 1 tablespoon cream cheese
- ◄ ¾ teaspoon dried rosemary
- ◄ 2 ounces (57 g) Parmesan, grated
- ◄ 1 teaspoon butter

1. Whisk the beaten eggs until homogenous. Add the cream cheese, dried rosemary, and dill. 2. Grease the springform with the butter and place the haddock inside. 3. Pour the egg mixture over the fish and add sprinkle with Parmesan. 4. Set the Manual mode (High Pressure) and cook for 5 minutes. Then make a natural release pressure for 5 minutes.

Per Serving:

calories: 380 | fat: 16g | protein: 56g | carbs: 18g | net carbs: 18g | fiber: 0g

Basil Halibut Red Pepper Packets

Prep time: 10 minutes | Cook time: 20 minutes | Serves 4

- ◄ 2 cups cauliflower florets
- ◄ 1 cup roasted red pepper strips
- ◄ ½ cup sliced sun-dried tomatoes
- ◄ 4 (4-ounce) halibut fillets
- ◄ ¼ cup chopped fresh basil
- ◄ Juice of 1 lemon
- ◄ ¼ cup good-quality olive oil
- ◄ Sea salt, for seasoning
- ◄ Freshly ground black pepper, for seasoning

1. Preheat the oven. Set the oven temperature to 400°F. Cut four (12-inch) square pieces of aluminum foil. Have a baking sheet ready. 2. Make the packets. Divide the cauliflower, red pepper strips, and sun-dried tomato between the four pieces of foil, placing the vegetables in the middle of each piece. Top each pile with 1 halibut fillet, and top each fillet with equal amounts of the basil, lemon juice, and olive oil. Fold and crimp the foil to form sealed packets of fish and vegetables and place them on the baking sheet. 3. Bake. Bake the packets for about 20 minutes, until the fish flakes with a fork. Be careful of the steam when you open the packet! 4. Serve. Transfer the vegetables and halibut to four plates, season with salt and pepper, and serve immediately.

Per Serving:

calories: 294 | fat: 18g | protein: 25g | carbs: 8g | net carbs: 5g | fiber: 3g

Ginger Cod

Prep time: 10 minutes | Cook time: 20 minutes | Serves 2

- ◄ 1 teaspoon ginger paste
- ◄ 8 ounces (227 g) cod fillet, chopped
- ◄ 1 tablespoon coconut oil
- ◄ ¼ cup coconut milk

1. Melt the coconut oil in the instant pot on Sauté mode. 2. Then add ginger paste and coconut milk and bring the mixture to boil. 3. Add chopped cod and sauté the meal for 12 minutes. Stir the fish cubes with the help of the spatula from time to time.

Per Serving:

calories: 222 | fat: 15g | protein: 21g | carbs: 2g | net carbs: 1g | fiber: 1g

Ahi Tuna and Cherry Tomato Salad

Prep time: 5 minutes | Cook time: 4 minutes | Serves 4

- ◄ 1 cup water
- ◄ 2 sprigs thyme
- ◄ 2 sprigs rosemary
- ◄ 2 sprigs parsley
- ◄ 1 lemon, sliced
- ◄ 1 pound (454 g) ahi tuna
- ◄ ⅓ teaspoon ground black pepper
- ◄ 1 head lettuce
- ◄ 1 cup cherry tomatoes, halved
- ◄ 1 red bell pepper, julienned
- ◄ 2 tablespoons extra-virgin olive oil
- ◄ 1 teaspoon Dijon mustard
- ◄ Sea salt, to taste

1. Pour the water into your Instant Pot. Add the thyme, rosemary, parsley, and lemon and insert a trivet. 2. Lay the fish on the trivet and season with the ground black pepper. 3. Lock the lid. Select the Manual mode and set the cooking time for 4 minutes at High Pressure. 4. When the timer beeps, perform a quick pressure release. Carefully remove the lid. 5. In a salad bowl, place the remaining ingredients and toss well. Add the flaked tuna and toss again. 6. Serve chilled.

Per Serving:

calories: 253 | fat: 14g | protein: 28g | carbs: 5g | net carbs: 4g | fiber: 1g

Salmon Cakes

Prep time: 10 minutes | Cook time: 15 minutes | Serves 4

- ◁ 1 (16-ounce / 454-g) can pink salmon, drained and bones removed
- ◁ ¼ cup almond flour
- ◁ ¼ cup crushed pork rinds
- ◁ 2 scallions, diced
- ◁ 1 large egg
- ◁ 3 tablespoons mayonnaise
- ◁ 1 teaspoon garlic salt
- ◁ 1 teaspoon freshly ground black pepper
- ◁ 2 tablespoons extra-virgin olive oil

1. Line a plate with paper towels and set aside. 2. In a bowl, combine the salmon, almond flour, pork rinds, scallions, egg, mayonnaise, garlic salt, and pepper, and mix together well, using your hands or a spatula. 3. Form 8 small patties or 4 large patties. If the patties seem too dry, add a little more mayonnaise. If they seem too wet, add a little more almond flour or pork rinds. 4. In a skillet over medium heat, heat the oil. Cook the patties for 4 to 5 minutes on each side, until crispy. Larger patties may need to cook a little longer. 5. Transfer the patties to the lined plate to drain.

Per Serving:

2 small patties: calories: 313 | fat: 21g | protein: 26g | carbs: 5g | net carbs: 5g | fiber: 0g

Mouthwatering Cod over Creamy Leek Noodles

Prep time: 10 minutes | Cook time: 24 minutes | Serves 4

- ◁ 1 small leek, sliced into long thin noodles (about 2 cups)
- ◁ ½ cup heavy cream
- ◁ 2 cloves garlic, minced
- ◁ 1 teaspoon fine sea salt, Coating:
- ◁ ¼ cup grated Parmesan cheese
- ◁ 2 tablespoons mayonnaise
- ◁ 2 tablespoons unsalted butter, softened
- divided
- ◁ 4 (4-ounce / 113-g) cod fillets (about 1 inch thick)
- ◁ ½ teaspoon ground black pepper
- ◁ 1 tablespoon chopped fresh thyme, or ½ teaspoon dried thyme leaves, plus more for garnish

1. Preheat the air fryer to 350°F (177°C). 2. Place the leek noodles in a casserole dish or a pan that will fit in your air fryer. 3. In a small bowl, stir together the cream, garlic, and ½ teaspoon of the salt. Pour the mixture over the leeks and cook in the air fryer for 10 minutes, or until the leeks are very tender. 4. Pat the fish dry and season with the remaining ½ teaspoon of salt and the pepper. When the leeks are ready, open the air fryer and place the fish fillets on top of the leeks. Air fry for 8 to 10 minutes, until the fish flakes easily with a fork (the thicker the fillets, the longer this will take). 5. While the fish cooks, make the coating: In a small bowl, combine the Parmesan, mayo, butter, and thyme. 6. When the fish is ready, remove it from the air fryer and increase the heat to 425°F

(218°C) (or as high as your air fryer can go). Spread the fillets with a ½-inch-thick to ¾-inch-thick layer of the coating. 7. Place the fish back in the air fryer and air fry for 3 to 4 minutes, until the coating browns. 8. Garnish with fresh or dried thyme, if desired. Store leftovers in an airtight container in the refrigerator for up to 3 days. Reheat in a casserole dish in a preheated 350°F (177°C) air fryer for 6 minutes, or until heated through.

Per Serving:

calories: 380 | fat: 28g | protein: 24g | carbs: 6g | net carbs: 5g | fiber: 1g

Pecan-Crusted Salmon

Prep time: 5 minutes | Cook time: 15 minutes | Serves 4

- ◁ 1 tablespoon butter, melted, plus more for greasing the pan
- ◁ 12 ounces (340 g) fresh salmon
- ◁ ½ cup finely chopped pecans
- ◁ 4 tablespoons grated
- Parmesan cheese
- ◁ 2 tablespoons cream cheese, at room temperature
- ◁ 1 teaspoon garlic salt
- ◁ 1 teaspoon freshly ground black pepper

1. Preheat the oven to 425°F (220°C). Lightly grease a 13-by-9-inch baking dish. 2. Place the salmon skin-side down in the dish. 3. In a small bowl, mix the pecans, Parmesan cheese, cream cheese, melted butter, garlic salt, and pepper, and spread evenly over the top of the salmon. 4. Bake for about 15 minutes or until the salmon flakes easily with a fork.

Per Serving:

3 ounces: calories: 303 | fat: 24g | protein: 21g | carbs: 3g | net carbs: 2g | fiber: 1g

Turmeric Salmon

Prep time: 10 minutes | Cook time: 4 minutes | Serves 3

- ◁ 1 pound (454 g) salmon fillet
- ◁ 1 teaspoon ground black pepper
- ◁ ½ teaspoon salt
- ◁ 1 teaspoon ground turmeric
- ◁ 1 teaspoon lemon juice
- ◁ 1 cup water

1. In the shallow bowl, mix up salt, ground black pepper, and ground turmeric. 2. Sprinkle the salmon fillet with lemon juice and rub with the spice mixture. 3. Then pour water in the instant pot and insert the steamer rack. 4. Wrap the salmon fillet in the foil and place it on the rack. 5. Close and seal the lid. 6. Cook the fish on Manual mode (High Pressure) for 4 minutes. 7. Make a quick pressure release and cut the fish on servings.

Per Serving:

calories: 205 | fat: 9g | protein: 30g | carbs: 1g | net carbs: 1g | fiber: 0g

Sushi

Prep time: 15 minutes | Cook time: 3 to 5 minutes | Serves 2 to 4

- 4 cups cauliflower rice
- 2 tablespoons grass-fed gelatin
- 1 tablespoon apple cider vinegar
- 1 teaspoon salt
- 2 to 4 nori sheets
- ½ pound (227 g) sushi-grade fish, thinly sliced
- 1 small avocado, halved, pitted, peeled, and thinly sliced

- 1 small cucumber (or any other vegetable you'd like), thinly sliced
- Sesame seeds, for topping (optional)
- Coconut aminos or tamari, wasabi, sugar-free pickled ginger, sliced avocado, and/ or avocado oil mayonnaise mixed with sugar-free hot sauce, for serving (optional)

1. In a shallow pot with a lid, combine the cauliflower with 3 tablespoons of water. Turn the heat to medium, cover the pot, and steam for 3 to 5 minutes. 2. Drain the cauliflower and transfer to a mixing bowl. Stir in the gelatin, vinegar, and salt. Stir together until the mixture is smooth and sticky. Set aside. 3. Fold a dish towel in half lengthwise and place it on your counter. Cover the towel in plastic wrap. 4. Place a nori sheet on top of the plastic wrap, then spread with a layer of the cauliflower rice. 5. Layer slices of fish, avocado, and cucumber over the cauliflower on the end of the nori sheet closest to you. 6. Starting at the end closest to you, gently roll the nori sheet over all the ingredients, using the towel as your rolling aid. (Emphasis on the word "gently" because you don't want to tear the nori sheet.) When you're done rolling, remove the towel and plastic wrap as you slide the roll onto a plate or cutting board. Using a sharp knife, cut the roll into equal pieces. Repeat steps 4 through 7 with the remaining nori and filling ingredients. 7. Sprinkle sesame seeds on top of your sushi, if desired, and serve with any of the other optional ingredients you'd like.

Per Serving:

calories: 295 | fat: 15g | protein: 30g | carbs: 10g | net carbs: 2g | fiber: 8g

Garlic Lemon Scallops

Prep time: 5 minutes | Cook time: 10 minutes | Serves 4

- 4 tablespoons salted butter, melted
- 4 teaspoons peeled and finely minced garlic
- ½ small lemon, zested and juiced

- 8 (1-ounce / 28-g) sea scallops, cleaned and patted dry
- ¼ teaspoon salt
- ¼ teaspoon ground black pepper

1. In a small bowl, mix butter, garlic, lemon zest, and lemon juice. Place scallops in an ungreased round nonstick baking dish. Pour butter mixture over scallops, then sprinkle with salt and pepper. 2. Place dish into air fryer basket. Adjust the temperature to 360°F

(182ºC) and bake for 10 minutes. Scallops will be opaque and firm, and have an internal temperature of 135ºF (57ºC) when done. Serve warm.

Per Serving:

calories: 113 | fat: 9g | protein: 4g | carbs: 3g | net carbs: 2g | fiber: 0g

Pork Rind Salmon Cakes

Prep time: 10 minutes | Cook time: 10 minutes | Serves 2

- 6 ounces canned Alaska wild salmon, drained
- 2 tablespoons crushed pork rinds
- 1 egg, lightly beaten
- 3 tablespoons mayonnaise,

- divided
- Pink Himalayan salt
- Freshly ground black pepper
- 1 tablespoon ghee
- ½ tablespoon Dijon mustard

1. In a medium bowl, mix to combine the salmon, pork rinds, egg, and 1½ tablespoons of mayonnaise, and season with pink Himalayan salt and pepper. 2. With the salmon mixture, form patties the size of hockey pucks or smaller. Keep patting the patties until they keep together. 3. In a medium skillet over medium-high heat, melt the ghee. When the ghee sizzles, place the salmon patties in the pan. Cook for about 3 minutes per side, until browned. Transfer the patties to a paper towel–lined plate. 4. In a small bowl, mix together the remaining 1½ tablespoons of mayonnaise and the mustard. 5. Serve the salmon cakes with the mayo-mustard dipping sauce.

Per Serving:

calories: 362 | fat: 31g | protein: 24g | carbs: 1g | net carbs: 1g | fiber: 0g

Grandma Bev's Ahi Poke

Prep time: 10 minutes | Cook time: 0 minutes | Serves 6

- 3 scallions, diced
- ½ cup soy sauce
- 2 teaspoons sesame oil
- 1 tablespoon sesame seeds
- ¼ teaspoon ground ginger

- 1 teaspoon garlic powder
- 1 teaspoon salt
- 2 pounds (907 g) fresh ahi tuna, cut into ½-inch cubes

1. In a medium bowl, mix the scallions, soy sauce, sesame oil, sesame seeds, ginger, garlic powder, and salt. 2. Combine the soy sauce mixture with the tuna, and toss well. Serve immediately. 3. If not serving immediately, store the tuna and the soy sauce mixture separately in the refrigerator until ready to serve.

Per Serving:

⅙ recipe: calories: 241 | fat: 9g | protein: 38g | carbs: 2g | net carbs: 1g | fiber: 1g

Crunchy Fish Sticks

Prep time: 30 minutes | Cook time: 9 minutes | Serves 4

- ◄ 1 pound (454 g) cod fillets
- ◄ 1½ cups finely ground blanched almond flour
- ◄ 2 teaspoons Old Bay seasoning
- ◄ ½ teaspoon paprika
- ◄ Sea salt and freshly ground
- black pepper, to taste
- ◄ ¼ cup sugar-free mayonnaise
- ◄ 1 large egg, beaten
- ◄ Avocado oil spray
- ◄ Tartar sauce, for serving

1. Cut the fish into ¾-inch-wide strips. 2. In a shallow bowl, stir together the almond flour, Old Bay seasoning, paprika, and salt and pepper to taste. In another shallow bowl, whisk together the mayonnaise and egg. 3. Dip the cod strips in the egg mixture, then the almond flour, gently pressing with your fingers to help adhere to the coating. 4. Place the coated fish on a parchment paper-lined baking sheet and freeze for 30 minutes. 5. Spray the air fryer basket with oil. Set the air fryer to 400°F (204°C). Place the fish in the basket in a single layer, and spray each piece with oil. 6. Cook for 5 minutes. Flip and spray with more oil. Cook for 4 minutes more, until the internal temperature reaches 140°F (60°C). Serve with the tartar sauce.

Per Serving:

calories: 500 | fat: 38g | protein: 33g | carbs: 12g | net carbs: 6g | fiber: 6g

Souvlaki Spiced Salmon Bowls

Prep time: 10 minutes | Cook time: 20 minutes | Serves 4

For The Salmon
- ◄ ¼ cup good-quality olive oil
- ◄ Juice of 1 lemon
- ◄ 2 tablespoons chopped fresh oregano
- ◄ 1 tablespoon minced garlic
- ◄ 1 tablespoon balsamic vinegar

For The Bowls
- ◄ 2 tablespoons good-quality olive oil
- ◄ 1 red bell pepper, cut into strips
- ◄ 1 yellow bell pepper, cut into strips
- ◄ 1 zucchini, cut into ½-inch strips lengthwise

- ◄ 1 tablespoon smoked sweet paprika
- ◄ ½ teaspoon sea salt
- ◄ ¼ teaspoon freshly ground black pepper
- ◄ 4 (4-ounce) salmon fillets

- ◄ 1 cucumber, diced
- ◄ 1 large tomato, chopped
- ◄ ½ cup sliced Kalamata olives
- ◄ 6 ounces feta cheese, crumbled
- ◄ ½ cup sour cream

Make The Salmon: 1. Marinate the fish. In a medium bowl, stir together the olive oil, lemon juice, oregano, garlic, vinegar, paprika, salt, and pepper. Add the salmon and turn to coat it well with the marinade. Cover the bowl and let the salmon sit marinating for 15 to 20 minutes. 2. Grill the fish. Preheat the grill to medium-high heat and grill the fish until just cooked through, 4 to 5 minutes per side. Set the fish aside on a plate. Make The Bowls: 1. Grill the vegetables. In a medium bowl, toss together the oil, red and yellow bell peppers, and zucchini. Grill the vegetables, turning once, until they're lightly charred and soft, about 3 minutes per side. 2. Assemble and serve. Divide the grilled vegetables between four bowls. Top each bowl with cucumber, tomato, olives, feta cheese, and the sour cream. Place one salmon fillet on top of each bowl and serve immediately.

Per Serving:

calories: 553 | fat: 44g | protein: 30g | carbs: 10g | net carbs: 7g | fiber: 3g

Prosciutto-Wrapped Haddock

Prep time: 10 minutes | Cook time: 15 minutes | Serves 4

- ◄ 4 (4 ounces) haddock fillets, about 1 inch thick
- ◄ Sea salt, for seasoning
- ◄ Freshly ground black pepper, for seasoning
- ◄ 4 slices prosciutto (2 ounces)
- ◄ 3 tablespoons garlic-infused olive oil
- ◄ Juice and zest of 1 lemon

1. Preheat the oven. Set the oven temperature to 350°F. Line a baking sheet with parchment paper. 2. Prepare the fish. Pat the fish dry with paper towels and season it lightly on both sides with salt and pepper. Wrap the prosciutto around the fish tightly but carefully so it doesn't rip. 3. Bake the fish. Place the fish on the baking sheet and drizzle it with the olive oil. Bake for 15 to 17 minutes until the fish flakes easily with a fork. 4. Serve. Divide the fish between four plates and top with the lemon zest and a drizzle of lemon juice.

Per Serving:

calories: 282 | fat: 18g | protein: 29g | carbs: 1g | net carbs: 1g | fiber: 0g

Parmesan Mackerel with Coriander

Prep time: 10 minutes | Cook time: 7 minutes | Serves 2

- ◄ 12 ounces (340 g) mackerel fillet
- ◄ 2 ounces (57 g) Parmesan,
- grated
- ◄ 1 teaspoon ground coriander
- ◄ 1 tablespoon olive oil

1. Sprinkle the mackerel fillet with olive oil and put it in the air fryer basket. 2. Top the fish with ground coriander and Parmesan. 3. Cook the fish at 390°F (199°C) for 7 minutes.

Per Serving:

calories: 504 | fat: 36g | protein: 42g | carbs: 3g | net carbs: 2g | fiber: 0g

Cajun Cod Fillet

Prep time: 10 minutes | Cook time: 4 minutes | Serves 2

- ◄ 10 ounces (283 g) cod fillet
- ◄ 1 tablespoon olive oil
- ◄ 1 teaspoon Cajun seasoning
- ◄ 2 tablespoons coconut aminos

1. Sprinkle the cod fillet with coconut aminos and Cajun seasoning. 2. Then heat up olive oil in the instant pot on Sauté mode. 3. Add the spiced cod fillet and cook it for 4 minutes from each side. 4. Then cut it into halves and sprinkle with the oily liquid from the instant pot.

Per Serving:

calories: 189 | fat: 8g | protein: 25g | carbs: 3g | net carbs: 3g | fiber: 0g

Cod with Avocado

Prep time: 30 minutes | Cook time: 10 minutes | Serves 2

- ◄ 1 cup shredded cabbage
- ◄ ¼ cup full-fat sour cream
- ◄ 2 tablespoons full-fat mayonnaise
- ◄ ¼ cup chopped pickled jalapeños
- ◄ 2 (3-ounce / 85-g) cod fillets
- ◄ 1 teaspoon chili powder
- ◄ 1 teaspoon cumin
- ◄ ½ teaspoon paprika
- ◄ ¼ teaspoon garlic powder
- ◄ 1 medium avocado, peeled, pitted, and sliced
- ◄ ½ medium lime

1. In a large bowl, place cabbage, sour cream, mayonnaise, and jalapeños. Mix until fully coated. Let sit for 20 minutes in the refrigerator. 2. Sprinkle cod fillets with chili powder, cumin, paprika, and garlic powder. Place each fillet into the air fryer basket. 3. Adjust the temperature to 370ºF (188ºC) and set the timer for 10 minutes. 4. Flip the fillets halfway through the cooking time. When fully cooked, fish should have an internal temperature of at least 145ºF (63ºC). 5. To serve, divide slaw mixture into two serving bowls, break cod fillets into pieces and spread over the bowls, and top with avocado. Squeeze lime juice over each bowl. Serve immediately.

Per Serving:

calories: 550 | fat: 43g | protein: 28g | carbs: 18g | net carbs: 9g | fiber: 9g

Blackened Red Snapper

Prep time: 13 minutes | Cook time: 8 to 10 minutes | Serves 4

- ◄ 1½ teaspoons black pepper
- ◄ ¼ teaspoon thyme
- ◄ ¼ teaspoon garlic powder
- ◄ ⅛ teaspoon cayenne pepper
- ◄ 1 teaspoon olive oil
- ◄ 4 (4 ounces / 113 g) red snapper fillet portions, skin on
- ◄ 4 thin slices lemon
- ◄ Cooking spray

1. Mix the spices and oil together to make a paste. Rub into both sides of the fish. 2. Spray the air fryer basket with nonstick cooking spray and lay snapper steaks in basket, skin-side down. 3. Place a lemon slice on each piece of fish. 4. Roast at 390ºF (199ºC) for 8 to 10 minutes. The fish will not flake when done, but it should be white through the center.

Per Serving:

calories: 134 | fat: 3g | protein: 22g | carbs: 2g | net carbs: 1g | fiber: 1g

Chapter 7

Snacks and Appetizers

Chapter 7
Snacks and Appetizers

Snappy Bacon Asparagus

Prep time: 20 minutes | Cook time: 25 minutes | Serves 6

◀ 24 asparagus spears
◀ 6 strips no-sugar-added bacon, uncooked
◀ 2 tablespoons olive oil
◀ ⅛ teaspoon salt

1. My favorite part of preparing asparagus is the SNAP. Grab the "nonpointed" end of stalk and bend until it breaks. This usually happens about an inch from the end with the cut. Now, line up asparagus and cut entire bunch at "snapping" point, making all of your stalks uniform in length. Fancy, right? 2. On a microwave-safe plate, microwave asparagus 2 minutes to soften. Let cool 5 minutes. 3. Lay strip of bacon on a cutting board at 45-degree angle. Lay four asparagus spears centered on bacon in an "up and down" position. 4. Pick up bacon and asparagus where they meet and wrap two ends of bacon around asparagus in opposite directions. 5. Wrap bacon tightly and secure, pinning bacon to asparagus at ends with toothpicks. Don't worry if bacon doesn't cover entire spears. 6. Brush asparagus with olive oil and sprinkle with salt. 7. Heat a medium nonstick skillet over medium heat. Cook asparagus/bacon 3–5 minutes per side while turning to cook thoroughly. Continue flipping until bacon is brown and crispy.

Per Serving:

calories: 90 | fat: 7g | protein: 5g | carbs: 3g | net carbs: 3g | fiber: 1g

Bacon-Pepper Fat Bombs

Prep time: 10 minutes | Cook time: 0 minutes | Makes 12 fat bombs

◀ 2 ounces goat cheese, at room temperature
◀ 2 ounces cream cheese, at room temperature
◀ ¼ cup butter, at room
temperature
◀ 8 bacon slices, cooked and chopped
◀ Pinch freshly ground black pepper

1. Line a small baking sheet with parchment paper and set aside. 2. In a medium bowl, stir together the goat cheese, cream cheese, butter, bacon, and pepper until well combined. 3. Use a tablespoon to drop mounds of the bomb mixture on the baking sheet and place

the sheet in the freezer until the fat bombs are very firm but not frozen, about 1 hour. 4. Store the fat bombs in a sealed container in the refrigerator for up to 2 weeks.

Per Serving:

1 fat bomb: calories: 89 | fat: 8g | protein: 3g | carbs: 0g | net carbs: 0g | fiber: 0g

Broccoli Cheese Dip

Prep time: 5 minutes | Cook time: 10 minutes | Serves 6

◀ 4 tablespoons butter
◀ ½ medium onion, diced
◀ 1½ cups chopped broccoli
◀ 8 ounces (227 g) cream cheese
◀ ½ cup mayonnaise
◀ ½ cup chicken broth
◀ 1 cup shredded Cheddar cheese

1. Press the Sauté button and then press the Adjust button to set heat to Less. Add butter to Instant Pot. Add onion and sauté until softened, about 5 minutes. Press the Cancel button. 2. Add broccoli, cream cheese, mayo, and broth to pot. Press the Manual button and adjust time for 4 minutes. 3. When timer beeps, quick-release the pressure and stir in Cheddar. Serve warm.

Per Serving:

calories: 411 | fat: 37g | protein: 8g | carbs: 4g | net carbs: 3g | fiber: 1g

Cream Cheese and Berries

Prep time: 5 minutes | Cook time: 0 minutes | Serves 1

◀ 2 ounces (57 g) cream cheese
◀ 2 large strawberries, cut into
thin slices or chunks
◀ 5 blueberries
◀ ⅛ cup chopped pecans

1. Place the cream cheese on a small plate or in a bowl. 2. Pour the berries and chopped pecans on top. Enjoy!

Per Serving:

calories: 330 | fat: 31g | protein: 6g | carbs: 7g | net carbs: 5g | fiber: 2g

Ketone Gummies

Prep time: 10 minutes | Cook time: 5 minutes | Makes 8 gummies

- ◄ ½ cup (120 ml) lemon juice
- ◄ 8 hulled strawberries (fresh or frozen and defrosted)
- ◄ 2 tablespoons unflavored

Special Equipment (optional):
- ◄ Silicone mold with eight 2-tablespoon or larger cavities

- gelatin
- ◄ 2 teaspoons exogenous ketones

1. Have on hand your favorite silicone mold. I like to use a large silicone ice cube tray and spoon 2 tablespoons of the mixture into each cavity, If you do not have a silicone mold, you can use an 8-inch (20-cm) square silicone or metal baking pan; if using a metal pan, line it with parchment paper, draping some over the sides for easy removal. 2. Place the lemon juice, strawberries, and gelatin in a blender or food processor and pulse until smooth. Transfer the mixture to a small saucepan and set over low heat for 5 minutes, or until it becomes very liquid-y and begins to simmer. 3. Remove from the heat and stir in the exogenous ketones. 4. Divide the mixture evenly among 8 cavities of the mold or pour into the baking pan. Transfer to the fridge and allow to set for 30 minutes. If using a baking pan, cut into 8 squares.

Per Serving:

calories: 19 | fat: 0g | protein: 3g | carbs: 1g | net carbs: 1g | fiber: 0g

Roasted Spiced Nut Mix

Prep time: 10 minutes | Cook time: 10 minutes | Serves 8

- ◄ 1 teaspoon vanilla extract
- ◄ 1 teaspoon ground cinnamon
- ◄ 1 teaspoon ground allspice
- ◄ ½ teaspoon ground ginger
- ◄ ½ teaspoon ground nutmeg
- ◄ 1 teaspoon liquid stevia

- (optional)
- ◄ 4 tablespoons butter
- ◄ 1 cup pecans
- ◄ ½ cup almonds
- ◄ ½ cup macadamia nuts

1. Preheat the oven to 375ºF (190ºC). 2. In a small bowl, combine the vanilla, cinnamon, allspice, ginger, nutmeg, and stevia (if using). Set aside. 3. In a large nonstick skillet over medium-low heat, melt the butter. 4. Add the pecans, almonds, and macadamias. Sprinkle the spice mixture over the nuts and stir to combine, ensuring the nuts are thoroughly coated in butter and spices. Cook for about 10 minutes or until the nuts are golden brown. Remove from the heat and cool slightly before serving. 5. Store in an airtight container on the counter for a few days or refrigerate for up to 1 week.

Per Serving:

¼ cup: calories: 279 | fat: 27g | protein: 4g | carbs: 5g | net carbs: 2g | fiber: 3g

Bacon-Studded Pimento Cheese

Prep time: 10 minutes | Cook time: 5 minutes | Serves 6

- ◄ 2 ounces (57 g) bacon (about 4 thick slices)
- ◄ 4 ounces (113 g) cream cheese, room temperature
- ◄ ¼ cup mayonnaise
- ◄ ¼ teaspoon onion powder

- ◄ ¼ teaspoon cayenne pepper (optional)
- ◄ 1 cup thick-shredded extra-sharp Cheddar cheese
- ◄ 2 ounces (57 g) jarred diced pimentos, drained

1. Chop the raw bacon into ½-inch-thick pieces. Cook in a small skillet over medium heat until crispy, 3 to 4 minutes. Use a slotted spoon to transfer the bacon onto a layer of paper towels. Reserve the rendered fat. 2. In a large bowl, combine the cream cheese, mayonnaise, onion powder, and cayenne (if using), and beat with an electric mixer or by hand until smooth and creamy. 3. Add the rendered bacon fat, Cheddar cheese, and pimentos and mix until well combined. 4. Refrigerate for at least 30 minutes before serving to allow flavors to blend. Serve cold with raw veggies.

Per Serving:

calories: 216 | fat: 20g | protein: 8g | carbs: 2g | net carbs: 0g | fiber: 2

Broccoli with Garlic-Herb Cheese Sauce

Prep time: 5 minutes | Cook time: 3 minutes | Serves 4

- ◄ ½ cup water
- ◄ 1 pound (454 g) broccoli (frozen or fresh)
- ◄ ½ cup heavy cream
- ◄ 1 tablespoon butter
- ◄ ½ cup shredded Cheddar

- cheese
- ◄ 3 tablespoons garlic and herb cheese spread
- ◄ Pinch of salt
- ◄ Pinch of black pepper

1. Add the water to the pot and place the trivet inside. 2. Put the steamer basket on top of the trivet. Place the broccoli in the basket. 3. Close the lid and seal the vent. Cook on Low Pressure for 1 minute. Quick release the steam. Press Cancel. 4. Carefully remove the steamer basket from the pot and drain the water. If you steamed a full bunch of broccoli, pull the florets off the stem. (Chop the stem into bite-size pieces, it's surprisingly creamy.) 5. Turn the pot to Sauté mode. Add the cream and butter. Stir continuously while the butter melts and the cream warms up. 6. When the cream begins to bubble on the edges, add the Cheddar cheese, cheese spread, salt, and pepper. Whisk continuously until the cheeses are melted and a sauce consistency is reached, 1 to 2 minutes. 7. Top one-fourth of the broccoli with 2 tablespoons cheese sauce.

Per Serving:

calories: 134 | fat: 12g | protein:4 g | carbs: 5g | net carbs: 3g | fiber: 2g

English Cucumber Tea Sandwiches

Prep time: 10 minutes | Cook time: 0 minutes | Makes 12 snacks

◄ 1 large cucumber, peeled (approximately 10 ounces / 283 g)
◄ 4 ounces (113 g) cream cheese, softened

◄ 2 tablespoons finely chopped fresh dill
◄ Freshly ground black pepper, to taste

1. Slice the cucumbers into 24 rounds approximately ¼ inch (6 mm) thick. Place in a single layer between two kitchen towels. Put a cutting board on top. Allow to sit about 5 minutes. 2. Mix the cream cheese and dill. 3. Spread 2 teaspoons cream cheese on half the cucumber slices. Grind black pepper over the cheese. Place another slice of cucumber on top of each and secure with a toothpick, if desired.

Per Serving:

calories: 96 | fat: 8g | protein: 3g | carbs: 3g | net carbs: 1g | fiber: 2g

Sweet Pepper Nacho Bites

Prep time: 5 minutes | Cook time: 5 minutes | Makes 24 bites

◄ 12 mini sweet peppers (approximately 8 ounces / 227 g)
◄ ½ cup shredded Monterey

Jack cheese
◄ ½ cup guacamole
◄ Juice of 1 lime

1. Preheat the oven to 400ºF (205ºC). 2. Carefully cut each pepper in half lengthwise and remove the seeds. Place them cut side up on a rimmed baking sheet so they aren't touching. Place 1 teaspoon of shredded cheese inside each. Bake 3 to 5 minutes, until the cheese starts to melt. 3. Remove from the oven and top each with 1 teaspoon of guacamole. Squeeze the lime juice over top. Serve immediately.

Per Serving:

calories: 137 | fat: 12g | protein: 4g | carbs: 5g | net carbs: 3g | fiber: 2g

Candied Georgia Pecans

Prep time: 10 minutes | Cook time: 1 hour | Serves 12

◄ 12 ounces raw pecan halves
◄ 1 large egg white
◄ 1 teaspoon water
◄ 2 teaspoons vanilla extract
◄ ½ teaspoon plus 10 drops of

liquid stevia
◄ 1 teaspoon ground cinnamon
◄ 1 teaspoon pink Himalayan salt

1. Preheat the oven to 250°F. Line a rimmed baking sheet with parchment paper. 2. Spread the pecan halves on the prepared

baking sheet in an even layer. 3. In a small bowl, whisk together the egg white, water, vanilla extract, stevia, cinnamon, and salt until combined. Pour the mixture over the pecans and toss with your hands or a spoon until the pecans are evenly coated. 4. Flatten out the pecans into a single layer and bake for 45 to 60 minutes, tossing every 15 minutes. The pecans are done when they have fully dried out and browned.

Per Serving:

calories: 202 | fat: 24g | protein: 3g | carbs: 4g | net carbs: 3g | fiber: 3g

Herbed Zucchini Slices

Prep time: 5 minutes | Cook time: 5 minutes | Serves 4

◄ 2 tablespoons olive oil
◄ 2 garlic cloves, chopped
◄ 1 pound (454 g) zucchini, sliced
◄ ½ cup water

◄ ½ cup sugar-free tomato purée
◄ 1 teaspoon dried thyme
◄ ½ teaspoon dried rosemary
◄ ½ teaspoon dried oregano

1. Set your Instant Pot to Sauté and heat the olive oil. 2. Add the garlic and sauté for 2 minutes until fragrant. 3. Add the remaining ingredients to the Instant Pot and stir well. 4. Lock the lid. Select the Manual mode and set the cooking time for 3 minutes at Low Pressure. 5. When the timer beeps, perform a quick pressure release. Carefully remove the lid. 6. Serve warm.

Per Serving:

calories: 87 | fat: 8g | protein: 2g | carbs: 5g | net carbs: 3g | fiber: 2g

Cubed Tofu Fries

Prep time: 25 minutes | Cook time: 20 minutes | Serves 4

◄ 1 (12 ounces) package extra-firm tofu
◄ 2 tablespoons sesame oil
◄ ⅛ teaspoon salt, divided

◄ ⅛ teaspoon black pepper, divided
◄ ⅛ teaspoon creole seasoning, divided

1. Remove tofu from packaging and wrap in paper towel. Set on a clean plate. Place a second plate on top and put a 3- to 5-pound weight on top. Let sit 20 minutes. Drain excess water. 2. Unwrap tofu and slice into small cubes no larger than ½" square (a little larger than sugar cubes). 3. In a large skillet over medium heat, heat oil. 4. Combine salt, pepper, and creole seasoning in a small bowl. Sprinkle one-third of spice mixture evenly into skillet and add tofu evenly. 5. Sprinkle one-third of spices on top and let fry 5 minutes on each side, flipping three times (for the four sides), browning all four sides. 6. Dust tofu with remaining spice mixture. 7. Remove from heat. Enjoy while hot!

Per Serving:

calories: 160 | fat: 13g | protein: 8g | carbs: 2g | net carbs: 2g | fiber: 0g

Parmesan Artichoke

Prep time: 1 minute | Cook time: 30 minutes | Serves 2

- 1 large artichoke
- 1 cup water
- ¼ cup grated Parmesan
- cheese
- ¼ teaspoon salt
- ¼ teaspoon red pepper flakes

1. Trim artichoke. Remove stem, outer leaves and top. Gently spread leaves. 2. Add water to Instant Pot and place steam rack on bottom. Place artichoke on steam rack and sprinkle with Parmesan, salt, and red pepper flakes. Click lid closed. Press the Steam button and adjust time for 30 minutes. 3. When timer beeps, allow a 15-minute natural release and then quick-release the remaining pressure. Enjoy warm topped with additional Parmesan.

Per Serving:

calories: 90 | fat: 3g | protein: 6g | carbs: 10g | net carbs: 6g | fiber: 4g

Oregano Sausage Balls

Prep time: 10 minutes | Cook time: 16 minutes | Serves 10

- 15 ounces (425 g) ground pork sausage
- 1 teaspoon dried oregano
- 4 ounces (113 g) Mozzarella, shredded
- 1 cup coconut flour
- 1 garlic clove, grated
- 1 teaspoon coconut oil, melted

1. In the bowl mix up ground pork sausages, dried oregano, shredded Mozzarella, coconut flour, and garlic clove. 2. When the mixture is homogenous, make the balls. 3. After this, pour coconut oil in the instant pot. 4. Arrange the balls in the instant pot and cook them on Sauté mode for 8 minutes from each side.

Per Serving:

calories: 310 | fat: 23g | protein: 17g | carbs: 10g | net carbs: 5g | fiber: 5g

Bacon-Wrapped Jalapeños

Prep time: 10 minutes | Cook time: 20 minutes | Serves 4

- 10 jalapeños
- 8 ounces cream cheese, at room temperature
- 1 pound bacon (you will use about half a slice per popper)

1. Preheat the oven to 450°F. Line a baking sheet with aluminum foil or a silicone baking mat. 2. Halve the jalapeños lengthwise, and remove the seeds and membranes (if you like the extra heat, leave them in). Place them on the prepared pan cut-side up. 3. Spread some of the cream cheese inside each jalapeño half. 4. Wrap a jalapeño half with a slice of bacon (depending on the size of the jalapeño, use a whole slice of bacon, or half). 5. Secure the bacon around each jalapeño with 1 to 2 toothpicks so it stays put while baking. 6. Bake for 20 minutes, until the bacon is done and crispy. 7. Serve hot or at room temperature. Either way, they are delicious!

Per Serving:

calories: 164 | fat: 13g | protein: 9g | carbs: 1g | net carbs: 1g | fiber 0g

Cheese and Charcuterie Board

Prep time: 15 minutes | Cook time: 0 minutes | Serves 7

- 4 ounces prosciutto, sliced
- 4 ounces Calabrese salami, sliced
- 4 ounces capicola, sliced
- 7 ounces Parrano Gouda cheese
- 7 ounces aged Manchego
- cheese
- 7 ounces Brie cheese
- ½ cup roasted almonds
- ½ cup mixed olives
- 12 cornichons (small, tart pickles)

1. Sprig fresh rosemary or other herbs of choice, for garnish. Arrange the meats, cheeses, and almonds on a large wooden cutting board. 2. Place the olives and pickles in separate bowls and set them on or alongside the cutting board. Garnish with a spring of rosemary or other fresh herbs of your choice.

Per Serving:

calories: 445 | fat: 35g | protein: 31g | carbs: 3g | net carbs: 2g fiber: 1g

Peanut Butter Keto Fudge

Prep time: 5 minutes | Cook time: 10 minutes | Serves 12

- ½ cup (1 stick) butter
- 8 ounces (227 g) cream cheese
- 1 cup unsweetened peanut butter
- 1 teaspoon vanilla extract (or the seeds from 1 vanilla bean)
- 1 teaspoon liquid stevia (optional)

1. Line an 8 or 9-inch square or 9-by-13-inch rectangular baking dish with parchment paper. Set aside. 2. In a saucepan over medium heat, melt the butter and cream cheese together, stirring frequently for about 5 minutes. 3. Add the peanut butter and continue to stir until smooth. Remove from the heat. 4. Stir in the vanilla and stevia (if using). Pour the mixture into the prepared dish and spread into an even layer. Refrigerate for about 1 hour until thickened and set enough to cut and handle. Cut into small squares and enjoy. Refrigerate, covered, for up to 1 week.

Per Serving:

1 fudge square: calories: 261 | fat: 24g | protein: 8g | carbs: 5g | net carbs: 4g | fiber: 1g

Sweet and Spicy Beef Jerky

Prep time: 15 minutes | Cook time: 4 to 6 hours | Serves 16

- ◄ 3 pounds flat-iron steak

Marinade:
- ◄ ½ cup soy sauce
- ◄ ½ cup apple cider vinegar
- ◄ ¼ cup Frank's RedHot sauce
- ◄ ½ teaspoon liquid stevia
- ◄ 2 teaspoons liquid smoke
- ◄ 2 teaspoons ground black pepper
- ◄ 1½ teaspoons garlic powder
- ◄ 1 teaspoon onion powder

Special equipment:
- ◄ 10 (12-inch) bamboo skewers

1. Marinate the steak: Slice the steak into thin jerky-sized strips, about ¼ inch thick, and put them in a gallon-sized ziptop plastic bag. Add the marinade ingredients, seal the bag, and shake to fully coat the meat. 2. Seal the bag tightly (removing any excess air) and place it in a bowl to catch any leakage. Place the bowl in the refrigerator for at least 4 hours or up to 24 hours. 3. Make the jerky: Adjust the racks in your oven so that one is in the highest position and one is in the lowest position. Preheat the oven to 190°F. 4. Remove the steak strips from the marinade and pat them as dry as possible using paper towels; discard the remaining marinade. 5. Using bamboo skewers, pierce the tip of each meat strip so that there are anywhere from 5 to 7 strips hanging on each skewer. Be sure to leave space between the strips so that air can circulate around them. Hang the skewers from the top oven rack and place a rimmed baking sheet on the lowest rack to catch any drippings. 6. Bake for 4 to 6 hours, until the jerky is dry to the touch. 7. Store in a zip-top plastic bag in the refrigerator for up to 10 days.

Per Serving:

calories: 150 | fat: 10g | protein: 16g | carbs: 1g | net carbs: 1g | fiber: 0g

Everything Bagel Cream Cheese Dip

Prep time: 10 minutes | Cook time: 0 minutes | Serves 4

- ◄ 1 (8-ounce / 227-g) package cream cheese, at room temperature
- ◄ ½ cup sour cream
- ◄ 1 tablespoon garlic powder
- ◄ 1 tablespoon dried onion, or onion powder
- ◄ 1 tablespoon sesame seeds
- ◄ 1 tablespoon kosher salt

1. In a small bowl, combine the cream cheese, sour cream, garlic powder, dried onion, sesame seeds, and salt. Stir well to incorporate everything together. Serve immediately or cover and refrigerate for up to 6 days.

Per Serving:

calories: 291 | fat: 27g | protein: 6g | carbs: 6g | net carbs: 5g | fiber: 1g

Creamed Onion Spinach

Prep time: 3 minutes | Cook time: 5 minutes | Serves 6

- ◄ 4 tablespoons butter
- ◄ ¼ cup diced onion
- ◄ 8 ounces (227 g) cream cheese
- ◄ 1 (12 ounces / 340 g) bag
- ◄ frozen spinach
- ◄ ½ cup chicken broth
- ◄ 1 cup shredded whole-milk Mozzarella cheese

1. Press the Sauté button and add butter. Once butter is melted, add onion to Instant Pot and sauté for 2 minutes or until onion begins to turn translucent. 2. Break cream cheese into pieces and add to Instant Pot. Press the Cancel button. Add frozen spinach and broth. Click lid closed. Press the Manual button and adjust time for 5 minutes. When timer beeps, quick-release the pressure and stir in shredded Mozzarella. If mixture is too watery, press the Sauté button and reduce for additional 5 minutes, stirring constantly.

Per Serving:

calories: 273 | fat: 24g | protein: 9g | carbs: 5g | net carbs: 3g | fiber: 2g

Salami Chips with Pesto

Prep time: 10 minutes | Cook time: 12 minutes | Serves 6

Chips:
- ◄ 6 ounces sliced Genoa salami

Pesto:
- ◄ 1 cup fresh basil leaves
- ◄ 3 cloves garlic
- ◄ ¼ cup grated Parmesan cheese
- ◄ ¼ cup raw walnuts
- ◄ ¼ teaspoon pink Himalayan salt
- ◄ ¼ teaspoon ground black pepper
- ◄ ½ cup extra-virgin olive oil

1. Make the chips: Preheat the oven to 375°F and line 2 rimmed baking sheets with parchment paper. 2. Arrange the salami in a single layer on the lined baking sheets. Bake for 10 to 12 minutes, until crisp. Transfer to a paper towel–lined plate to absorb the excess oil. Allow to cool and crisp up further. 3. Make the pesto: Put all the pesto ingredients, except for the olive oil, in a food processor and pulse until everything is roughly chopped and a coarse paste has formed. 4. With the food processor running, slowly pour in the olive oil. Process until all of the oil has been added and the ingredients are fully incorporated. Taste and season with additional salt and pepper, if desired. 5. Pour the pesto into a small serving bowl and serve the salami chips alongside. Store leftover pesto in a sealed container in the refrigerator for up to 2 weeks; store the chips in a zip-top plastic bag in the refrigerator for up to 5 days.

Per Serving:

calories: 202 | fat: 9g | protein: 8g | carbs: 1g | net carbs: 1g | fiber: 0g

Baked Crab Dip

Prep time: 15 minutes | Cook time: 25 minutes | Serves 4 to 6

- 4 ounces cream cheese, softened
- ½ cup shredded Parmesan cheese, plus ½ cup extra for topping (optional) ⅓ cup mayonnaise
- ¼ cup sour cream
- 1 tablespoon chopped fresh
- parsley
- 2 teaspoons fresh lemon juice
- 1½ teaspoons Sriracha sauce
- ½ teaspoon garlic powder
- 8 ounces fresh lump crabmeat
- Salt and pepper

1. Preheat the oven to 375°F. 2. Combine all the ingredients except for the crabmeat in a mixing bowl and use a hand mixer to blend until smooth. 3. Put the crabmeat in a separate bowl, check for shells, and rinse with cold water, if needed. Pat dry or allow to rest in a strainer until most of the water has drained. 4. Add the crabmeat to the bowl with the cream cheese mixture and gently fold to combine. Taste for seasoning and add salt and pepper to taste, if needed. Pour into an 8-inch round or square baking dish and bake for 25 minutes, until the cheese has melted and the dip is warm throughout. 5. If desired, top the dip with another ½ cup of Parmesan cheese and broil for 2 to 3 minutes, until the cheese has melted and browned slightly.

Per Serving:

calories: 275 | fat: 23g | protein: 16g | carbs: 1g | net carbs: 1g | fiber: 0g

Grandma's Meringues

Prep time: 10 minutes | Cook time: 1 hour | Makes 12 meringues

- 2 large egg whites, room temperature
- ¼ teaspoon cream of tartar
- Pinch of finely ground sea salt
- ½ cup (80 g) confectioners'-style erythritol
- ½ teaspoon vanilla extract
- For Serving:
- 24 fresh strawberries, sliced
- ¾ cup (190 g) coconut cream
- 12 fresh mint leaves

1. Preheat the oven to 225°F (108°C). Line a rimmed baking sheet with parchment paper or a silicone baking mat. 2. Place the egg whites, cream of tartar, and salt in a very clean large bowl. Make sure that the bowl does not have any oil residue in it. Using a handheld electric mixer or stand mixer, mix on low speed until the mixture becomes foamy. 3. Once foamy, increase the speed to high. Slowly add the erythritol, 1 tablespoon at a time, mixing all the while. Add a tablespoon about every 20 seconds. 4. Keep beating until the mixture is shiny and thick and peaks have formed; it should be nearly doubled in volume. (The peaks won't be as stiff as in a traditional meringue.) Fold in the vanilla. 5. Using a large spoon, dollop the meringue mixture onto the lined baking sheet, making a total of 12 meringues. 6. Bake for 1 hour without

opening the oven door. After 1 hour, turn off the oven and keep the meringues in the cooling oven for another hour, then remove. 7. To serve, place 2 meringues on each plate. Top each serving with 4 sliced strawberries, 2 tablespoons of coconut cream, and 2 mint leaves.

Per Serving:

calories: 100 | fat: 8g | protein: 2g | carbs: 6g | net carbs: 4g | fiber: 2g

Avocado Feta Dip

Prep time: 15 minutes | Cook time: 0 minutes | Serves 8

- 2 avocados, diced
- 2 Roma tomatoes, chopped
- ¼ medium red onion, finely chopped (about ½ cup)
- 2 garlic cloves, minced
- 2 tablespoons chopped fresh parsley (or cilantro)
- 2 tablespoons olive oil or avocado oil
- 2 tablespoons red wine
- vinegar
- 1 tablespoon freshly squeezed lemon or lime juice
- ½ teaspoon sea salt
- ¼ teaspoon freshly ground black pepper
- 8 ounces (227 g) feta cheese, crumbled

1. In a large bowl, gently stir together the avocados, tomatoes, onion, garlic, and parsley. 2. In a small bowl, whisk together the oil, vinegar, lemon juice, salt, and pepper. Pour the mixture over the avocado mixture. Fold in the cheese. 3. Cover and let chill in the refrigerator for 1 to 2 hours before serving.

Per Serving:

½ cup: calories: 190 | fat: 16g | protein: 6g | carbs: 6g | net carbs: 3g | fiber: 3g

Queso Dip

Prep time: 5 minutes | Cook time: 10 minutes | Serves 6

- ½ cup coconut milk
- ½ jalapeño pepper, seeded and diced
- 1 teaspoon minced garlic
- ½ teaspoon onion powder
- 2 ounces goat cheese
- 6 ounces sharp Cheddar cheese, shredded
- ¼ teaspoon cayenne pepper

1. Place a medium pot over medium heat and add the coconut milk, jalapeño, garlic, and onion powder. 2. Bring the liquid to a simmer and then whisk in the goat cheese until smooth. 3. Add the Cheddar cheese and cayenne and whisk until the dip is thick, 30 seconds to 1 minute. 4. Pour into a serving dish and serve with keto crackers or low-carb vegetables.

Per Serving:

calories: 213 | fat: 19g | protein: 10g | carbs: 2g | net carbs: 2g | fiber: 0g

Cookie Fat Bombs

Prep time: 10 minutes | Cook time: 0 minutes | serves 6

- 1 cup almond butter
- ½ cup coconut flour
- 1 teaspoon ground cinnamon
- ¼ cup cacao nibs or vegan keto chocolate chips

1. Line a baking sheet with parchment paper. If you don't have parchment paper, use aluminum foil or a greased pan. 2. In a mixing bowl, whisk together the almond butter, coconut flour, and cinnamon. 3. Fold in the cacao nibs. 4. Cover the bowl and put it in the freezer for 15 to 20 minutes. 5. Remove the bowl from the freezer and, using a spoon or cookie scoop, scoop out a dollop of mixture and roll it between your palms to form a ball. Repeat to use all the mixture. 6. Place the fat bombs on a baking sheet and put the sheet in the freezer to chill for 20 minutes until firm.

Per Serving:

calories: 319 | fat: 26g | protein: 8g | carbs: 18g | net carbs: 8g | fiber: 10g

Zucchini Cakes with Lemon Aioli

Prep time: 20 minutes | Cook time: 22 minutes | Makes 8 small cakes

Cakes:
- 3 lightly packed cups (450 g) shredded zucchini (about 3 medium zucchinis)
- 4 strips bacon (about 4 ounces/110 g)
- 1 teaspoon finely ground sea salt
- 1 large egg
- 1 tablespoon coconut flour

- 1 tablespoon arrowroot starch or tapioca starch
- ¾ teaspoon garlic powder
- ¾ teaspoon onion powder
- ½ teaspoon dried oregano leaves
- ¼ teaspoon ground black pepper

Lemon Aioli:
- ¼ cup (52 g) mayonnaise
- Grated zest of ½ lemon
- 1 tablespoon plus 1 teaspoon lemon juice
- 1 teaspoon Dijon mustard

- 1 clove garlic, minced
- ¼ teaspoon finely ground sea salt
- ⅛ teaspoon ground black pepper

1. Cut the cucumber in half lengthwise, scoop out the seeds, and then cut each piece in half crosswise. Set aside. 2. Place the remaining ingredients in a medium-sized bowl and mix until incorporated. 3. Spoon the tuna mixture into the hollowed-out cucumber pieces, piling it high. Set on a plate and 1. Place the shredded zucchini in a strainer set over the sink. Sprinkle with the salt and allow to sit for 15 minutes. 2. Meanwhile, cook the bacon in a large frying pan over medium heat until crispy, about 10 minutes. Remove the bacon from the pan, leaving the grease in the pan. When the bacon has cooled, crumble it. 3. While the bacon is cooking, make the aioli: Put the mayonnaise, lemon zest, lemon juice, mustard, garlic, salt, and pepper in a small bowl and whisk to incorporate. Set aside. 4. When the zucchini is ready, squeeze it

over and over again to get out as much of the water as you can. 5. Transfer the zucchini to a large mixing bowl and add the remaining ingredients for the cakes. Stir until fully incorporated. 6. Set the frying pan with the bacon grease over medium-low heat. Scoop up 2 tablespoons of the zucchini mixture, roll it into a ball between your hands, and place in the hot pan. Repeat with the remaining mixture, making a total of 8 balls. Press each ball with the back of a fork until the cakes are about ½ inch (1.25 cm) thick. 7. Cook the cakes for 4 to 6 minutes per side, until golden. Serve with the aioli.

Per Serving:

calories: 636 | fat: 53g | protein: 28g | carbs: 12g | net carbs: 9g | fiber: 3g

Citrus-Marinated Olives

Prep time: 10 minutes | Cook time: 0 minutes | Makes 2 cups

- 2 cups mixed green olives with pits
- ¼ cup red wine vinegar
- ¼ cup extra-virgin olive oil
- 4 garlic cloves, finely minced
- Zest and juice of 2

- clementines or 1 large orange
- 1 teaspoon red pepper flakes
- 2 bay leaves
- ½ teaspoon ground cumin
- ½ teaspoon ground allspice

1. In a large glass bowl or jar, combine the olives, vinegar, oil, garlic, orange zest and juice, red pepper flakes, bay leaves, cumin, and allspice and mix well. Cover and refrigerate for at least 4 hours or up to a week to allow the olives to marinate, tossing again before serving.

Per Serving:

¼ cup: calories: 100 | fat: 10g | protein: 1g | carbs: 3g | net carbs: 2g | fiber: 1g

Walnut Herb-Crusted Goat Cheese

Prep time: 10 minutes | Cook time: 0 minutes | Serves 4

- 6 ounces chopped walnuts
- 1 tablespoon chopped oregano
- 1 tablespoon chopped parsley

- 1 teaspoon chopped fresh thyme
- ¼ teaspoon freshly ground black pepper
- 1 (8 ounces) log goat cheese

1. Place the walnuts, oregano, parsley, thyme, and pepper in a food processor and pulse until finely chopped. 2. Pour the walnut mixture onto a plate and roll the goat cheese log in the nut mixture, pressing so the cheese is covered and the walnut mixture sticks to the log. 3. Wrap the cheese in plastic and store in the refrigerator for up to 1 week. 4. Slice and enjoy!

Per Serving:

calories: 304 | fat: 28g | protein: 12g | carbs: 4g | net carbs: 2g | fiber: 2g

Caponata Dip

Prep time: 15 minutes | Cook time: 35 minutes | Makes about 2 cups

- 1 large eggplant (about 1¼ pounds / 567 g), cut into ½-inch pieces
- 1 large yellow onion, cut into ½-inch pieces
- 4 large cloves garlic, peeled and smashed with the side of a knife
- 4 tablespoons extra-virgin olive oil, divided, plus extra

For Garnish:
- Extra-virgin olive oil
- Fresh cilantro leaves

For Serving (Optional):
- Low-carb flax crackers
- for garnish
- ½ teaspoon sea salt
- ¼ teaspoon ground black pepper
- ¼ teaspoon ground cumin
- 1 medium tomato, chopped into 1-inch chunks
- Juice of 1 lemon
- 2 tablespoons chopped fresh cilantro leaves
- Pinch of paprika (optional)
- Pine nuts (optional)
- Sliced vegetables

1. Preheat the oven to 375ºF (190ºC). 2. Place the eggplant, onion, garlic, 2 tablespoons of the olive oil, salt, pepper, and cumin in a large bowl and toss to combine. 3. Spread the mixture out on a rimmed baking sheet and bake for 30 to 35 minutes, until the eggplant is softened and browned, tossing halfway through. 4. Remove the eggplant mixture from the oven and transfer it to a food processor. Add the tomato, lemon juice, cilantro, and remaining 2 tablespoons of olive oil. Pulse until the mixture is just slightly chunky. Add salt and pepper to taste. 5. Scoop the dip into a serving dish and garnish with additional olive oil, cilantro, paprika (if desired), and pine nuts (optional). Serve with low-carb crackers and sliced vegetables, if desired.

Per Serving:

calories: 90 | fat: 7g | protein: 1g | carbs: 7g | net carbs: 4g | fiber: 3g

Bacon-Cheddar Dip Stuffed Mushrooms

Prep time: 10 minutes | Cook time: 35 minutes | Serves 12

- 24 ounces (680 g) baby portobello mushrooms
- 2 tablespoons avocado oil
- 3 ounces (85 g) cream cheese
- ¼ cup sour cream
- 2 cloves garlic, minced
- 1 tablespoon chopped fresh
- dill
- 1 tablespoon chopped fresh parsley
- ¾ cup (3 ounces / 85 g) shredded Cheddar cheese
- ⅓ cup cooked bacon bits
- 3 tablespoons sliced green onions

1. Preheat the oven to 400ºF (205ºC). Line a sheet pan with foil or parchment paper and grease lightly. 2. Remove the stems from the mushrooms and place cavity side up on the baking sheet. Drizzle with the avocado oil. 3. Roast the mushrooms for 15 to 20 minutes, until soft. 4. Meanwhile, in a microwave-safe bowl or a saucepan, melt the cream cheese in the microwave or over low heat on the stove until it's soft and easy to stir. Remove from the heat. 5. Stir the sour cream, garlic, dill, and parsley into the cream cheese. Stir in the Cheddar, bacon, and green onions. 6. When the mushrooms are soft, remove from the oven but leave the oven on. Drain any liquid from the pan and from inside the mushrooms. Pat the cavities dry with paper towels. Use a small cookie scoop or spoon to fill them with the dip mixture. 7. Bake the stuffed mushrooms for 10 to 15 minutes, until hot.

Per Serving:

calories: 107 | fat: 8g | protein: 4g | carbs: 3g | net carbs: 3g | fiber: 0g

Pecan Sandy Fat Bombs

Prep time: 15 minutes | Cook time: 0 minutes | Makes 8 fat bombs

- ½ cup (1 stick) unsalted butter, room temperature
- ¼ cup granulated sugar-free sweetener
- ½ teaspoon vanilla extract
- 1 cup almond flour
- ¾ cup chopped roasted unsalted pecans, divided

1. In a large bowl, use an electric mixer on medium speed to cream together the butter and sweetener until smooth. Add the vanilla and beat well. 2. Add the almond flour and ½ cup of chopped pecans and stir until well incorporated. Place the mixture in the refrigerator for 30 minutes, or until slightly hardened. Meanwhile, very finely chop the remaining ¼ cup of pecans. 3. Using a spoon or your hands, form the chilled mixture into 8 (1-inch) round balls and place on a baking sheet lined with parchment paper. Roll each ball in the finely chopped pecans, and refrigerate for at least 30 minutes before serving. Store in an airtight container in the refrigerator for up to 1 week or in the freezer for up to 2 months.

Per Serving:

calories: 242 | fat: 25g | protein: 4g | carbs: 4g | net carbs: 1g | fiber: 3g

Warm Herbed Olives

Prep time: 5 minutes | Cook time: 4 minutes | Serves 4

- ¼ cup good-quality olive oil
- 4 ounces green olives
- 4 ounces Kalamata olives
- ½ teaspoon dried thyme
- ¼ teaspoon fennel seeds
- Pinch red pepper flakes

1. Sauté the olives. In a large skillet over medium heat, warm the olive oil. Sauté the olives, thyme, fennel seeds, and red pepper flakes until the olives start to brown, 3 to 4 minutes. 2. Serve. Put the olives into a bowl and serve them warm.

Per Serving:

calories: 165 | fat: 17g | protein: 1g | carbs: 3g | net carbs: 2g | fiber: 1g

Cauliflower Popcorn

Prep time: 5 minutes | Cook time: 40 minutes | Serves 2 to 3

- ◄ Nonstick avocado oil cooking spray, for greasing
- ◄ 1 small to medium head cauliflower, florets with stems chopped into bite-size pieces
- ◄ ½ cup avocado oil
- ◄ ½ cup neutral-flavored
- ◄ grass-fed collagen protein powder (optional)
- ◄ Popcorn seasonings of choice: salt, freshly ground black pepper, garlic powder, onion powder, dried oregano, dried sage, and/or nutritional yeast

1. Preheat the oven to 400°F (205°C). Coat a broiling pan with nonstick avocado oil spray. (If you have an air fryer, you can make your Cauliflower Popcorn in there instead; just coat the fryer basket with nonstick spray.) 2. Put the cauliflower in a mixing bowl. Pour the avocado oil over the top and sprinkle in the protein powder. Add the seasonings of your choice to the bowl. Stir all together to evenly coat the cauliflower. 3. Spread the cauliflower in an even layer on the prepared pan and place in the oven (or pour into your air fryer). Cook for roughly 40 minutes, checking periodically and stirring every 10 minutes or so (same goes for the air fryer, if using). 4. Remove from the oven (or air fryer) and serve.

Per Serving:

calories: 389 | fat: 37g | protein: 4g | carbs: 10g | net carbs: 5g | fiber: 5g

Hushpuppies

Prep time: 10 minutes | Cook time: 15 minutes | Makes 10 hushpuppies

- ◄ High-quality oil, for frying
- ◄ 1 cup finely ground blanched almond flour
- ◄ 1 tablespoon coconut flour
- ◄ 1 teaspoon baking powder
- ◄ ½ teaspoon salt
- ◄ ¼ cup finely chopped onions
- ◄ ¼ cup heavy whipping cream
- ◄ 1 large egg, beaten

1. Attach a candy thermometer to a Dutch oven or other large heavy pot, then pour in 3 inches of oil and set over medium-high heat. Heat the oil to 375°F. 2. In a medium-sized bowl, stir together the almond flour, coconut flour, baking powder, and salt. Stir in the rest of the ingredients and mix until blended. Do not overmix. 3. Use a tablespoon-sized cookie scoop to gently drop the batter into the hot oil. Don't overcrowd the hushpuppies; cook them in two batches. Fry for 3 minutes, then use a mesh skimmer or slotted spoon to turn and fry them for 3 more minutes or until golden brown on all sides. 4. Use the skimmer or slotted spoon to remove the hushpuppies from the oil and place on a paper towel–lined plate to drain. They are best served immediately.

Per Serving:

calories: 172 | fat: 14g | protein: 6g | carbs: 5g | net carbs: 3g | fiber: 3g

Crispy Bacon Wrapped Onion Rings

Prep time: 15 minutes | Cook time: 40 minutes | Serves 6

- ◄ 1 extra-large (1 pound / 454 g) onion, sliced into ½-inch-thick rings
- ◄ 12 slices bacon, halved
- ◄ lengthwise
- ◄ Avocado oil cooking spray
- ◄ ½ cup (2 ounces / 57 g) grated Parmesan cheese

1. Preheat the oven to 400°F (205°C). Line a sheet pan with foil. If you have an ovenproof nonstick cooling rack, place it over the pan. (This is optional, but recommended for the crispiest bacon.) Grease the sheet pan or rack. 2. Wrap each onion ring tightly in a thin strip of bacon, trying to cover the whole ring without overlapping. As you finish each ring, place it on a large cutting board in a single layer. (You can also just use the baking sheet without the rack for this step and the next, then use the rack starting at step 5.) 3. Spray the onion rings with avocado oil spray, then sprinkle lightly with half of the grated Parmesan. Flip and repeat on the other side. 4. Place the onion rings on the prepared baking sheet. Bake for 30 to 35 minutes, flipping halfway through, until the bacon is cooked through and starting to get a little crispy on the edges. Drain the bacon grease from the pan occasionally if not using a rack. 5. Switch the oven to broil. Broil the onion rings for 3 to 5 minutes, until crispy. To crisp up more, let the onion rings cool from hot to warm.

Per Serving:

calories: 141 | fat: 8g | protein: 9g | carbs: 7g | net carbs: 6g | fiber: 1g

Almond and Chocolate Chia Pudding

Prep time: 10 minutes | Cook time: 0 minutes | Serves 4

- ◄ 1 (14 ounces / 397 g) can full-fat coconut milk
- ◄ ⅓ cup chia seeds
- ◄ 1 tablespoon unsweetened cocoa powder
- ◄ 2 tablespoons unsweetened almond butter
- ◄ 2 to 3 teaspoons granulated sugar-free sweetener of choice (optional)
- ◄ ½ teaspoon vanilla extract
- ◄ ½ teaspoon almond extract (optional)

1. Combine all the ingredients in a small bowl, whisking well to fully incorporate the almond butter. 2. Divide the mixture between four ramekins or small glass jars. 3. Cover and refrigerate for at least 6 hours, preferably overnight. Serve cold.

Per Serving:

calories: 335 | fat: 31g | protein: 7g | carbs: 13g | net carbs: 6g | fiber: 7g

Crunchy Granola Bars

Prep time: 15 minutes | Cook time: 15 minutes | Makes 16 bars

- ½ cup unsweetened almond butter
- 2 tablespoons coconut oil
- 2 to 4 tablespoons granulated sugar-free sweetener
- 1 egg white
- 1 teaspoon ground cinnamon
- 1 teaspoon vanilla extract
- ¼ teaspoon salt
- 2 tablespoons almond flour
- 1 cup unsweetened coconut flakes
- 1 cup slivered almonds
- 1 cup chopped roasted unsalted pecans
- 1 cup shelled pumpkin seeds

1. Preheat the oven to 350°F (180°C). Line an 8-inch square glass baking dish with parchment paper, letting the paper hang over the sides. 2. In a large glass bowl, combine the almond butter, coconut oil, and sweetener and microwave for 30 seconds, or until the coconut oil is melted. 3. Whisk in the egg white, cinnamon, vanilla extract, and salt until smooth and creamy. 4. Stir in the almond flour, coconut flakes, almonds, pecans, and pumpkin seeds until thoroughly combined. 5. Transfer the mixture into the prepared dish and press down firmly with a spatula to cover the bottom evenly. 6. Bake for 15 minutes, or until crispy and slightly browned around the edges. 7. Allow to cool completely before cutting into 16 bars. Bars can be stored tightly wrapped in the freezer for up to 3 months.

Per Serving:

calories: 215 | fat: 20g | protein: 6g | carbs: 6g | net carbs: 3g | fiber: 3g

Goat Cheese–Mackerel Pâté

Prep time: 10 minutes | Cook time: 0 minutes | Serves 4

- 4 ounces (113 g) olive oil-packed wild-caught mackerel
- 2 ounces (57 g) goat cheese
- Zest and juice of 1 lemon
- 2 tablespoons chopped fresh parsley
- 2 tablespoons chopped fresh arugula
- 1 tablespoon extra-virgin olive oil
- 2 teaspoons chopped capers
- 1 to 2 teaspoons fresh horseradish (optional)
- Crackers, cucumber rounds, endive spears, or celery, for serving (optional)

1. In a food processor, blender, or large bowl with immersion blender, combine the mackerel, goat cheese, lemon zest and juice, parsley, arugula, olive oil, capers, and horseradish (if using). Process or blend until smooth and creamy. 2. Serve with crackers, cucumber rounds, endive spears, or celery. 3. Store covered in the refrigerator for up to 1 week.

Per Serving:

calories: 190 | fat: 15g | protein: 11g | carbs: 3g | net carbs: 2g | fiber: 1g

Keto Antipasto

Prep time: 20 minutes | Cook time: 0 minutes | Serves 12

- 8 ounces (227 g) soppressata salami, diced
- 5 ounces (142 g) Calabrese salami, diced
- 4 ounces (113 g) sharp provolone or white Cheddar cheese, diced
- 4 ounces (113 g) Mozzarella, diced
- 4 celery stalks, diced
- ¼ medium red onion, finely chopped (about ½ cup)
- 24 large green olives (or 35 medium), pitted and
- chopped
- 10 pepperoncini peppers, diced
- ¼ cup fresh basil, chopped
- 1 tablespoon Italian seasoning
- 2 tablespoons olive oil
- 2 tablespoons red wine vinegar
- 1 teaspoon balsamic vinegar
- 1 teaspoon Dijon mustard
- Sea salt and freshly ground black pepper, to taste

1. In a large bowl, combine the soppressata, Calabrese, provolone, Mozzarella, celery, onion, olives, peppers, basil, and Italian seasoning. Mix until well combined. 2. In a small bowl, whisk together the olive oil, red wine vinegar, balsamic vinegar, and mustard. Add salt and pepper. 3. Pour the dressing over the meat and cheese mixture and stir well. 4. Serve immediately or transfer to an airtight container and store in the refrigerator for up to 1 week or in the freezer for up to 3 months.

Per Serving:

⅓ cup: calories: 206 | fat: 16g | protein: 12g | carbs: 3g | net carbs: 3g | fiber: 0g

Herbed Shrimp

Prep time: 5 minutes | Cook time: 5 minutes | Serves 4

- 2 tablespoons olive oil
- ¾ pound (340 g) shrimp, peeled and deveined
- 1 teaspoon paprika
- 1 teaspoon garlic powder
- 1 teaspoon onion powder
- 1 teaspoon dried parsley flakes
- ½ teaspoon dried oregano
- ½ teaspoon dried thyme
- ½ teaspoon dried basil
- ½ teaspoon dried rosemary
- ¼ teaspoon red pepper flakes
- Coarse sea salt and ground black pepper, to taste
- 1 cup chicken broth

1. Set your Instant Pot to Sauté and heat the olive oil. 2. Add the shrimp and sauté for 2 to 3 minutes. 3. Add the remaining ingredients to the Instant Pot and stir to combine. 4. Secure the lid. Select the Manual mode and set the cooking time for 2 minutes at Low Pressure. 5. When the timer beeps, perform a quick pressure release. Carefully remove the lid. 6. Transfer the shrimp to a plate and serve.

Per Serving:

calories: 146 | fat: 8g | protein: 19g | carbs: 3g | net carbs: 2g | fiber: 1g

Taco Beef Bites

Prep time: 10 minutes | Cook time: 15 minutes | Serves 6

- ◄ 10 ounces (283 g) ground beef
- ◄ 3 eggs, beaten
- ◄ ⅓ cup shredded Mozzarella
- cheese
- ◄ 1 teaspoon taco seasoning
- ◄ 1 teaspoon sesame oil

1. In the mixing bowl mix up ground beef, eggs, Mozzarella, and taco seasoning. 2. Then make the small meat bites from the mixture. 3. Heat up sesame oil in the instant pot. 4. Put the meat bites in the hot oil and cook them for 5 minutes from each side on Sauté mode.

Per Serving:

calories: 132 | fat: 6g | protein: 17g | carbs: 1g | net carbs: 1g | fiber: 0g

Cheesecake Balls

Prep time: 15 minutes | Cook time: 0 minutes | Makes 12 balls

Almond Flour Center:
- ◄ ½ cup (55 g) blanched almond flour
- ◄ 2 tablespoons coconut oil or

Cream Cheese Layer:
- ◄ 1 (8 ounces/225 g) package cream cheese (dairy-free or regular)
- ◄ 3 tablespoons coconut oil or ghee

Cinnamon Sugar Topping:
- ◄ ¼ cup (48 g) granulated erythritol

- ghee
- ◄ 1 tablespoon confectioners'-style erythritol

- ◄ ¼ cup plus 2 tablespoons (60 g) confectioners'-style erythritol
- ◄ 2 teaspoons ground cinnamon

- ◄ 2 teaspoons ground cinnamon

1. Line a rimmed baking sheet or tray that will fit into your freezer with parchment paper. 2. Make the almond flour center: Place the almond flour, oil, and erythritol in a small bowl. Knead with your hands until incorporated. Separate the mixture into 12 pieces and roll into balls. Place the balls on the lined baking sheet and place in the freezer. 3. Make the cream cheese layer: Place the cream cheese, oil, and erythritol in a small bowl and combine with a fork or handheld mixer. Divide the mixture evenly between 2 bowls. To one bowl, add the cinnamon and mix until incorporated. Place both bowls in the freezer until the cream cheese has hardened but is still workable and not completely frozen through, about 1 hour. 4. Place the ingredients for the cinnamon sugar topping in a small bowl and whisk with a fork to combine. Set aside. 5. Once the cream cheese mixtures have chilled sufficiently, scoop a teaspoon each of the cinnamon cream cheese mixture and the plain cream cheese mixture and place them side by side on the lined baking sheet. Take the almond flour balls out of the freezer and place one ball between a pair of cream cheese pieces. Pick up the pile and roll between your palms until the almond flour ball is in the middle and the cream cheese surrounds it. Roll the ball in the cinnamon sugar

mixture until coated. Place the coated ball back on the lined baking sheet and place in the freezer. 6. Repeat with the remaining almond flour balls, cream cheese mixtures, and cinnamon sugar topping, placing the coated balls on the baking sheet in the freezer as you complete them. 7. Place the coated balls in the freezer to chill for 20 minutes before enjoying.

Per Serving:

calories: 126 | fat: 13g | protein: 1g | carbs: 2g | net carbs: 1g | fiber: 1g

Zucchini and Cheese Tots

Prep time: 15 minutes | Cook time: 10 minutes | Serves 6

- ◄ 4 ounces (113 g) Parmesan, grated
- ◄ 4 ounces (113 g) Cheddar cheese, grated
- ◄ 1 zucchini, grated
- ◄ 1 egg, beaten
- ◄ 1 teaspoon dried oregano
- ◄ 1 tablespoon coconut oil

1. In the mixing bowl, mix up Parmesan, Cheddar cheese, zucchini, egg, and dried oregano. 2. Make the small tots with the help of the fingertips. 3. Then melt the coconut oil in the instant pot on Sauté mode. 4. Put the prepared zucchini tots in the hot coconut oil and cook them for 3 minutes from each side or until they are light brown. Cool the zucchini tots for 5 minutes.

Per Serving:

calories: 173 | fat: 13g | protein: 12g | carbs: 2g | net carbs: 2g | fiber: 0g

Pancetta Pizza Dip

Prep time: 10 minutes | Cook time: 4 minutes | Serves 10

- ◄ 10 ounces (283 g) Pepper Jack cheese
- ◄ 10 ounces (283 g) cream cheese
- ◄ 10 ounces (283 g) pancetta, chopped
- ◄ 1 pound (454 g) tomatoes, puréed
- ◄ 1 cup green olives, pitted and halved
- ◄ 1 teaspoon dried oregano
- ◄ ½ teaspoon garlic powder
- ◄ 1 cup chicken broth
- ◄ 4 ounces (113 g) Mozzarella cheese, thinly sliced

1. Mix together the Pepper Jack cheese, cream cheese, pancetta, tomatoes, olives, oregano, and garlic powder in the Instant Pot. Pour in the chicken broth. 2. Lock the lid. Select the Manual mode and set the cooking time for 4 minutes at High Pressure. 3. When the timer beeps, perform a quick pressure release. Carefully remove the lid. 4. Scatter the Mozzarella cheese on top. Cover and allow to sit in the residual heat. Serve warm.

Per Serving:

calories: 287 | fat: 21g | protein: 21g | carbs: 3g | net carbs: 2g | fiber: 1g

Baked Brie with Pecans

Prep time: 5 minutes | Cook time: 10 minutes | Serves 6

- 1 (¾ pound / 340 g) wheel Brie cheese
- 3 ounces (85 g) pecans, chopped
- 2 garlic cloves, minced
- 2 tablespoons minced fresh rosemary leaves
- 1½ tablespoons olive oil
- Salt and freshly ground black pepper, to taste

1. Preheat the oven to 400°F (205°C). 2. Line a baking sheet with parchment paper and place the Brie on it. 3. In a small bowl, stir together the pecans, garlic, rosemary, and olive oil. Season with salt and pepper. Spoon the mixture in an even layer over the Brie. Bake for about 10 minutes until the cheese is warm and the nuts are lightly browned. 4. Remove and let it cool for 1 to 2 minutes before serving.

Per Serving:

calories: 318 | fat: 29g | protein: 13g | carbs: 3g | net carbs: 2g | fiber: 1g

Mayo Chicken Celery

Prep time: 15 minutes | Cook time: 15 minutes | Serves 4

- 14 ounces (397 g) chicken breast, skinless, boneless
- 1 cup water
- 4 celery stalks
- 1 teaspoon salt
- ½ teaspoon onion powder
- 1 teaspoon mayonnaise

1. Combine all the ingredients except the mayo in the Instant Pot. 2. Secure the lid. Select the Manual mode and set the cooking time for 15 minutes at High Pressure. 3. Once cooking is complete, do a natural pressure release for 6 minutes, then release any remaining pressure. Carefully open the lid. 4. Remove the chicken and shred with two forks, then return to the Instant Pot. 5. Add the mayo and stir well. Serve immediately.

Per Serving:

calories: 119 | fat: 3g | protein: 21g | carbs: 1g | net carbs: 1g | fiber: 0g

Chapter 8

Vegetarian Mains

Chapter 8 Vegetarian Mains

Crustless Spanakopita

Prep time: 15 minutes | Cook time: 45 minutes | Serves 6

- ◄ 12 tablespoons extra-virgin olive oil, divided
- ◄ 1 small yellow onion, diced
- ◄ 1 (32-ounce / 907-g) bag frozen chopped spinach, thawed, fully drained, and patted dry (about 4 cups)
- ◄ 4 garlic cloves, minced
- ◄ ½ teaspoon salt
- ◄ ½ teaspoon freshly ground black pepper
- ◄ 1 cup whole-milk ricotta cheese
- ◄ 4 large eggs
- ◄ ¾ cup crumbled traditional feta cheese
- ◄ ¼ cup pine nuts

1. Preheat the oven to 375ºF (190ºC). 2. In a large skillet, heat 4 tablespoons olive oil over medium-high heat. Add the onion and sauté until softened, 6 to 8 minutes. 3. Add the spinach, garlic, salt, and pepper and sauté another 5 minutes. Remove from the heat and allow to cool slightly. 4. In a medium bowl, whisk together the ricotta and eggs. Add to the cooled spinach and stir to combine. 5. Pour 4 tablespoons olive oil in the bottom of a 9-by-13-inch glass baking dish and swirl to coat the bottom and sides. Add the spinach-ricotta mixture and spread into an even layer. 6. Bake for 20 minutes or until the mixture begins to set. Remove from the oven and crumble the feta evenly across the top of the spinach. Add the pine nuts and drizzle with the remaining 4 tablespoons olive oil. Return to the oven and bake for an additional 15 to 20 minutes, or until the spinach is fully set and the top is starting to turn golden brown. Allow to cool slightly before cutting to serve.

Per Serving:

calories: 440 | fat: 38g | protein: 17g | carbs: 9g | net carbs: 8g | fiber: 1g

Cheesy Cauliflower Pizza Crust

Prep time: 15 minutes | Cook time: 11 minutes | Serves 2

- ◄ 1 (12 ounces / 340 g) steamer bag cauliflower
- ◄ ½ cup shredded sharp Cheddar cheese
- ◄ 1 large egg
- ◄ 2 tablespoons blanched finely ground almond flour
- ◄ 1 teaspoon Italian blend seasoning

1. Cook cauliflower according to package instructions. Remove from bag and place into cheesecloth or paper towel to remove excess water. Place cauliflower into a large bowl. 2. Add cheese, egg, almond flour, and Italian seasoning to the bowl and mix well. 3. Cut a piece of parchment to fit your air fryer basket. Press cauliflower into 6-inch round circle. Place into the air fryer basket. 4. Adjust the temperature to 360ºF (182ºC) and air fry for 11 minutes. 5. After 7 minutes, flip the pizza crust. 6. Add preferred toppings to pizza. Place back into air fryer basket and cook an additional 4 minutes or until fully cooked and golden. Serve immediately.

Per Serving:

calories: 248 | fat: 18g | protein: 16g | carbs: 8g | net carbs: 4g | fiber: 4g

Cauliflower Tikka Masala

Prep time: 10 minutes | Cook time: 20 minutes | Serves 4

For The Cauliflower
- ◄ 1 head cauliflower, cut into small florets
- ◄ 1 tablespoon coconut oil,
For The Sauce
- ◄ 2 tablespoons coconut oil
- ◄ ½ onion, chopped
- ◄ 1 tablespoon minced garlic
- ◄ 1 tablespoon grated ginger
- ◄ 2 tablespoons garam masala
- ◄ 1 tablespoon tomato paste
- melted
- ◄ 1 teaspoon ground cumin
- ◄ ½ teaspoon ground coriander

- ◄ ½ teaspoon salt
- ◄ 1 cup crushed tomatoes
- ◄ 1 cup heavy (whipping) cream
- ◄ 1 tablespoon chopped fresh cilantro

Make The Cauliflower: 1. Preheat the oven. Set the oven temperature to 425°F. Line a baking sheet with aluminum foil. 2. Prepare the cauliflower. In a large bowl, toss the cauliflower with the coconut oil, cumin, and coriander. Spread the cauliflower on the baking sheet in a single layer and bake it for 20 minutes, until the cauliflower is tender. Make The Sauce: 1. Sauté the vegetables. While the cauliflower is baking, in a large skillet over medium-high heat, warm the coconut oil. Add the onion, garlic, and ginger and sauté until they've softened, about 3 minutes. 2. Finish the sauce. Stir in the garam masala, tomato paste, and salt until the vegetables are coated. Stir in the crushed tomatoes and bring to a boil, then reduce the heat to low and simmer the sauce for 10 minutes, stirring it often. Remove the skillet from the heat and stir in the cream and cilantro. 3. Assemble and serve. Add the cauliflower to the sauce, stirring to combine everything. Divide the mixture between four bowls and serve it hot.

Per Serving:

calories: 372 | fat: 32g | protein: 8g | carbs: 17g | net carbs: 10g | fiber: 7g

Cheese Stuffed Peppers

Prep time: 20 minutes | Cook time: 15 minutes | Serves 2

- 1 red bell pepper, top and seeds removed
- 1 yellow bell pepper, top and seeds removed
- Salt and pepper, to taste
- 1 cup Cottage cheese
- 4 tablespoons mayonnaise
- 2 pickles, chopped

1. Arrange the peppers in the lightly greased air fryer basket. Cook in the preheated air fryer at 400ºF (204ºC) for 15 minutes, turning them over halfway through the cooking time. 2. Season with salt and pepper. Then, in a mixing bowl, combine the cream cheese with the mayonnaise and chopped pickles. Stuff the pepper with the cream cheese mixture and serve. Enjoy!
Per Serving:
calories: 250 | fat: 20g | protein: 11g | carbs: 8g | net carbs: 6g | fiber: 2g

Parmesan Artichokes

Prep time: 10 minutes | Cook time: 10 minutes | Serves 4

- 2 medium artichokes, trimmed and quartered, center removed
- 2 tablespoons coconut oil
- 1 large egg, beaten
- ½ cup grated vegetarian
- Parmesan cheese
- ¼ cup blanched finely ground almond flour
- ½ teaspoon crushed red pepper flakes

1. In a large bowl, toss artichokes in coconut oil and then dip each piece into the egg. 2. Mix the Parmesan and almond flour in a large bowl. Add artichoke pieces and toss to cover as completely as possible, sprinkle with pepper flakes. Place into the air fryer basket. 3. Adjust the temperature to 400ºF (204ºC) and air fry for 10 minutes. 4. Toss the basket two times during cooking. Serve warm.

Per Serving:

calories: 220 | fat: 18g | protein: 10g | carbs: 9g | net carbs: 4g | fiber: 5g

Baked Zucchini

Prep time: 10 minutes | Cook time: 8 minutes | Serves 4

- 2 tablespoons salted butter
- ¼ cup diced white onion
- ½ teaspoon minced garlic
- ½ cup heavy whipping cream
- 2 ounces (57 g) full-fat
- cream cheese
- 1 cup shredded sharp Cheddar cheese
- 2 medium zucchini, spiralized

1. In a large saucepan over medium heat, melt butter. Add onion and sauté until it begins to soften, 1 to 3 minutes. Add garlic and

sauté for 30 seconds, then pour in cream and add cream cheese. 2. Remove the pan from heat and stir in Cheddar. Add the zucchini and toss in the sauce, then put into a round baking dish. Cover the dish with foil and place into the air fryer basket. 3. Adjust the temperature to 370ºF (188ºC) and set the timer for 8 minutes. 4. After 6 minutes remove the foil and let the top brown for remaining cooking time. Stir and serve.

Per Serving:

calories: 346 | fat: 32g | protein: 11g | carbs: 6g | net carbs: 5g | fiber: 1g

Loaded Cauliflower Steak

Prep time: 5 minutes | Cook time: 7 minutes | Serves 4

- 1 medium head cauliflower
- ¼ cup hot sauce
- 2 tablespoons salted butter,
- melted
- ¼ cup blue cheese crumbles
- ¼ cup full-fat ranch dressing

1. Remove cauliflower leaves. Slice the head in ½-inch-thick slices. 2. In a small bowl, mix hot sauce and butter. Brush the mixture over the cauliflower. 3. Place each cauliflower steak into the air fryer, working in batches if necessary. 4. Adjust the temperature to 400ºF (204ºC) and air fry for 7 minutes. 5. When cooked, edges will begin turning dark and caramelized. 6. To serve, sprinkle steaks with crumbled blue cheese. Drizzle with ranch dressing.

Per Serving:

calories: 140 | fat: 12g | protein: 5g | carbs: 6g | net carbs: 5g | fiber: 1g

Pesto Vegetable Skewers

Prep time: 30 minutes | Cook time: 8 minutes | Makes 8 skewers

- 1 medium zucchini, trimmed and cut into ½-inch slices
- ½ medium yellow onion, peeled and cut into 1-inch squares
- 1 medium red bell pepper, seeded and cut into 1-inch
- squares
- 16 whole cremini mushrooms
- ⅓ cup basil pesto
- ½ teaspoon salt
- ¼ teaspoon ground black pepper

1. Divide zucchini slices, onion, and bell pepper into eight even portions. Place on 6-inch skewers for a total of eight kebabs. Add 2 mushrooms to each skewer and brush kebabs generously with pesto. 2. Sprinkle each kebab with salt and black pepper on all sides, then place into ungreased air fryer basket. Adjust the temperature to 375ºF (191ºC) and air fry for 8 minutes, turning kebabs halfway through cooking. Vegetables will be browned at the edges and tender-crisp when done. Serve warm.

Per Serving:

calories: 50 | fat: 4g | protein: 2g | carbs: 4g | net carbs: 3g | fiber: 1g

Cheesy Garden Veggie Crustless Quiche

Prep time: 5 minutes | Cook time: 25 minutes | Serves 4

- ◀ 1 tablespoon grass-fed butter, divided
- ◀ 6 eggs
- ◀ ¾ cup heavy (whipping) cream
- ◀ 3 ounces goat cheese, divided
- ◀ ½ cup sliced mushrooms, chopped
- ◀ 1 scallion, white and green parts, chopped
- ◀ 1 cup shredded fresh spinach
- ◀ 10 cherry tomatoes, cut in half

1. Preheat the oven. Set the oven temperature to 350°F. Grease a 9-inch pie plate with ½ teaspoon of the butter and set it aside. 2. Mix the quiche base. In a medium bowl, whisk the eggs, cream, and 2 ounces of the cheese until it's all well blended. Set it aside. 3. Sauté the vegetables. In a small skillet over medium-high heat, melt the remaining butter. Add the mushrooms and scallion and sauté them until they've softened, about 2 minutes. Add the spinach and sauté until it's wilted, about 2 minutes. 4. Assemble and bake. Spread the vegetable mixture in the bottom of the pie plate and pour the egg-and-cream mixture over the vegetables. Scatter the cherry tomatoes and the remaining 1 ounce of goat cheese on top. Bake for 20 to 25 minutes until the quiche is cooked through, puffed, and lightly browned. 5. Serve. Cut the quiche into wedges and divide it between four plates. Serve it warm or cold.

Per Serving:

calories: 355 | fat: 30g | protein: 18g | carbs: 5g | net carbs: 4g | fiber: 1g

Herbed Ricotta–Stuffed Mushrooms

Prep time: 10 minutes | Cook time: 30 minutes | Serves 4

- ◀ 6 tablespoons extra-virgin olive oil, divided
- ◀ 4 portobello mushroom caps, cleaned and gills removed
- ◀ 1 cup whole-milk ricotta cheese
- ◀ ⅓ cup chopped fresh herbs (such as basil, parsley,
- rosemary, oregano, or thyme)
- ◀ 2 garlic cloves, finely minced
- ◀ ½ teaspoon salt
- ◀ ¼ teaspoon freshly ground black pepper

1. Preheat the oven to 400°F (205°C). 2. Line a baking sheet with parchment or foil and drizzle with 2 tablespoons olive oil, spreading evenly. Place the mushroom caps on the baking sheet, gill-side up. 3. In a medium bowl, mix together the ricotta, herbs, 2 tablespoons olive oil, garlic, salt, and pepper. Stuff each mushroom cap with one-quarter of the cheese mixture, pressing down if needed. Drizzle with remaining 2 tablespoons olive oil and bake until golden brown and the mushrooms are soft, 30 to 35 minutes, depending on the size of the mushrooms.

Per Serving:

calories: 400 | fat: 36g | protein: 12g | carbs: 7g | net carbs: 6g | fiber: 1g

Eggplant and Zucchini Bites

Prep time: 30 minutes | Cook time: 30 minutes | Serves 8

- ◀ 2 teaspoons fresh mint leaves, chopped
- ◀ 1½ teaspoons red pepper chili flakes
- ◀ 2 tablespoons melted butter
- ◀ 1 pound (454 g) eggplant, peeled and cubed
- ◀ 1 pound (454 g) zucchini, peeled and cubed
- ◀ 3 tablespoons olive oil

1. Toss all the above ingredients in a large-sized mixing dish. 2. Roast the eggplant and zucchini bites for 30 minutes at 325°F (163°C) in your air fryer, turning once or twice. 3. Serve with a homemade dipping sauce.

Per Serving:

calories: 140 | fat: 12g | protein: 2g | carbs: 8g | net carbs: 6g | fiber 2g

Almond-Cauliflower Gnocchi

Prep time: 5 minutes | Cook time: 25 to 30 minutes | Serves 4

- ◀ 5 cups cauliflower florets
- ◀ ⅔ cup almond flour
- ◀ ½ teaspoon salt
- ◀ ¼ cup unsalted butter,
- melted
- ◀ ¼ cup grated Parmesan cheese

1. In a food processor fitted with a metal blade, pulse the cauliflower until finely chopped. Transfer the cauliflower to a large microwave-safe bowl and cover it with a paper towel. Microwave for 5 minutes. Spread the cauliflower on a towel to cool. 2. When cool enough to handle, draw up the sides of the towel and squeeze tightly over a sink to remove the excess moisture. Return the cauliflower to the food processor and whirl until creamy. Sprinkle in the flour and salt and pulse until a sticky dough comes together. 3. Transfer the dough to a workspace lightly floured with almond flour. Shape the dough into a ball and divide into 4 equal sections. Roll each section into a rope 1 inch thick. Slice the dough into squares with a sharp knife. 4. Preheat the air fryer to 400°F (204°C). 5. Working in batches if necessary, place the gnocchi in a single layer in the basket of the air fryer and spray generously with olive oil. Pausing halfway through the cooking time to turn the gnocchi, air fry for 25 to 30 minutes until golden brown and crispy on the edges. Transfer to a large bowl and toss with the melted butter and Parmesan cheese.

Per Serving:

calories: 220 | fat: 20g | protein: 7g | carbs: 8g | net carbs: 5g | fiber 3g

Green Vegetable Stir-Fry with Tofu

Prep time: 15 minutes | Cook time: 15 minutes | Serves 2

◄ 3 tablespoons avocado oil, divided
◄ 1 cup Brussels sprouts, halved
◄ ½ onion, diced
◄ ½ leek, white and light green parts diced
◄ ½ head green cabbage, diced
◄ ¼ cup water, plus more if needed
◄ ½ cup kale, coarsely chopped
◄ 1 cup spinach, coarsely chopped
◄ 8 ounces (227 g) tofu, diced
◄ 2 teaspoons garlic powder
◄ Salt and freshly ground black pepper, to taste
◄ ½ avocado, pitted, peeled, and diced
◄ MCT oil (optional)

1. In a large skillet with a lid (or a wok if you have one), heat 2 tablespoons of avocado oil over medium-high heat. Add the Brussels sprouts, onion, leek, and cabbage and stir together. Add the water, cover, lower the heat to medium, and cook for about 5 minutes. 2. Toss in the kale and spinach and cook for 3 minutes, stirring constantly, until the onion, leek, and cabbage are caramelized. 3. Add the tofu to the stir-fry, then season with the garlic, salt, pepper, and the remaining tablespoon of avocado oil. 4. Turn the heat back up to medium-high and cook for about 10 minutes, stirring constantly, until the tofu is nice and caramelized on all sides. If you experience any burning, turn down the heat and add 2 to 3 tablespoons of water. 5. Divide the stir-fry between two plates and sprinkle with diced avocado. Feel free to drizzle algae oil or MCT oil over the top for a little extra fat.

Per Serving:

calories: 473 | fat: 33g | protein: 17g | carbs: 27g | net carbs: 15g | fiber: 12g

Zucchini Pasta with Spinach, Olives, and Asiago

Prep time: 10 minutes | Cook time: 10 minutes | Serves 4

◄ 3 tablespoons good-quality olive oil
◄ 1 tablespoon grass-fed butter
◄ 1½ tablespoons minced garlic
◄ 1 cup packed fresh spinach
◄ ½ cup sliced black olives
◄ ½ cup halved cherry tomatoes
◄ 2 tablespoons chopped fresh basil
◄ 3 zucchini, spiralized
◄ Sea salt, for seasoning
◄ Freshly ground black pepper, for seasoning
◄ ½ cup shredded Asiago cheese

1. Sauté the vegetables. In a large skillet over medium-high heat, warm the olive oil and butter. Add the garlic and sauté until it's tender, about 2 minutes. Stir in the spinach, olives, tomatoes, and basil and sauté until the spinach is wilted, about 4 minutes. Stir in the zucchini noodles, toss to combine them with the sauce, and cook until the zucchini is tender, about 2 minutes. 2. Serve. Season with salt and pepper. Divide the mixture between four bowls and serve topped with the Asiago.

Per Serving:

calories: 199 | fat: 18g | protein: 6g | carbs: 4g | net carbs: 3g | fiber: 1g

Vegetable Vodka Sauce Bake

Prep time: 10 minutes | Cook time: 30 minutes | Serves 4

◄ 3 tablespoons melted grass-fed butter, divided
◄ 4 cups mushrooms, halved
◄ 4 cups cooked cauliflower florets
◄ 1½ cups purchased vodka sauce
◄ ¾ cup heavy (whipping) cream
◄ ½ cup grated Asiago cheese
◄ Sea salt, for seasoning
◄ Freshly ground black pepper, for seasoning
◄ 1 cup shredded provolone cheese
◄ 2 tablespoons chopped fresh oregano

1. Preheat the oven. Set the oven temperature to 350°F and use 1 tablespoon of the melted butter to grease a 9-by-13-inch baking dish. 2. Mix the vegetables. In a large bowl, combine the mushrooms, cauliflower, vodka sauce, cream, Asiago, and the remaining 2 tablespoons of butter. Season the vegetables with salt and pepper. 3. Bake. Transfer the vegetable mixture to the baking dish and top it with the provolone cheese. Bake for 30 to 35 minutes until it's bubbly and heated through. 4. Serve. Divide the mixture between four plates and top with the oregano.

Per Serving:

calories: 537 | fat: 45g | protein: 19g | carbs: 14g | net carbs: 8g | fiber: 19g

Whole Roasted Lemon Cauliflower

Prep time: 5 minutes | Cook time: 15 minutes | Serves 4

◄ 1 medium head cauliflower
◄ 2 tablespoons salted butter, melted
◄ 1 medium lemon
◄ ½ teaspoon garlic powder
◄ 1 teaspoon dried parsley

1. Remove the leaves from the head of cauliflower and brush it with melted butter. Cut the lemon in half and zest one half onto the cauliflower. Squeeze the juice of the zested lemon half and pour it over the cauliflower. 2. Sprinkle with garlic powder and parsley. Place cauliflower head into the air fryer basket. 3. Adjust the temperature to 350ºF (177ºC) and air fry for 15 minutes. 4. Check cauliflower every 5 minutes to avoid overcooking. It should be fork tender. 5. To serve, squeeze juice from other lemon half over cauliflower. Serve immediately.

Per Serving:

calories: 90 | fat: 7g | protein: 3g | carbs: 6g | net carbs: 4g | fiber: 2g

Broccoli-Cheese Fritters

Prep time: 5 minutes | Cook time: 20 to 25 minutes | Serves 4

- 1 cup broccoli florets
- 1 cup shredded Mozzarella cheese
- ¾ cup almond flour
- ½ cup flaxseed meal, divided
- 2 teaspoons baking powder
- 1 teaspoon garlic powder
- Salt and freshly ground black pepper, to taste
- 2 eggs, lightly beaten
- ½ cup ranch dressing

1. Preheat the air fryer to 400ºF (204ºC). 2. In a food processor fitted with a metal blade, pulse the broccoli until very finely chopped. 3. Transfer the broccoli to a large bowl and add the Mozzarella, almond flour, ¼ cup of the flaxseed meal, baking powder, and garlic powder. Stir until thoroughly combined. Season to taste with salt and black pepper. Add the eggs and stir again to form a sticky dough. Shape the dough into 1¼-inch fritters. 4. Place the remaining ¼ cup flaxseed meal in a shallow bowl and roll the fritters in the meal to form an even coating. 5. Working in batches if necessary, arrange the fritters in a single layer in the basket of the air fryer and spray generously with olive oil. Pausing halfway through the cooking time to shake the basket, air fry for 20 to 25 minutes until the fritters are golden brown and crispy. Serve with the ranch dressing for dipping.

Per Serving:

calories: 638 | fat: 54g | protein: 28g | carbs: 16g | net carbs: 9g | fiber: 7g

Garlic White Zucchini Rolls

Prep time: 20 minutes | Cook time: 20 minutes | Serves 4

- 2 medium zucchini
- 2 tablespoons unsalted butter
- ¼ white onion, peeled and diced
- ½ teaspoon finely minced roasted garlic
- ¼ cup heavy cream
- 2 tablespoons vegetable broth
- ⅛ teaspoon xanthan gum
- ½ cup full-fat ricotta cheese
- ¼ teaspoon salt
- ½ teaspoon garlic powder
- ¼ teaspoon dried oregano
- 2 cups spinach, chopped
- ½ cup sliced baby portobello mushrooms
- ¾ cup shredded Mozzarella cheese, divided

1. Using a mandoline or sharp knife, slice zucchini into long strips lengthwise. Place strips between paper towels to absorb moisture. Set aside. 2. In a medium saucepan over medium heat, melt butter. Add onion and sauté until fragrant. Add garlic and sauté 30 seconds. 3. Pour in heavy cream, broth, and xanthan gum. Turn off heat and whisk mixture until it begins to thicken, about 3 minutes. 4. In a medium bowl, add ricotta, salt, garlic powder, and oregano and mix well. Fold in spinach, mushrooms, and ½ cup Mozzarella. 5. Pour half of the sauce into a round baking pan. To assemble the rolls, place two strips of zucchini on a work surface. Spoon 2 tablespoons of ricotta mixture onto the slices and roll up. Place

seam side down on top of sauce. Repeat with remaining ingredients. 6. Pour remaining sauce over the rolls and sprinkle with remaining Mozzarella. Cover with foil and place into the air fryer basket. 7. Adjust the temperature to 350ºF (177ºC) and bake for 20 minutes. 8. In the last 5 minutes, remove the foil to brown the cheese. Serve immediately.

Per Serving:

calories: 270 | fat: 21g | protein: 14g | carbs: 7g | net carbs: 5g | fiber: 2g

Broccoli with Garlic Sauce

Prep time: 19 minutes | Cook time: 15 minutes | Serves 4

- 2 tablespoons olive oil
- Kosher salt and freshly ground black pepper, to

Dipping Sauce:
- 2 teaspoons dried rosemary, crushed
- 3 garlic cloves, minced
- ⅓ teaspoon dried marjoram,

- taste
- 1 pound (454 g) broccoli florets

- crushed
- ¼ cup sour cream
- ⅓ cup mayonnaise

1. Lightly grease your broccoli with a thin layer of olive oil. Season with salt and ground black pepper. 2. Arrange the seasoned broccoli in the air fryer basket. Bake at 395ºF (202ºC) for 15 minutes, shaking once or twice. In the meantime, prepare the dipping sauce by mixing all the sauce ingredients. Serve warm broccoli with the dipping sauce and enjoy!

Per Serving:

calories: 250 | fat: 23g | protein: 3g | carbs: 10g | net carbs: 9g | fiber: 1g

Tangy Asparagus and Broccoli

Prep time: 25 minutes | Cook time: 22 minutes | Serves 4

- ½ pound (227 g) asparagus, cut into 1½-inch pieces
- ½ pound (227 g) broccoli, cut into 1½-inch pieces
- 2 tablespoons olive oil
- Salt and white pepper, to taste
- ½ cup vegetable broth
- 2 tablespoons apple cider vinegar

1. Place the vegetables in a single layer in the lightly greased air fryer basket. Drizzle the olive oil over the vegetables. 2. Sprinkle with salt and white pepper. 3. Cook at 380ºF (193ºC) for 15 minutes, shaking the basket halfway through the cooking time. 4. Add ½ cup of vegetable broth to a saucepan; bring to a rapid boil and add the vinegar. Cook for 5 to 7 minutes or until the sauce has reduced by half. 5. Spoon the sauce over the warm vegetables and serve immediately. Bon appétit!

Per Serving:

calories: 89 | fat: 7g | protein: 3g | carbs: 7g | net carbs: 4g | fiber: 3g

Greek Vegetable Briam

Prep time: 10 minutes | Cook time: 30 minutes | Serves 4

- ⅓ cup good-quality olive oil, divided
- 1 onion, thinly sliced
- 1 tablespoon minced garlic
- ¾ small eggplant, diced
- 2 zucchini, diced
- 2 cups chopped cauliflower
- 1 red bell pepper, diced
- 2 cups diced tomatoes
- 2 tablespoons chopped fresh

- parsley
- 2 tablespoons chopped fresh oregano
- Sea salt, for seasoning
- Freshly ground black pepper, for seasoning
- 1½ cups crumbled feta cheese
- ¼ cup pumpkin seeds

1. Preheat the oven. Set the oven to broil and lightly grease a 9-by-13-inch casserole dish with olive oil. 2. Sauté the aromatics. In a medium stockpot over medium heat, warm 3 tablespoons of the olive oil. Add the onion and garlic and sauté until they've softened, about 3 minutes. 3. Sauté the vegetables. Stir in the eggplant and cook for 5 minutes, stirring occasionally. Add the zucchini, cauliflower, and red bell pepper and cook for 5 minutes. Stir in the tomatoes, parsley, and oregano and cook, giving it a stir from time to time, until the vegetables are tender, about 10 minutes. Season it with salt and pepper. 4. Broil. Transfer the vegetable mixture to the casserole dish and top with the crumbled feta. Broil for about 4 minutes until the cheese is golden. 5. Serve. Divide the casserole between four plates and top it with the pumpkin seeds. Drizzle with the remaining olive oil.

Per Serving:

calories: 356 | fat: 28g | protein: 11g | carbs: 18g | net carbs: 11g | fiber: 7g

Eggplant Parmesan

Prep time: 15 minutes | Cook time: 17 minutes | Serves 4

- 1 medium eggplant, ends trimmed, sliced into ½-inch rounds
- ¼ teaspoon salt
- 2 tablespoons coconut oil
- ½ cup grated Parmesan cheese

- 1 ounce (28 g) 100% cheese crisps, finely crushed
- ½ cup low-carb marinara sauce
- ½ cup shredded Mozzarella cheese

1. Sprinkle eggplant rounds with salt on both sides and wrap in a kitchen towel for 30 minutes. Press to remove excess water, then drizzle rounds with coconut oil on both sides. 2. In a medium bowl, mix Parmesan and cheese crisps. Press each eggplant slice into mixture to coat both sides. 3. Place rounds into ungreased air fryer basket. Adjust the temperature to 350ºF (177ºC) and air fry for 15 minutes, turning rounds halfway through cooking. They will be crispy around the edges when done. 4. Spoon marinara over rounds and sprinkle with Mozzarella. Continue cooking an additional 2

minutes at 350ºF (177ºC) until cheese is melted. Serve warm.

Per Serving:

calories: 330 | fat: 24g | protein: 18g | carbs: 13g | net carbs: 9g | fiber: 4g

Crispy Eggplant Rounds

Prep time: 15 minutes | Cook time: 10 minutes | Serves 4

- 1 large eggplant, ends trimmed, cut into ½-inch slices
- ½ teaspoon salt
- 2 ounces (57 g) Parmesan

- 100% cheese crisps, finely ground
- ½ teaspoon paprika
- ¼ teaspoon garlic powder
- 1 large egg

1. Sprinkle eggplant rounds with salt. Place rounds on a kitchen towel for 30 minutes to draw out excess water. Pat rounds dry. 2. In a medium bowl, mix cheese crisps, paprika, and garlic powder. In a separate medium bowl, whisk egg. Dip each eggplant round in egg, then gently press into cheese crisps to coat both sides. 3. Place eggplant rounds into ungreased air fryer basket. Adjust the temperature to 400ºF (204ºC) and air fry for 10 minutes, turning rounds halfway through cooking. Eggplant will be golden and crispy when done. Serve warm.

Per Serving:

calories: 133 | fat: 8g | protein: 10g | carbs: 6g | net carbs: 4g | fiber: 3g

Pesto Spinach Flatbread

Prep time: 10 minutes | Cook time: 8 minutes | Serves 4

- 1 cup blanched finely ground almond flour
- 2 ounces (57 g) cream cheese
- 2 cups shredded Mozzarella

- cheese
- 1 cup chopped fresh spinach leaves
- 2 tablespoons basil pesto

1. Place flour, cream cheese, and Mozzarella in a large microwave-safe bowl and microwave on high 45 seconds, then stir. 2. Fold in spinach and microwave an additional 15 seconds. Stir until a soft dough ball forms. 3. Cut two pieces of parchment paper to fit air fryer basket. Separate dough into two sections and press each out on ungreased parchment to create 6-inch rounds. 4. Spread 1 tablespoon pesto over each flatbread and place rounds on parchment into ungreased air fryer basket. Adjust the temperature to 350ºF (177ºC) and air fry for 8 minutes, turning crusts halfway through cooking. Flatbread will be golden when done. 5. Let cool 5 minutes before slicing and serving.

Per Serving:

calories: 506 | fat: 43g | protein: 27g | carbs: 9g | net carbs: 5g | fiber: 4g

Caprese Eggplant Stacks

Prep time: 5 minutes | Cook time: 12 minutes | Serves 4

- ◀ 1 medium eggplant, cut into ¼-inch slices
- ◀ 2 large tomatoes, cut into ¼-inch slices
- ◀ 4 ounces (113 g) fresh

Mozzarella, cut into ½-ounce / 14-g slices
- ◀ 2 tablespoons olive oil
- ◀ ¼ cup fresh basil, sliced

1. In a baking dish, place four slices of eggplant on the bottom. Place a slice of tomato on top of each eggplant round, then Mozzarella, then eggplant. Repeat as necessary. 2. Drizzle with olive oil. Cover dish with foil and place dish into the air fryer basket. 3. Adjust the temperature to 350°F (177°C) and bake for 12 minutes. 4. When done, eggplant will be tender. Garnish with fresh basil to serve.

Per Serving:

calories: 203 | fat: 16g | protein: 8g | carbs: 10g | net carbs: 7g | fiber: 3g

Cauliflower Steak with Gremolata

Prep time: 15 minutes | Cook time: 25 minutes | Serves 4

- ◀ 2 tablespoons olive oil
- ◀ 1 tablespoon Italian seasoning
- ◀ 1 large head cauliflower, outer leaves removed and

Gremolata:
- ◀ 1 bunch Italian parsley (about 1 cup packed)
- ◀ 2 cloves garlic
- ◀ Zest of 1 small lemon, plus 1

sliced lengthwise through the core into thick "steaks"
- ◀ Salt and freshly ground black pepper, to taste
- ◀ ¼ cup Parmesan cheese

to 2 teaspoons lemon juice
- ◀ ½ cup olive oil
- ◀ Salt and pepper, to taste

1. Preheat the air fryer to 400°F (204°C). 2. In a small bowl, combine the olive oil and Italian seasoning. Brush both sides of each cauliflower "steak" generously with the oil. Season to taste with salt and black pepper. 3. Working in batches if necessary, arrange the cauliflower in a single layer in the air fryer basket. Pausing halfway through the cooking time to turn the "steaks," air fry for 15 to 20 minutes until the cauliflower is tender and the edges begin to brown. Sprinkle with the Parmesan and air fry for 5 minutes longer. 4. To make the gremolata: In a food processor fitted with a metal blade, combine the parsley, garlic, and lemon zest and juice. With the motor running, add the olive oil in a steady stream until the mixture forms a bright green sauce. Season to taste with salt and black pepper. Serve the cauliflower steaks with the gremolata spooned over the top.

Per Serving:

calories: 257 | fat: 23g | protein: 6g | carbs: 9g | net carbs: 7g | fiber: 4g

Sweet Pepper Nachos

Prep time: 10 minutes | Cook time: 5 minutes | Serves 2

- ◀ 6 mini sweet peppers, seeded and sliced in half
- ◀ ¾ cup shredded Colby jack cheese
- ◀ ¼ cup sliced pickled

jalapeños
- ◀ ½ medium avocado, peeled, pitted, and diced
- ◀ 2 tablespoons sour cream

1. Place peppers into an ungreased round nonstick baking dish. Sprinkle with Colby and top with jalapeños. 2. Place dish into air fryer basket. Adjust the temperature to 350°F (177°C) and bake for 5 minutes. Cheese will be melted and bubbly when done. 3. Remove dish from air fryer and top with avocado. Drizzle with sour cream. Serve warm.

Per Serving:

calories: 255 | fat: 21g | protein: 11g | carbs: 9g | net carbs: 5g | fiber: 4g

Mediterranean Filling Stuffed Portobello Mushrooms

Prep time: 10 minutes | Cook time: 35 minutes | Serves 4

- ◀ 4 large portobello mushroom caps
- ◀ 3 tablespoons good-quality olive oil, divided
- ◀ 1 cup chopped fresh spinach
- ◀ 1 red bell pepper, chopped
- ◀ 1 celery stalk, chopped
- ◀ ½ cup chopped sun-dried tomato

- ◀ ¼ onion, chopped
- ◀ 2 teaspoons minced garlic
- ◀ 1 teaspoon chopped fresh oregano
- ◀ 2 cups chopped pecans
- ◀ ¼ cup balsamic vinaigrette
- ◀ Sea salt, for seasoning
- ◀ Freshly ground black pepper for seasoning

1. Preheat the oven. Set the oven temperature to 350°F. Line a baking sheet with parchment paper. 2. Prepare the mushrooms. Use a spoon to scoop the black gills out of the mushrooms. Massage 2 tablespoons of the olive oil all over the mushroom caps and place the mushrooms on the prepared baking sheet. Set them aside. 3. Prepare the filling. In a large skillet over medium-high heat, warm the remaining 1 tablespoon of olive oil. Add the spinach, red bell pepper, celery, sun-dried tomato, onion, garlic, and oregano and sauté until the vegetables are tender, about 10 minutes. Stir in the pecans and balsamic vinaigrette and season the mixture with salt and pepper. 4. Assemble and bake. Stuff the mushroom caps with the filling and bake for 20 to 25 minutes until they're tender and golden. 5. Serve. Place one stuffed mushroom on each of four plates and serve them hot.

Per Serving:

calories: 595 | fat: 56g | protein: 10g | carbs: 18g | net carbs: 9g | fiber: 9g

Cauliflower Rice-Stuffed Peppers

Prep time: 10 minutes | Cook time: 15 minutes | Serves 4

- 2 cups uncooked cauliflower rice
- ¾ cup drained canned petite diced tomatoes
- 2 tablespoons olive oil
- 1 cup shredded Mozzarella cheese
- ¼ teaspoon salt
- ¼ teaspoon ground black pepper
- 4 medium green bell peppers, tops removed, seeded

1. In a large bowl, mix all ingredients except bell peppers. Scoop mixture evenly into peppers. 2. Place peppers into ungreased air fryer basket. Adjust the temperature to 350ºF (177ºC) and air fry for 15 minutes. Peppers will be tender and cheese will be melted when done. Serve warm.

Per Serving:

calories: 309 | fat: 23g | protein: 16g | carbs: 11g | net carbs: 7g | fiber: 4g

Italian Baked Egg and Veggies

Prep time: 10 minutes | Cook time: 10 minutes | Serves 2

- 2 tablespoons salted butter
- 1 small zucchini, sliced lengthwise and quartered
- ½ medium green bell pepper, seeded and diced
- 1 cup fresh spinach, chopped
- 1 medium Roma tomato, diced
- 2 large eggs
- ¼ teaspoon onion powder
- ¼ teaspoon garlic powder
- ½ teaspoon dried basil
- ¼ teaspoon dried oregano

1. Grease two ramekins with 1 tablespoon butter each. 2. In a large bowl, toss zucchini, bell pepper, spinach, and tomatoes. Divide the mixture in two and place half in each ramekin. 3. Crack an egg on top of each ramekin and sprinkle with onion powder, garlic powder, basil, and oregano. Place into the air fryer basket. 4. Adjust the temperature to 330ºF (166ºC) and bake for 10 minutes. 5. Serve immediately.

Per Serving:

calories: 260 | fat: 21g | protein: 10g | carbs: 8g | net carbs: 5g | fiber: 3g

Chapter 9

Desserts

Chapter 9 Desserts

Cocoa Custard

Prep time: 5 minutes | Cook time: 7 minutes | Serves 4

◄ 2 cups heavy cream (or full-fat coconut milk for dairy-free)
◄ 4 large egg yolks
◄ ¼ cup Swerve, or more to taste

◄ 1 tablespoon plus 1 teaspoon unsweetened cocoa powder, or more to taste
◄ ½ teaspoon almond extract
◄ Pinch of fine sea salt
◄ 1 cup cold water

1. Heat the cream in a pan over medium-high heat until hot, about 2 minutes. 2. Place the remaining ingredients except the water in a blender and blend until smooth. 3. While the blender is running, slowly pour in the hot cream. Taste and adjust the sweetness to your liking. Add more cocoa powder, if desired. 4. Scoop the custard mixture into four ramekins with a spatula. Cover the ramekins with aluminum foil. 5. Place a trivet in the Instant Pot and pour in the water. Place the ramekins on the trivet. 6. Lock the lid. Select the Manual mode and set the cooking time for 5 minutes at High Pressure. 7. When the timer beeps, use a quick pressure release. Carefully remove the lid. 8. Remove the foil and set the foil aside. Let the custard cool for 15 minutes. Cover the ramekins with the foil again and place in the refrigerator to chill completely, about 2 hours. 9. Serve.

Per Serving:

calories: 269 | fat: 27g | protein: 4g | carbs: 4g | net carbs: 4g | fiber: 0g

Easy Truffles

Prep time: 15 minutes | Cook time: 0 minutes | Makes 18 truffles

◄ 1 cup sugar-free chocolate chips
◄ ½ cup heavy whipping cream
◄ Suggested Coatings:

◄ Cocoa powder
◄ Unsweetened shredded coconut
◄ Crushed nuts (raw or roasted) of choice

1. Put the chocolate chips in small bowl. 2. In a small saucepan over low heat, bring the cream to a simmer. 3. Pour the hot cream over the chocolate. Allow to sit for a few minutes, until the chocolate begins to melt, then stir until smooth. Allow to cool, then refrigerate the mixture for 2 hours. 4. Line a small sheet pan or tray with parchment paper. 5. To make the truffles, scoop a teaspoon-sized ball of the chocolate mixture. Quickly roll it between the palms of your hands. Then roll it in the coating of your choice and place the ball on the lined pan. Repeat with the rest of the truffle mixture and coating. 6. Refrigerate for at least 1 hour before serving. Allow the truffles to sit out for 10 minutes to soften before eating. Store in an airtight container in the refrigerator for up to a week.

Per Serving:

calories: 149 | fat: 6g | protein: 1g | carbs: 6g | net carbs: 2g | fiber: 3g

Snickerdoodle Cream Cheesecake

Prep time: 5 minutes | Cook time: 90 minutes | Serves 1

Filling:
◄ 1 tablespoon cream cheese, room temperature
◄ 1 teaspoon powdered

erythritol
◄ 1 teaspoon ground cinnamon

Cake:
◄ 1½ tablespoons coconut flour
◄ 1 tablespoon golden flax meal
◄ ¼ teaspoon baking powder
◄ ⅛ teaspoon cream of tartar

◄ 2 tablespoons unsalted butter, melted but not hot
◄ 1 large egg
◄ ½ teaspoon vanilla extract
◄ ¼ teaspoon plus 15 drops of liquid stevia

For Garnish (optional):
◄ Ground cinnamon

◄ Powdered erythritol

1. Make the filling: Place a piece of plastic wrap in a small bowl and put the cream cheese, erythritol, and cinnamon in the center. Use a spoon to combine the ingredients, then wrap the plastic wrap around the mixture to enclose it securely. Using your hands, form the filling into a small disc, 1 inch in diameter and ½ inch thick. Place in the freezer for 30 minutes. 2. Make the cake: In a small bowl, use a fork to whisk together the coconut flour, flax meal, baking powder, and cream of tartar. In another small bowl, whisk together the melted butter, egg, vanilla extract, and stevia. 3. Slowly add the dry mixture to the wet mixture and whisk together until it has a thick batterlike consistency. 4. Grease a 4- or 5-ounce microwave-safe ramekin with coconut oil spray. Pour half of the batter into the ramekin. Remove the cream cheese disc from the freezer, unwrap, and place in the center of the ramekin. Gently press it down, but do not let it hit the bottom. Pour the rest of the batter on top of the filling and spread, fully covering the disc and creating an even surface. 5. Microwave for 90 seconds. Flip the cake over onto a plate and, if desired, dust with ground cinnamon and powdered erythritol. Enjoy!

Per Serving:

calories: 403 | fat: 36g | protein: 11g | carbs: 12g | net carbs: 5g | fiber: 7g

Thai Pandan Coconut Custard

Prep time: 10 minutes | Cook time: 30 minutes | Serves 4

- ◄ Nonstick cooking spray
- ◄ 1 cup unsweetened coconut milk
- ◄ 3 eggs
- ◄ ⅓ cup Swerve
- ◄ 3 to 4 drops pandan extract, or use vanilla extract if you must

1. Grease a 6-inch heatproof bowl with the cooking spray. 2. In a large bowl, whisk together the coconut milk, eggs, Swerve, and pandan extract. Pour the mixture into the prepared bowl and cover it with aluminum foil. 3. Pour 2 cups of water into the inner cooking pot of the Instant Pot, then place a trivet in the pot. Place the bowl on the trivet. 4. Lock the lid into place. Select Manual and adjust the pressure to High. Cook for 30 minutes. When the cooking is complete, let the pressure release naturally. Unlock the lid. 5. Remove the bowl from the pot and remove the foil. A knife inserted into the custard should come out clean. Cool in the refrigerator for 6 to 8 hours, or until the custard is set.

Per Serving:

calories: 202 | fat: 18g | protein: 6g | carbs: 4g | net carbs: 3g | fiber: 1g

Trail Mix with Dried Coconut and Strawberries

Prep time: 15 minutes | Cook time: 3 hours 30 minutes | Makes 7 cups

- ◄ 10 medium strawberries, hulled and halved
- ◄ 2 tablespoons coconut oil
- ◄ 1 teaspoon ground cinnamon
- ◄ ½ teaspoon vanilla extract
- ◄ Sweetener of choice (optional)
- ◄ 2 cups chopped pecans
- ◄ 2 cups walnut halves,
- chopped
- ◄ 1 cup unsweetened coconut flakes
- ◄ ½ cup macadamia nuts
- ◄ ½ cup sliced almonds
- ◄ 3 Brazil nuts, chopped
- ◄ 3 tablespoons hulled pumpkin seeds

1. Preheat the oven to 200ºF (93ºC). Line a baking sheet with parchment paper. 2. Arrange the strawberries cut-side up on the prepared baking sheet and bake for 3 hours, rotating the baking sheet every hour. Remove from the oven and let cool for 30 minutes. If they are still moist, cook for another 30 minutes. 3. While the strawberries are cooling, increase the oven heat to 375ºF (190ºC). 4. In a microwave-safe bowl, melt the coconut oil in the microwave. Stir in the cinnamon, vanilla, and sweetener (if using). In another bowl, combine the pecans, walnuts, coconut flakes, macadamia nuts, almonds, Brazil nuts, and pumpkin seeds. Drizzle the coconut oil mixture over the nuts until everything is lightly coated but not soaked. 5. Line two more baking sheets with parchment paper and spread the nut mixture over the sheets evenly. Bake for 15 to 30 minutes until the nuts begin to brown. Remove from the oven and pour onto a paper towel to dry. 6. Once all the

ingredients have cooled, toss the nuts and strawberries together and eat right away. 7. If not eating right away, store the strawberries and nuts separately. Both will store safely in an airtight container for 1 week. If moisture develops in your strawberry container, bake for another 30 minutes at 200°F.

Per Serving:

½ cup: calories: 388 | fat: 36g | protein: 7g | carbs: 9g | net carbs: 4g | fiber: 5g

Lemonade Fat Bomb

Prep time: 10 minutes | Cook time: 0 minutes | Serves 2

- ◄ ½ lemon
- ◄ 4 ounces cream cheese, at room temperature
- ◄ 2 ounces butter, at room temperature
- ◄ 2 teaspoons Swerve natural sweetener or 2 drops liquid stevia
- ◄ Pinch pink Himalayan salt

1. Zest the lemon half with a very fine grater into a small bowl. Squeeze the juice from the lemon half into the bowl with the zest. 2. In a medium bowl, combine the cream cheese and butter. Add the sweetener, lemon zest and juice, and pink Himalayan salt. Using a hand mixer, beat until fully combined. 3. Spoon the mixture into the fat bomb molds. (I use small silicone cupcake molds. If you don't have molds, you can use cupcake paper liners that fit into the cups of a muffin tin.) 4. Freeze for at least 2 hours, unmold, and eat. Keep extras in your freezer in a zip-top bag so you and your loved ones can have them anytime you are craving a sweet treat. They will keep in the freezer for up to 3 months.

Per Serving:

calories: 404 | fat: 43g | protein: 4g | carbs: 8g | net carbs: 4g | fiber: 1g

Lime Muffins

Prep time: 10 minutes | Cook time: 15 minutes | Serves 6

- ◄ 1 teaspoon lime zest
- ◄ 1 tablespoon lemon juice
- ◄ 1 teaspoon baking powder
- ◄ 1 cup almond flour
- ◄ 2 eggs, beaten
- ◄ 1 tablespoon Swerve
- ◄ ¼ cup heavy cream
- ◄ 1 cup water, for cooking

1. In the mixing bowl, mix up lemon juice, baking powder, almond flour, eggs, Swerve, and heavy cream. 2. When the muffin batter is smooth, add lime zest and mix it up. 3. Fill the muffin molds with batter. 4. Then pour water and insert the rack in the instant pot. 5. Place the muffins on the rack. Close and seal the lid. 6. Cook the muffins on Manual (High Pressure) for 15 minutes. 7. Then allow the natural pressure release.

Per Serving:

calories: 153 | fat: 12g | protein: 6g | carbs: 5g | net carbs: 3g | fiber: 2g

Cinnamon Toast Crunch Nuts

Prep time: 1 minutes | Cook time: 5 minutes | Serves 1

- 1 tablespoon unsalted butter, softened
- ¼ cup pecan halves
- ¼ teaspoon pure vanilla extract
- 4 tablespoons 0g net carb sweetener
- ⅛ teaspoon ground cinnamon

1. In a small saucepan over low heat, toss all ingredients starting with the butter until well coated and toasted (up to 5 minutes). 2. Spread out and let cool on wax or parchment paper to prevent sticking together.

Per Serving:

calories: 275 | fat: 28g | protein: 2g | carbs: 4g | net carbs: 1g | fiber: 3g

Peanut Butter Mousse

Prep time: 10 minutes | Cook time: 0 minutes | Serves 4

- 1 cup heavy (whipping) cream
- ¼ cup natural peanut butter
- 1 teaspoon alcohol-free pure vanilla extract
- 4 drops liquid stevia

1. In a medium bowl, beat together the heavy cream, peanut butter, vanilla, and stevia until firm peaks form, about 5 minutes. 2. Spoon the mousse into 4 bowls and place in the refrigerator to chill for 30 minutes. 3. Serve.

Per Serving:

calories: 280 | fat: 28g | protein: 6g | carbs: 4g | net carbs: 3g | fiber: 1g

Traditional Cheesecake

Prep time: 30 minutes | Cook time: 45 minutes | Serves 8

For Crust:
- 1½ cups almond flour
- 4 tablespoons butter, melted
- 1 tablespoon Swerve
- 1 tablespoon granulated

For Filling:
- 16 ounces (454 g) cream cheese, softened
- ½ cup granulated erythritol
- 2 eggs

- erythritol
- ½ teaspoon ground cinnamon

- 1 teaspoon vanilla extract
- ½ teaspoon lemon extract
- 1½ cups water

1. To make the crust: In a medium bowl, combine the almond flour, butter, Swerve, erythritol, and cinnamon. Use a fork to press it all together. When completed, the mixture should resemble wet sand.

2. Spray the springform pan with cooking spray and line the bottom with parchment paper. 3. Press the crust evenly into the pan. Work the crust up the sides of the pan, about halfway from the top, and make sure there are no bare spots on the bottom. 4. Place the crust in the freezer for 20 minutes while you make the filling. 5. To make the filling: In the bowl of a stand mixer using the whip attachment, combine the cream cheese and erythritol on medium speed until the cream cheese is light and fluffy, 2 to 3 minutes. 6. Add the eggs, vanilla extract, and lemon extract. Mix until well combined. 7. Remove the crust from the freezer and pour in the filling. Cover the pan tightly with aluminum foil and place it on the trivet. 8. Add the water to the pot and carefully lower the trivet into the pot. 9. Close the lid. Select Manual mode and set cooking time for 45 minutes on High Pressure. 10. When timer beeps, use a quick pressure release and open the lid. 11. Remove the trivet and cheesecake from the pot. Remove the foil from the pan. The center of the cheesecake should still be slightly jiggly. If the cheesecake is still very jiggly in the center, cook for an additional 5 minutes on High pressure until the appropriate doneness is reached. 12. Let the cheesecake cool for 30 minutes on the counter before placing it in the refrigerator to set. Leave the cheesecake in the refrigerator for at least 6 hours before removing the sides of the pan, slicing, and serving.

Per Serving:

calories: 437 | fat: 35g | protein: 10g | carbs: 7g | net carbs: 4g | fiber: 2g

Hearty Crème Brûlée

Prep time: 5 minutes | Cook time: 30 minutes | Serves 4

- 5 egg yolks
- 5 tablespoons powdered erythritol
- 1½ cups heavy cream
- 2 teaspoons vanilla extract
- 2 cups water

1. In a small bowl, use a fork to break up the egg yolks. Stir in the erythritol. 2. Pour the cream into a small saucepan over medium-low heat and let it warm up for 3 to 4 minutes. Remove the saucepan from the heat. 3. Temper the egg yolks by slowly adding a small spoonful of the warm cream, keep whisking. Do this three times to make sure the egg yolks are fully tempered. 4. Slowly add the tempered eggs to the cream, whisking the whole time. Add the vanilla and whisk again. 5. Pour the cream mixture into the ramekins. Each ramekin should have ½ cup liquid. Cover each with aluminum foil. 6. Place the trivet inside the Instant Pot. Add the water. Carefully place the ramekins on top of the trivet. 7. Close the lid. Select Manual mode and set cooking time for 11 minutes on High Pressure. 8. When timer beeps, use a natural release for 15 minutes, then release any remaining pressure. Open the lid. 9. Carefully remove a ramekin from the pot. Remove the foil and check for doneness. The custard should be mostly set with a slightly jiggly center. 10. Place all the ramekins in the fridge for 2 hours to chill and set. Serve chilled.

Per Serving:

calories: 229 | fat: 22g | protein: 4g | carbs: 2g | net carbs: 2g | fiber: 0g

Keto Brownies

Prep time: 15 minutes | Cook time: 15 minutes | Serves 8

- ◀ 1 cup coconut flour
- ◀ 1 tablespoon cocoa powder
- ◀ 1 tablespoon coconut oil
- ◀ 1 teaspoon vanilla extract
- ◀ 1 teaspoon baking powder
- ◀ 1 teaspoon apple cider vinegar
- ◀ ⅓ cup butter, melted
- ◀ 1 tablespoon erythritol
- ◀ 1 cup water, for cooking

1. In the mixing bowl, mix up erythritol, melted butter, apple cider vinegar, baking powder, vanilla extract, coconut oil, cocoa powder, and coconut flour. 2. Whisk the mixture until smooth and pour it in the baking pan. Flatten the surface of the batter. 3. Pour water and insert the steamer rack in the instant pot. 4. Put the pan with brownie batter on the rack. Close and seal the lid. 5. Cook the brownie on Manual mode (High Pressure) for 15 minutes. 6. Then allow the natural pressure release for 5 minutes. 7. Cut the cooked brownies into the bars.

Per Serving:

calories: 146 | fat: 11g | protein: 2g | carbs: 9g | net carbs: 5g | fiber: 4g

Cinnamon Roll Cheesecake

Prep time: 15 minutes | Cook time: 35 minutes | Serves 12

Crust:
- ◀ 3½ tablespoons unsalted butter or coconut oil
- ◀ 1½ ounces (43 g) unsweetened baking chocolate, chopped
- ◀ 1 large egg, beaten

Filling:
- ◀ 4 (8-ounce / 227-g) packages cream cheese, softened
- ◀ ¾ cup Swerve
- ◀ ½ cup unsweetened almond milk (or hemp milk for nut-free)

Cinnamon Swirl:
- ◀ 6 tablespoons (¾ stick) unsalted butter (or butter flavored coconut oil for dairy-free)
- ◀ ½ cup Swerve
- ◀ Seeds scraped from ½ vanilla bean (about 8 inches

- ◀ ⅓ cup Swerve
- ◀ 2 teaspoons ground cinnamon
- ◀ 1 teaspoon vanilla extract
- ◀ ¼ teaspoon fine sea salt

- ◀ 1 teaspoon vanilla extract
- ◀ ¼ teaspoon almond extract (omit for nut-free)
- ◀ ¼ teaspoon fine sea salt
- ◀ 3 large eggs

long), or 1 teaspoon vanilla extract
- ◀ 1 tablespoon ground cinnamon
- ◀ ¼ teaspoon fine sea salt
- ◀ 1 cup cold water

1. Line a baking pan with two layers of aluminum foil. 2. Make the crust: Melt the butter in a pan over medium-low heat. Slowly add the chocolate and stir until melted. Stir in the egg, sweetener, cinnamon, vanilla extract, and salt. 3. Transfer the crust mixture to the prepared baking pan, spreading it with your hands to cover the bottom completely. 4. Make the filling: In the bowl of a stand mixer, add the cream cheese, sweetener, milk, extracts, and salt and mix until well blended. Add the eggs, one at a time, mixing on low speed after each addition just until blended. Then blend until the filling is smooth. Pour half of the filling over the crust. 5. Make the cinnamon swirl: Heat the butter over high heat in a pan until the butter froths and brown flecks appear, stirring occasionally. Stir in the sweetener, vanilla seeds, cinnamon, and salt. Remove from the heat and allow to cool slightly. 6. Spoon half of the cinnamon swirl on top of the cheesecake filling in the baking pan. Use a knife to cut the cinnamon swirl through the filling several times for a marbled effect. Top with the rest of the cheesecake filling and cinnamon swirl. Cut the cinnamon swirl through the cheesecake filling again several times. 7. Place a trivet in the bottom of the Instant Pot and pour in the water. Use a foil sling to lower the baking pan onto the trivet. Cover the cheesecake with 3 large sheets of paper towel to ensure that condensation doesn't leak onto it. Tuck in the sides of the sling. 8. Lock the lid. Select the Manual mode and set the cooking time for 26 minutes at High Pressure. 9. When the timer beeps, use a natural pressure release for 10 minutes. Carefully remove the lid. 10. Use the foil sling to lift the pan out of the Instant Pot. 11. Let the cheesecake cool, then place in the refrigerator for 4 hours to chill and set completely before slicing and serving.

Per Serving:

calories: 363 | fat: 34g | protein: 7g | carbs: 8g | net carbs: 6g | fiber: 1g

Fluffy Coconut Mousse

Prep time: 15 minutes | Cook time: 5 minutes | Serves 4

- ◀ ¼ cup cold water
- ◀ 2 teaspoons granulated gelatin
- ◀ 1 cup coconut milk
- ◀ 3 egg yolks
- ◀ ½ cup monk fruit sweetener, granulated form
- ◀ 1 cup heavy (whipping) cream

1. Prepare the gelatin. Pour the cold water into a small bowl, sprinkle the gelatin on top, and set it aside for 10 minutes. 2. Heat the coconut milk. Place a small saucepan over medium heat and pour in the coconut milk. Bring the coconut milk to a boil then remove the pan from the heat. 3. Thicken the base. Whisk the eggs and sweetener in a medium bowl. Pour the coconut milk into the yolks and whisk it to blend. Pour the yolk mixture back into the saucepan and place it over medium heat. Whisk until the base thickens, about 5 minutes. Remove the pan from the heat and whisk in the gelatin mixture. 4. Cool. Transfer the mixture to a medium bowl and cool it completely in the refrigerator, about 1 hour. 5. Make the mousse. When the coconut milk mixture is cool, whisk the cream in a large bowl until it's thick and fluffy, about 3 minutes. Fold the whipped cream into the coconut mixture until the mousse is well combined and fluffy. 6. Serve. Divide the mousse between four bowls and serve it immediately.

Per Serving:

calories: 261 | fat: 27g | protein: 5g | carbs: 3g | net carbs: 3g | fiber: 0g

Blackberry Crisp

Prep time: 5 minutes | Cook time: 5 minutes | Serves 1

◁ 10 blackberries
◁ ½ teaspoon vanilla extract
◁ 2 tablespoons powdered erythritol
◁ ⅛ teaspoon xanthan gum
◁ 1 tablespoon butter
◁ ¼ cup chopped pecans
◁ 3 teaspoons almond flour
◁ ½ teaspoon cinnamon
◁ 2 teaspoons powdered erythritol
◁ 1 cup water

1. Place blackberries, vanilla, erythritol, and xanthan gum in 4-inch ramekin. Stir gently to coat blackberries. 2. In small bowl, mix remaining ingredients. Sprinkle over blackberries and cover with foil. Press the Manual button and set time for 4 minutes. When timer beeps, quick-release the pressure. Serve warm. Feel free to add scoop of whipped cream on top.

Per Serving:

calories: 346 | fat: 31g | protein: 3g | carbs: 13g | net carbs: 5g | fiber: 8g

Mixed Berry Cobbler

Prep time: 10 minutes | Cook time: 35 minutes | Serves 4

Filling:
◁ 2 cups frozen mixed berries
◁ 1 tablespoon granulated erythritol
◁ ½ teaspoon water
Crust:
◁ ½ cup coconut flour
◁ 2 tablespoons granulated erythritol
◁ ½ teaspoon xanthan gum
Topping:
◁ 1 teaspoon granulated erythritol
◁ ¼ teaspoon freshly squeezed lemon juice
◁ ¼ teaspoon vanilla extract

◁ ½ teaspoon baking powder
◁ 6 tablespoons butter, cold
◁ ¼ cup heavy (whipping) cream

◁ ¼ teaspoon ground cinnamon

1. Preheat the oven to 350°F (180°C). 2. To make the filling: In a 9-inch round pie dish, combine the berries, erythritol, water, lemon juice, and vanilla. 3. To make the crust: In a food processor, pulse to combine the coconut flour, erythritol, xanthan gum, and baking powder. 4. Add the butter and cream, and pulse until pea-sized pieces of dough form. Don't overprocess. 5. Form 5 equal balls of dough, then flatten them to between ¼- and ½-inch thickness. 6. Place the dough rounds on the top of the berries so that they are touching, but not overlapping. 7. To make the topping: In a small bowl, combine the erythritol and cinnamon. Sprinkle the mixture over the dough. 8. Bake for 30 to 35 minutes, until the topping is beginning to brown, then let cool for 10 minutes before serving.

Per Serving:

calories: 317 | fat: 25g | protein: 4g | carbs: 19g | net carbs: 12g | fiber: 7g

Strawberry Shake

Prep time: 10 minutes | Cook time: 0 minutes | Serves 2

◁ ¾ cup heavy (whipping) cream
◁ 2 ounces cream cheese, at room temperature
◁ 1 tablespoon Swerve natural
◁ sweetener
◁ ¼ teaspoon vanilla extract
◁ 6 strawberries, sliced
◁ 6 ice cubes

1. In a food processor (or blender), combine the heavy cream, cream cheese, sweetener, and vanilla. Mix on high to fully combine. 2. Add the strawberries and ice, and blend until smooth. 3. Pour into two tall glasses and serve.

Per Serving:

calories: 407 | fat: 42g | protein: 4g | carbs: 13g | net carbs: 6g | fiber: 1g

Keto Cheesecake with Hazelnut Crust

Prep time: 10 minutes | Cook time: 1 hour 45 minutes | Serves 10

◁ 4 tablespoons butter, melted, plus more for the pan
◁ 1 cup finely crushed hazelnuts
◁ 1 cup almond flour
◁ 5 (8-ounce / 227-g) blocks
◁ cream cheese, at room temperature
◁ 1½ cups Swerve
◁ 4 eggs
◁ 1 teaspoon vanilla extract
◁ 1 cup sour cream

1. Preheat the oven to 375°F (190°C). 2. Grease a 10-inch springform pan with melted butter. 3. In a large bowl, stir together the hazelnuts and almond flour. Pour the melted butter over them and stir until the nut mixture becomes wet and crumbly. Scrape the crust into the prepared pan, pressing firmly with your fingers. Bake for about 15 minutes or until the crust begins to brown. Remove from the oven and let it cool completely. 4. Reduce the oven temperature to 325°F (163°C). 5. In a bowl, beat the cream cheese with a handheld mixer until fluffy. Continue to beat as you add the Swerve. 6. Add the eggs one at a time, beating well after each addition. 7. Continue to beat while adding the vanilla followed by the sour cream. 8. Fill a large deeply rimmed baking sheet halfway with hot water. Carefully transfer the springform pan with the crust to the water bath and pour the cheesecake filling into the crust. Bake for 1 hour, 30 minutes or until you can slide a knife in and it comes out clean. Let the cheesecake cool then refrigerate for several hours, preferably overnight.

Per Serving:

calories: 578 | fat: 58g | protein: 12g | carbs: 7g | net carbs: 6g | fiber: 1g

Cardamom Rolls with Cream Cheese

Prep time: 20 minutes | Cook time: 18 minutes | Serves 5

- ½ cup coconut flour
- 1 tablespoon ground cardamom
- 2 tablespoon Swerve
- 1 egg, whisked
- ¼ cup almond milk
- 1 tablespoon butter, softened
- 1 tablespoon cream cheese
- ⅓ cup water

1. Combine together coconut flour, almond milk, and softened butter. 2. Knead the smooth dough. 3. Roll up the dough with the help of the rolling pin. 4. Then combine together Swerve and ground cardamom. 5. Sprinkle the surface of the dough with the ground cardamom mixture. 6. Roll the dough into one big roll and cut them into servings. 7. Place the rolls into the instant pot round mold. 8. Pour water in the instant pot (⅓ cup) and insert the mold inside. 9. Set Manual mode (High Pressure) for 18 minutes. 10. Then use the natural pressure release method for 15 minutes. 11. Chill the rolls to the room temperature and spread with cream cheese.

Per Serving:

calories: 128 | fat: 6g | protein: 5g | carbs: 12g | net carbs: 8g | fiber: 4g

Pecan Pumpkin Pie

Prep time: 5 minutes | Cook time: 40 minutes | Serves 5 to 6

Base:
- 2 tablespoons grass-fed butter, softened
Topping:
- ½ cup Swerve, or more to taste
- ⅓ cup heavy whipping cream
- ½ teaspoon ground cinnamon
- ½ teaspoon ginger, finely
- 1 cup blanched almond flour
- ½ cup chopped pecans grated
- ½ teaspoon ground nutmeg
- ½ teaspoon ground cloves
- 1 (14-ounce / 397-g) can organic pumpkin purée
- 1 egg

1. Pour 1 cup of filtered water into the inner pot of the Instant Pot, then insert the trivet. Using an electric mixer, combine the butter, almond flour, and pecans. Mix thoroughly. Transfer this mixture into a well-greased, Instant Pot-friendly pan, and form a crust at the bottom of the pan, with a slight coating of the mixture also on the sides. Freeze for 15 minutes. In a large bowl, thoroughly combine the topping ingredients. 2. Take the pan from the freezer, add the topping evenly, and then place the pan onto the trivet. Cover loosely with aluminum foil. Close the lid, set the pressure release to Sealing, and select Manual. Set the Instant Pot to 40 minutes on High Pressure, and let cook. 3. Once cooked, let the pressure

naturally disperse from the Instant Pot for about 10 minutes, then carefully switch the pressure release to Venting. 4. Open the Instant Pot and remove the pan. Cool in the refrigerator for 4 to 5 hours, serve, and enjoy!

Per Serving:

calories: 152 | fat: 14g | protein: 3g | carbs: 6g | net carbs: 4g | fiber: 2g

After-Dinner Parfait

Prep time: 10 minutes | Cook time: 0 minutes | Serves 4

- 1 small (9-gram) package sugar-free Jell-O, any flavor
- 1 cup boiling water
- 1 cup cold water
- 4 ounces full-fat cream
- cheese, softened
- 2 tablespoons canned whipped cream
- 1 tablespoon crushed salty peanuts

1. In a medium bowl, add Jell-O to boiling water. Stir in cold water until mixture starts to thicken, 2–3 minutes. Refrigerate until firm, about 30 minutes. 2. Using a mixer in a medium mixing bowl, beat softened cream cheese until smooth. Going slowly at first, combine firm Jell-O with cream cheese. Gradually increase speed until desired consistency is reached. 3. Scoop into serving bowls and top with whipped cream and dusting of crushed peanuts.

Per Serving:

calories: 122 | fat: 10g | protein: 3g | carbs: 2g | net carbs: 2g | fiber: 0g

Vanilla Egg Custard

Prep time: 10 minutes | Cook time: 30 minutes | Serves 2

- 1 cup heavy whipping cream, plus ¼ cup for topping if desired
- 2 large egg yolks
- 2 teaspoons vanilla extract
- ½ teaspoon liquid stevia

1. Preheat the oven to 300°F. 2. Put the 1 cup of cream, egg yolks, vanilla extract, and stevia in a medium-sized mixing bowl and beat with a hand mixer until combined. Pour into two 6-ounce ramekins. Place the ramekins in a baking dish and fill the baking dish with boiling water so that it goes two-thirds of the way up the sides of the ramekins. 3. Bake for 30 minutes, or until the edges of the custard are just starting to brown. It should not be completely baked through and firm. Place in the refrigerator to chill and set for at least 2 hours before serving. 4. If making the topping, put the ¼ cup of cream in a medium-sized mixing bowl and whip using the hand mixer until soft peaks form. Top the custard with the whipped cream prior to serving.

Per Serving:

calories: 568 | fat: 59g | protein: 5g | carbs: 4g | net carbs: 4g | fiber: 0g

Chocolate Chip Brownies

Prep time: 10 minutes | Cook time: 33 minutes | Serves 8

◄ 1½ cups almond flour
◄ ⅓ cup unsweetened cocoa powder
◄ ¾ cup granulated erythritol
◄ 1 teaspoon baking powder
◄ 2 eggs

◄ 1 tablespoon vanilla extract
◄ 5 tablespoons butter, melted
◄ ¼ cup sugar-free chocolate chips
◄ ½ cup water

1. In a large bowl, add the almond flour, cocoa powder, erythritol, and baking powder. Use a hand mixer on low speed to combine and smooth out any lumps. 2. Add the eggs and vanilla and mix until well combined. 3. Add the butter and mix on low speed until well combined. Scrape the bottom and sides of the bowl and mix again if needed. Fold in the chocolate chips. 4. Grease a baking dish with cooking spray. Pour the batter into the dish and smooth with a spatula. Cover tightly with aluminum foil. 5. Pour the water into the pot. Place the trivet in the pot and carefully lower the baking dish onto the trivet. 6. Close the lid. Select Manual mode and set cooking time for 33 minutes on High Pressure. 7. When timer beeps, use a quick pressure release and open the lid. 8. Use the handles to carefully remove the trivet from the pot. Remove the foil from the dish. 9. Let the brownies cool for 10 minutes before turning out onto a plate.

Per Serving:

calories: 235 | fat: 20g | protein: 7g | carbs: 7g | net carbs: 3g | fiber: 4g

Pumpkin Walnut Cheesecake

Prep time: 15 minutes | Cook time: 50 minutes | Serves 6

◄ 2 cups walnuts
◄ 3 tablespoons melted butter
◄ 1 teaspoon cinnamon
◄ 16 ounces (454 g) cream cheese, softened
◄ 1 cup powdered erythritol

◄ ⅓ cup heavy cream
◄ ⅔ cup pumpkin purée
◄ 2 teaspoons pumpkin spice
◄ 1 teaspoon vanilla extract
◄ 2 eggs
◄ 1 cup water

1. Preheat oven to 350ºF (180ºC). Add walnuts, butter, and cinnamon to food processor. Pulse until ball forms. Scrape down sides as necessary. Dough should hold together in ball. 2. Press into greased 7-inch springform pan. Bake for 10 minutes or until it begins to brown. Remove and set aside. While crust is baking, make cheesecake filling. 3. In large bowl, stir cream cheese until completely smooth. Using rubber spatula, mix in erythritol, heavy cream, pumpkin purée, pumpkin spice, and vanilla. 4. In small bowl, whisk eggs. Slowly add them into large bowl, folding gently until just combined. 5. Pour mixture into crust and cover with foil. Pour water into Instant Pot and place steam rack on bottom. Place pan onto steam rack and click lid closed. Press the Cake button and press the Adjust button to set heat to More. Set timer

for 40 minutes. 6. When timer beeps, allow a full natural release. When pressure indicator drops, carefully remove pan and place on counter. Remove foil. Let cool for additional hour and then refrigerate. Serve chilled.

Per Serving:

calories: 578 | fat: 54g | protein: 12g | carbs: 11g | net carbs: 8g | fiber: 3g

New York Cheesecake

Prep time: 1 hour | Cook time: 37 minutes | Serves 8

◄ 1½ cups almond flour
◄ 3 ounces (85 g) Swerve
◄ ½ stick butter, melted
◄ 20 ounces (567 g) full-fat cream cheese

◄ ½ cup heavy cream
◄ 1¼ cups granulated Swerve
◄ 3 eggs, at room temperature
◄ 1 tablespoon vanilla essence
◄ 1 teaspoon grated lemon zest

1. Coat the sides and bottom of a baking pan with a little flour. 2. In a mixing bowl, combine the almond flour and Swerve. Add the melted butter and mix until your mixture looks like bread crumbs. 3. Press the mixture into the bottom of the prepared pan to form an even layer. Bake at 330ºF (166ºC) for 7 minutes until golden brown. Allow it to cool completely on a wire rack. 4. Meanwhile, in a mixer fitted with the paddle attachment, prepare the filling by mixing the soft cheese, heavy cream, and granulated Swerve; beat until creamy and fluffy. 5. Crack the eggs into the mixing bowl, one at a time; add the vanilla and lemon zest and continue to mix until fully combined. 6. Pour the prepared topping over the cooled crust and spread evenly. 7. Bake in the preheated air fryer at 330ºF (166ºC) for 25 to 30 minutes; leave it in the air fryer to keep warm for another 30 minutes. 8. Cover your cheesecake with plastic wrap. Place in your refrigerator and allow it to cool at least 6 hours or overnight. Serve well chilled.

Per Serving:

calories: 409 | fat: 38g | protein: 10g | carbs: 7g | net carbs: 5g | fiber: 2g

Vanilla Butter Curd

Prep time: 5 minutes | Cook time: 6 hours | Serves 3

◄ 4 egg yolks, whisked
◄ 2 tablespoon butter
◄ 1 tablespoon erythritol

◄ ½ cup organic almond milk
◄ 1 teaspoon vanilla extract

1. Set the instant pot to Sauté mode and when the "Hot" is displayed, add butter. 2. Melt the butter but not boil it and add whisked egg yolks, almond milk, and vanilla extract. 3. Add erythritol. Whisk the mixture. 4. Cook the meal on Low for 6 hours.

Per Serving:

calories: 154 | fat: 14g | protein: 4g | carbs: 7g | net carbs: 7g | fiber: 0g

Coffee Ice Pops

Prep time: 5 minutes | Cook time: 0 minutes | Serves 4

- 2 cups brewed coffee, cold
- ¾ cup coconut cream, ¾ cup unsweetened full-fat coconut milk, or ¾ cup heavy (whipping) cream
- 2 teaspoons Swerve natural sweetener or 2 drops liquid stevia
- 2 tablespoons sugar-free chocolate chips (I use Lily's)

1. In a food processor (or blender), mix together the coffee, coconut cream, and sweetener until thoroughly blended. 2. Pour into ice pop molds, and drop a few chocolate chips into each mold. 3. Freeze for at least 2 hours before serving.

Per Serving:

calories: 105 | fat: 10g | protein: 1g | carbs: 7g | net carbs: 2g | fiber: 2g

Chocolate Chip-Pecan Biscotti

Prep time: 15 minutes | Cook time: 20 to 22 minutes | Serves 10

- 1¼ cups finely ground blanched almond flour
- ¾ teaspoon baking powder
- ½ teaspoon xanthan gum
- ¼ teaspoon sea salt
- 3 tablespoons unsalted butter, at room temperature
- ⅓ cup Swerve
- 1 large egg, beaten
- 1 teaspoon pure vanilla extract
- ⅓ cup chopped pecans
- ¼ cup stevia-sweetened chocolate chips, such as Lily's Sweets brand
- Melted stevia-sweetened chocolate chips and chopped pecans, for topping (optional)

1. In a large bowl, combine the almond flour, baking powder, xanthan gum, and salt. 2. Line a cake pan that fits inside your air fryer with parchment paper. 3. In the bowl of a stand mixer, beat together the butter and Swerve. Add the beaten egg and vanilla, and beat for about 3 minutes. 4. Add the almond flour mixture to the butter-and-egg mixture; beat until just combined. 5. Stir in the pecans and chocolate chips. 6. Transfer the dough to the prepared pan, and press it into the bottom. 7. Set the air fryer to 325ºF (163ºC) and bake for 12 minutes. Remove from the air fryer and let cool for 15 minutes. Using a sharp knife, cut the cookie into thin strips, then return the strips to the cake pan with the bottom sides facing up. 8. Set the air fryer to 300ºF (149ºC). Bake for 8 to 10 minutes. 9. Remove from the air fryer and let cool completely on a wire rack. If desired, dip one side of each biscotti piece into melted chocolate chips, and top with chopped pecans.

Per Serving:

calories: 193 | fat: 18g | protein: 4g | carbs: 6g | net carbs: 3g | fiber: 3g

Chapter 10

Stews and Soups

Chapter 10   Stews and Soups

Thai Tum Yum Soup

Prep time: 10 minutes | Cook time: 20 minutes | serves 8

- 8 cups vegetable broth
- 1-inch knob fresh ginger, peeled and diced
- 2 garlic cloves, diced
- 1 teaspoon galangal
- 2 kefir lime leaves
- 1 cup coconut cream
- 1 cup sliced mushrooms
- 1 Roma tomato, coarsely chopped

- ½ yellow onion, coarsely chopped
- 1 cup coarsely chopped broccoli
- 1 cup coarsely chopped cauliflower
- 1 cup chopped fresh cilantro, for garnish
- 1 lime, cut into wedges, for garnish

1. In a large stockpot over medium heat, bring the broth to a simmer with the ginger, garlic, galangal, and lime leaves. 2. Pour in the coconut cream, followed by the mushrooms, tomato, onion, broccoli, and cauliflower. Simmer until tender. 3. Remove the pot from the heat and serve the soup garnished with the cilantro and a lime slice.

Per Serving:

calories: 97 | fat: 7g | protein: 1g | carbs: 9g | net carbs: 6g | fiber: 3g

Tomato-Basil Parmesan Soup

Prep time: 5 minutes | Cook time: 12 minutes | Serves 12

- 2 tablespoons unsalted butter or coconut oil
- ½ cup finely diced onions
- Cloves squeezed from 1 head roasted garlic , or 2 cloves garlic, minced
- 1 tablespoon dried basil leaves
- 1 teaspoon dried oregano leaves
- 1 (8 ounces / 227 g) package cream cheese, softened

- 4 cups chicken broth
- 2 (14½ ounces / 411 g) cans diced tomatoes
- 1 cup shredded Parmesan cheese, plus more for garnish
- 1 teaspoon fine sea salt
- ¼ teaspoon ground black pepper
- Fresh basil leaves, for garnish

1. Place the butter in the Instant Pot and press Sauté. Once melted, add the onions, garlic, basil, and oregano and cook, stirring often, for 4 minutes, or until the onions are soft. Press Cancel to stop the Sauté. 2. Add the cream cheese and whisk to loosen. (If you don't use a whisk to loosen the cream cheese, you will end up with clumps in your soup.) Slowly whisk in the broth. Add the tomatoes, Parmesan, salt, and pepper and stir to combine. 3. Seal the lid, press Manual, and set the timer for 8 minutes. Once finished, turn the valve to venting for a quick release. 4. Remove the lid and purée the soup with a stick blender, or transfer the soup to a regular blender or food processor and process until smooth. If using a regular blender, you may need to blend the soup in two batches; if you overfill the blender jar, the soup will not purée properly. 5 Season with salt and pepper to taste, if desired. Ladle the soup into bowls and garnish with more Parmesan and basil leaves.

Per Serving:

calories: 146 | fat: 10g | protein: 8g | carbs: 4g | net carbs: 3g | fiber: 1g

Cioppino Seafood Soup

Prep time: 10 minutes | Cook time: 30 minutes | Serves 6

- 2 tablespoons olive oil
- ½ onion, chopped
- 2 celery stalks, sliced
- 1 red bell pepper, chopped
- 1 tablespoon minced garlic
- 2 cups fish stock
- 1 (15-ounce) can coconut milk
- 1 cup crushed tomatoes
- 2 tablespoons tomato paste
- 1 tablespoon chopped fresh basil
- 2 teaspoons chopped fresh

- oregano
- ½ teaspoon sea salt
- ½ teaspoon freshly ground black pepper
- ¼ teaspoon red pepper flakes
- 10 ounces salmon, cut into 1-inch pieces
- ½ pound shrimp, peeled and deveined
- 12 clams or mussels, cleaned and debearded but in the shell

1. Sauté the vegetables. In a large stockpot over medium-high heat, warm the olive oil. Add the onion, celery, red bell pepper, and garlic and sauté until they've softened, about 4 minutes. 2. Make the soup base. Stir in the fish stock, coconut milk, crushed tomatoes, tomato paste, basil, oregano, salt, pepper, and red pepper flakes. Bring the soup to a boil, then reduce the heat to low and simmer the soup for 10 minutes. 3. Add the seafood. Stir in the salmon and simmer until it goes opaque, about 5 minutes. Add the shrimp and simmer until they're almost cooked through, about 3 minutes. Add the mussels and let them simmer until they open, about 3 minutes. Throw out any mussels that don't open. 4. Serve. Ladle the soup into bowls and serve it hot.

Per Serving:

calories: 377 | fat: 29g | protein: 24g | carbs: 9g | net carbs: 7g | fiber: 2g

Chicken and Asparagus Soup

Prep time: 7 minutes | Cook time: 11 minutes | Serves 8

- 1 tablespoon unsalted butter (or coconut oil for dairy-free)
- ¼ cup finely chopped onions
- 2 cloves garlic, minced
- 1 (14-ounce / 397-g) can full-fat coconut milk
- 1 (14-ounce / 397-g) can sugar-free tomato sauce
- 1 cup chicken broth
- 1 tablespoon red curry paste
- 1 teaspoon fine sea salt
- ½ teaspoon ground black pepper
- 2 pounds (907 g) boneless, skinless chicken breasts, cut into ½-inch chunks
- 2 cups asparagus, trimmed and cut into 2-inch pieces
- Fresh cilantro leaves, for garnish
- Lime wedges, for garnish

1. Place the butter in the Instant Pot and press Sauté. Once melted, add the onions and garlic and sauté for 4 minutes, or until the onions are soft. Press Cancel to stop the Sauté. 2. Add the coconut milk, tomato sauce, broth, curry paste, salt, and pepper and whisk to combine well. Stir in the chicken and asparagus. 3. Seal the lid, press Manual, and set the timer for 7 minutes. Once finished, turn the valve to venting for a quick release. 4. Remove the lid and stir well. Taste and adjust the seasoning to your liking. Ladle the soup into bowls and garnish with cilantro. Serve with lime wedges or a squirt of lime juice.

Per Serving:

calories: 235 | fat: 13g | protein: 24g | carbs: 8g | net carbs: 6g | fiber: 2g

Avocado and Serrano Chile Soup

Prep time: 10 minutes | Cook time: 7 minutes | Serves 4

- 2 avocados
- 1 small fresh tomatillo, quartered
- 2 cups chicken broth
- 2 tablespoons avocado oil
- 1 tablespoon butter
- 2 tablespoons finely minced onion
- 1 clove garlic, minced
- ½ Serrano chile, deseeded and ribs removed, minced, plus thin slices for garnish
- ¼ teaspoon sea salt
- Pinch of ground white pepper
- ½ cup full-fat coconut milk
- Fresh cilantro sprigs, for garnish

1. Scoop the avocado flesh into a food processor. Add the tomatillo and chicken broth and purée until smooth. Set aside. 2. Set the Instant Pot to Sauté mode and add the avocado oil and butter. When the butter melts, add the onion and garlic and sauté for a minute or until softened. Add the Serrano chile and sauté for 1 minute more. 3. Pour the puréed avocado mixture into the pot, add the salt and pepper, and stir to combine. 4. Secure the lid. Press the Manual button and set cooking time for 5 minutes on High Pressure. 5. When timer beeps, use a quick pressure release. Open the lid and stir in the coconut milk. 6. Serve hot topped with thin slices of Serrano chile, and cilantro sprigs.

Per Serving:

calories: 333 | fat: 32g | protein: 4g | carbs: 15g | net carbs: 7g | fiber: 8g

OG Zuppa Toscana Soup

Prep time: 20 minutes | Cook time: 51 minutes | Serves 8

- 1 pound loose Italian sausage
- 1 tablespoon unsalted butter
- 1½ cups chopped onion
- 3 cloves garlic, peeled and minced
- 8 cups water
- 2 (1 teaspoon) chicken bouillon cubes
- ½ pound no-sugar-added bacon, cooked and crumbled
- 4 cups chopped cauliflower, chopped into bite-sized chunks
- 4 cups chopped kale
- 1½ cups heavy whipping cream

1. In a medium-sized skillet over medium heat, cook sausage 10–15 minutes while stirring until brown. Drain fat. 2. In a large soup pot over medium heat, melt butter and then add onion. Sauté 3–5 minutes until soft and clear. Add garlic and cook 1 more minute. Add water and bouillon cubes. 3. Add crumbled bacon, cauliflower, and cooked sausage to pot. 4. When water reaches boil, reduce heat to low, cover pot, and simmer 15–20 minutes, stirring regularly until cauliflower reaches desired softness. 5. Add kale and cream. Cook, stirring regularly, for 10 minutes. 6. Let cool 10 minutes and then serve.

Per Serving:

calories: 488 | fat: 39g | protein: 21g | carbs: 10g | net carbs: 8g | fiber: 2g

Mushroom Pizza Soup

Prep time: 10 minutes | Cook time: 22 minutes | Serves 3

- 1 teaspoon coconut oil
- ¼ cup cremini mushrooms, sliced
- 5 ounces (142 g) Italian sausages, chopped
- ½ jalapeño pepper, sliced
- ½ teaspoon Italian seasoning
- 1 teaspoon unsweetened tomato purée
- 1 cup water
- 4 ounces (113 g) Mozzarella, shredded

1. Melt the coconut oil in the Instant Pot on Sauté mode. 2. Add the mushrooms and cook for 10 minutes. 3. Add the chopped sausages, sliced jalapeño, Italian seasoning, and unsweetened tomato purée. Pour in the water and stir to mix well. 4. Close the lid and select Manual mode. Set cooking time for 12 minutes on High Pressure. 5. When timer beeps, use a quick pressure release and open the lid. 6. Ladle the soup in the bowls. Top it with Mozzarella. Serve warm.

Per Serving:

calories: 289 | fat: 23g | protein: 18g | carbs: 3g | net carbs: 2g | fiber: 0g

Coconut Curry Broccoli Soup

Prep time: 10 minutes | Cook time: 20 minutes | Serves 4

◁ 4 tablespoons butter
◁ 1 celery stalk, diced
◁ 1 carrot, diced
◁ ½ onion, diced
◁ 1 garlic clove, minced
◁ 2 tablespoons curry powder

◁ 1 teaspoon red pepper flakes
◁ 3 cups chicken broth
◁ 2 cups broccoli florets
◁ 1 cup canned coconut cream
◁ Salt and freshly ground black pepper, to taste

1. In a large saucepan over medium heat, melt the butter. 2. Add the celery, carrot, onion, garlic, curry powder, and red pepper flakes. Stir to combine. Sauté for 5 to 7 minutes until the vegetables soften. 3. Stir in the chicken broth and bring to a simmer. 4. Add the broccoli and simmer for 5 to 7 minutes. 5. Stir in the coconut cream and simmer for 5 to 10 minutes more until the broccoli is cooked. Season well with salt and pepper and serve hot. Refrigerate leftovers in an airtight container for up to 1 week.

Per Serving:

calories: 274 | fat: 25g | protein: 7g | carbs: 11g | net carbs: 8g | fiber: 3g

Bacon Soup

Prep time: 10 minutes | Cook time: 1 hour 20 minutes | Serves 6

◁ ⅓ cup (69 g) lard
◁ 1 pound (455 g) pork stewing pieces
◁ ¾ cup (110 g) sliced shallots
◁ 10 strips bacon (about 10 ounces/285 g), cut into about ½-inch (1.25-cm) pieces
◁ 1¾ cups (415 ml) chicken bone broth
◁ 3 medium turnips (about 12½ ounces/355 g), cubed
◁ ¼ cup (60 ml) white wine, such as Pinot Grigio,

Sauvignon Blanc, or
◁ unoaked Chardonnay
◁ 1 tablespoon prepared yellow mustard
◁ 4 sprigs fresh thyme
◁ ½ cup (120 ml) full-fat coconut milk
◁ 2 tablespoons apple cider vinegar
◁ 2 tablespoons unflavored gelatin
◁ 1 tablespoon dried tarragon leaves

1. Melt the lard in a large saucepan over medium heat. Once the lard has melted, add the pork pieces and cook for 8 minutes, or until lightly browned on the outside. 2. Add the sliced shallots and bacon pieces. Sauté for an additional 5 minutes or until the shallots become fragrant. 3. Add the bone broth, turnips, wine, mustard, and thyme sprigs. Cover and bring to a boil, then reduce the heat to medium-low and cook until the meat and turnips are fork-tender, about 1 hour. 4. Remove the thyme sprigs and add the coconut milk, vinegar, gelatin, and tarragon. Increase the heat to medium and boil, covered, for another 10 minutes. 5. Divide the soup among 6 small bowls and serve.

Per Serving:

calories: 571 | fat: 41g | protein: 40g | carbs: 10g | net carbs: 9g | fiber: 1g

Blue Cheese Mushroom Soup

Prep time: 15 minutes | Cook time: 20 minutes | Serves 4

◁ 2 cups chopped white mushrooms
◁ 3 tablespoons cream cheese
◁ 4 ounces (113 g) scallions, diced
◁ 4 cups chicken broth

◁ 1 teaspoon olive oil
◁ ½ teaspoon ground cumin
◁ 1 teaspoon salt
◁ 2 ounces (57 g) blue cheese, crumbled

1. Combine the mushrooms, cream cheese, scallions, chicken broth, olive oil, and ground cumin in the Instant Pot. 2. Seal the lid. Select Manual mode and set cooking time for 20 minutes on High Pressure. 3. When timer beeps, use a quick pressure release and open the lid. 4. Add the salt and blend the soup with an immersion blender. 5. Ladle the soup in the bowls and top with blue cheese. Serve warm.

Per Serving:

calories: 142 | fat: 9g | protein: 10g | carbs: 5g | net carbs: 4g | fiber: 1g

Loaded Cauliflower Soup

Prep time: 5 minutes | Cook time: 25 minutes | Serves 3

◁ 2 bacon strips, roughly chopped
◁ ¼ medium onion, chopped
◁ 1½ cups chicken broth
◁ 1½ cups chopped cauliflower florets
◁ ½ teaspoon pink Himalayan sea salt
◁ ½ teaspoon freshly ground

black pepper
◁ ¼ teaspoon garlic powder
◁ 1 cup heavy (whipping) cream
◁ 1 cup shredded Cheddar cheese
◁ 3 tablespoons sour cream
◁ 2 tablespoons chopped fresh chives

1. In a medium saucepan, cook the bacon over medium-high heat for 8 to 10 minutes, until crispy. Transfer the bacon to a paper towel-lined plate. 2. Add the onion to the saucepan and cook for 8 to 10 minutes, until tender. 3. Add the broth, cauliflower, salt, pepper, and garlic powder. Bring to a simmer and cook for about 5 minutes, until the cauliflower is tender. 4. Reduce the heat and stir in the cream. Slowly stir in the cheese. 5. Divide the soup among 3 serving bowls. Top each bowl with 1 tablespoon of sour cream and equal portions of the bacon crumbles and chives.

Per Serving:

calories: 510 | fat: 48g | protein: 15g | carbs: 7g | net carbs: 6g | fiber: 1g

Summer Vegetable Soup

Prep time: 10 minutes | Cook time: 6 minutes | Serves 6

- 3 cups finely sliced leeks
- 6 cups chopped rainbow chard, stems and leaves separated
- 1 cup chopped celery
- 2 tablespoons minced garlic, divided
- 1 teaspoon dried oregano
- 1 teaspoon salt
- 2 teaspoons freshly ground
- black pepper
- 3 cups chicken broth, plus more as needed
- 2 cups sliced yellow summer squash, ½-inch slices
- ¼ cup chopped fresh parsley
- ¾ cup heavy (whipping) cream
- 4 to 6 tablespoons grated Parmesan cheese

1. Put the leeks, chard, celery, 1 tablespoon of garlic, oregano, salt, pepper, and broth into the inner cooking pot of the Instant Pot. 2. Lock the lid into place. Select Manual and adjust the pressure to High. Cook for 3 minutes. When the cooking is complete, quick-release the pressure. Unlock the lid. 3. Add more broth if needed. 4. Turn the pot to Sauté and adjust the heat to high. Add the yellow squash, parsley, and remaining 1 tablespoon of garlic. 5. Allow the soup to cook for 2 to 3 minutes, or until the squash is softened and cooked through. 6. Stir in the cream and ladle the soup into bowls. Sprinkle with the Parmesan cheese and serve.

Per Serving:

calories: 210 | fat: 14g | protein: 10g | carbs: 12g | net carbs: 8g | fiber: 4g

Venison and Tomato Stew

Prep time: 12 minutes | Cook time: 42 minutes | Serves 8

- 1 tablespoon unsalted butter
- 1 cup diced onions
- 2 cups button mushrooms, sliced in half
- 2 large stalks celery, cut into ¼-inch pieces
- Cloves squeezed from 2 heads roasted garlic or 4 cloves garlic, minced
- 2 pounds (907 g) boneless venison or beef roast, cut into 4 large pieces
- 5 cups beef broth
- 1 (14½-ounce / 411-g) can diced tomatoes
- 1 teaspoon fine sea salt
- 1 teaspoon ground black pepper
- ½ teaspoon dried rosemary, or 1 teaspoon fresh rosemary, finely chopped
- ½ teaspoon dried thyme leaves, or 1 teaspoon fresh thyme leaves, finely chopped
- ½ head cauliflower, cut into large florets
- Fresh thyme leaves, for garnish

1. Place the butter in the Instant Pot and press Sauté. Once melted, add the onions and sauté for 4 minutes, or until soft. 2. Add the mushrooms, celery, and garlic and sauté for another 3 minutes, or until the mushrooms are golden brown. Press Cancel to stop the Sauté. Add the roast, broth, tomatoes, salt, pepper, rosemary,

and thyme. 3. Seal the lid, press Manual, and set the timer for 30 minutes. Once finished, turn the valve to venting for a quick release. 4. Add the cauliflower. Seal the lid, press Manual, and set the timer for 5 minutes. Once finished, let the pressure release naturally. 5. Remove the lid and shred the meat with two forks. Taste the liquid and add more salt, if needed. Ladle the stew into bowls. Garnish with thyme leaves.

Per Serving:

calories: 359 | fat: 21g | protein: 32g | carbs: 9g | net carbs: 6g | fiber: 3g

Pork and Daikon Stew

Prep time: 15 minutes | Cook time: 3 minutes | Serves 6

- 1 pound (454 g) pork tenderloin, chopped
- 1 ounce (28 g) green onions, chopped
- ½ cup daikon, chopped
- 1 lemon slice
- 1 tablespoon heavy cream
- 1 tablespoon butter
- 1 teaspoon ground black pepper
- 3 cups water

1. Put all ingredients in the Instant Pot and stir to mix with a spatula. 2. Seal the lid. Set Manual mode and set cooking time for 20 minutes on High Pressure. 3. When cooking is complete, use a natural pressure release for 15 minutes, then release any remaining pressure. Open the lid. 4. Serve warm.

Per Serving:

calories: 137 | fat: 6g | protein: 20g | carbs: 1g | net carbs: 1g | fiber: 0g

Beef and Spinach Stew

Prep time: 20 minutes | Cook time: 30 minutes | Serves 4

- 1 pound (454 g) beef sirloin, chopped
- 2 cups spinach, chopped
- 3 cups chicken broth
- 1 cup coconut milk
- 1 teaspoon allspices
- 1 teaspoon coconut aminos

1. Put all ingredients in the Instant Pot. Stir to mix well. 2. Close the lid. Set the Manual mode and set cooking time for 30 minutes on High Pressure. 3. When timer beeps, use a natural pressure release for 10 minutes, then release any remaining pressure. Open the lid. 4. Blend with an immersion blender until smooth. 5. Serve warm.

Per Serving:

calories: 383 | fat: 22g | protein: 40g | carbs: 5g | net carbs: 3g | fiber: 2g

Easy Chili

Prep time: 10 minutes | Cook time: 35 minutes | Serves 6 to 8

- 2 pounds ground beef
- 2 tablespoons dried minced onions
- 2 teaspoons minced garlic
- 1 (15 ounces) can tomato sauce
- 1 (14½ ounces) can petite

Suggested Toppings:
- Sour cream
- Sliced green onions or

- diced tomatoes
- 1 cup water
- 2 tablespoons chili powder
- 1 tablespoon ground cumin
- ½ teaspoon salt
- ½ teaspoon ground black pepper

- chopped white onions
- Shredded cheddar cheese

1. Cook the ground beef, onions, and garlic in a stockpot over medium heat, crumbling the meat with a large spoon as it cooks, until the meat is browned, about 10 minutes. Drain the fat, if necessary. 2. Add the tomato sauce, tomatoes, water, chili powder, cumin, salt, and pepper to the pot. Bring to a boil, then reduce the heat to low and simmer for 20 minutes to allow the flavors to develop and the chili to thicken slightly. 3. Garnish with the chili topping(s) of your choice and serve. Leftovers can be stored in an airtight container in the refrigerator for up to 5 days.

Per Serving:

calories: 429 | fat: 31g | protein: 27g | carbs: 9g | net carbs: 6g | fiber: 3g

Chicken Poblano Pepper Soup

Prep time: 10 minutes | Cook time: 20 minutes | Serves 8

- 1 cup diced onion
- 3 poblano peppers, chopped
- 5 garlic cloves
- 2 cups diced cauliflower
- 1½ pounds (680 g) chicken breast, cut into large chunks
- ¼ cup chopped fresh cilantro
- 1 teaspoon ground coriander

- 1 teaspoon ground cumin
- 1 to 2 teaspoons salt
- 2 cups water
- 2 ounces (57 g) cream cheese, cut into small chunks
- 1 cup sour cream

1. To the inner cooking pot of the Instant Pot, add the onion, poblanos, garlic, cauliflower, chicken, cilantro, coriander, cumin, salt, and water. 2. Lock the lid into place. Select Manual and adjust the pressure to High. Cook for 15 minutes. When the cooking is complete, let the pressure release naturally for 10 minutes, then quick-release any remaining pressure. Unlock the lid. 3. Remove the chicken with tongs and place in a bowl. 4. Tilting the pot, use an immersion blender to roughly purée the vegetable mixture. It should still be slightly chunky. 5. Turn the Instant Pot to Sauté and adjust to high heat. When the broth is hot and bubbling, add the cream cheese and stir until it melts. Use a whisk to blend in the cream cheese if needed. 6. Shred the chicken and stir it back into the pot. Once it is heated through, serve, topped with sour cream,

and enjoy.

Per Serving:

calories: 202 | fat: 10g | protein: 20g | carbs: 8g | net carbs: 5g | fiber: 3g

Beef and Cauliflower Soup

Prep time: 10 minutes | Cook time: 14 minutes | Serves 4

- 1 cup ground beef
- ½ cup cauliflower, shredded
- 1 teaspoon unsweetened tomato purée
- ¼ cup coconut milk

- 1 teaspoon minced garlic
- 1 teaspoon dried oregano
- ½ teaspoon salt
- 4 cups water

1. Put all ingredients in the Instant Pot and stir well. 2. Close the lid. Select Manual mode and set cooking time for 14 minutes on High Pressure. 3. When timer beeps, make a quick pressure release and open the lid. 4. Blend with an immersion blender until smooth 5. Serve warm.

Per Serving:

calories: 106 | fat: 8g | protein: 7g | carbs: 2g | net carbs: 1g | fiber 1g

Keto Pho with Shirataki Noodles

Prep time: 20 minutes | Cook time: 10 minutes | Makes 4 bowls

- 8 ounces (227 g) sirloin, very thinly sliced
- 3 tablespoons coconut oil (or butter or ghee)
- 2 garlic cloves, minced
- 2 tablespoons liquid or coconut aminos
- 2 tablespoons fish sauce
- 1 teaspoon freshly grated or

- ground ginger
- 8 cups bone broth
- 4 (7-ounce / 198-g) packages shirataki noodles, drained and rinsed
- 1 cup bean sprouts
- 1 scallion, chopped
- 1 tablespoon toasted sesame seeds (optional)

1. Put the sirloin in the freezer while you prepare the broth and other ingredients (about 15 to 20 minutes). This makes it easier to slice. 2. In a large pot over medium heat, melt the coconut oil. Add the garlic and cook for 3 minutes. Then add the aminos, fish sauce, ginger, and bone broth. Bring to a boil. 3. Remove the beef from the freezer and slice it very thin. 4. Divide the noodles, beef, and bean sprouts evenly among four serving bowls. Carefully ladle 2 cups of broth into each bowl. Cover the bowls with plates and let sit for 3 to 5 minutes to cook the meat. 5. Serve garnished with the chopped scallion and sesame seeds (if using).

Per Serving:

1 bowl: calories: 385 | fat: 29g | protein: 23g | carbs: 8g | net carbs 4g | fiber: 4g

Cheesy Cauliflower Soup

Prep time: 5 minutes | Cook time: 20 minutes | Serves 4

◄ 1 tablespoon butter
◄ ½ onion, chopped
◄ 2 cups riced/shredded cauliflower (I buy it pre-riced at Trader Joe's)
◄ 1 cup chicken broth
◄ 2 ounces cream cheese
◄ 1 cup heavy (whipping) cream
◄ Pink Himalayan salt
◄ Freshly ground pepper
◄ ½ cup shredded Cheddar cheese (I use sharp Cheddar)

1. In a medium saucepan over medium heat, melt the butter. Add the onion and cook, stirring occasionally, until softened, about 5 minutes. 2. Add the cauliflower and chicken broth, and allow the mixture to come to a boil, stirring occasionally. 3. Lower the heat to medium-low and simmer until the cauliflower is soft enough to mash, about 10 minutes. 4. Add the cream cheese, and mash the mixture. 5. Add the cream and purée the mixture with an immersion blender (or you can pour the soup into the blender, blend it, and then pour it back into the pan and reheat it a bit). 6. Season the soup with pink Himalayan salt and pepper. 7. Pour the soup into four bowls, top each with the shredded Cheddar cheese, and serve.

Per Serving:

calories: 372 | fat: 35g | protein: 9g | carbs: 9g | net carbs: 6g | fiber: 3g

Avocado-Lime Soup

Prep time: 5 minutes | Cook time: 20 minutes | serves 8

◄ 2 tablespoons cold-pressed olive oil
◄ ½ yellow onion, chopped
◄ 1 teaspoon ground cumin
◄ 1 teaspoon ground coriander
◄ 1 teaspoon chili powder
◄ ¼ cup hemp hearts
◄ 1 medium tomato, chopped
◄ 1 cup chopped cabbage (set
some aside for garnish)
◄ ½ cup chopped fresh cilantro
◄ ½ cup chopped celery
◄ ½ jalapeño pepper, chopped
◄ 8 cups vegetable broth
◄ Juice of 2 limes
◄ 1 avocado, peeled, pitted, and cut into cubes
◄ 3 flax crackers

1. Heat the olive oil in a large stockpot over medium heat and add the onion, cumin, coriander, and chili powder. Sauté, stirring occasionally, until the onion becomes tender, about 5 minutes. 2. Add the hemp hearts, tomato, cabbage, cilantro, celery, and jalapeño to the pot. Stir to coat the spices and allow to cook for 4 minutes. 3. Pour the broth into the pot and simmer on low for 20 minutes. 4. Remove the pot from the heat and stir in the lime juice. 5. Divide the avocado equally among 4 serving bowls. 6. Pour the soup over the avocado in the bowls and garnish with additional cabbage and cilantro. 7. Break the flax crackers over the top of the soup to create a "tortilla soup" vibe.

Per Serving:

calories: 130 | fat: 9g | protein: 3g | carbs: 9g | net carbs: 5g | fiber: 4g

Curried Chicken Soup

Prep time: 10 minutes | Cook time: 10 minutes | Serves 6

◄ 1 pound (454 g) boneless, skinless chicken thighs
◄ 1½ cups unsweetened coconut milk
◄ ½ onion, finely diced
◄ 3 or 4 garlic cloves, crushed
◄ 1 (2-inch) piece ginger, finely chopped
◄ 1 cup sliced mushrooms,
such as cremini and shiitake
◄ 4 ounces (113 g) baby spinach
◄ 1 teaspoon salt
◄ ½ teaspoon ground turmeric
◄ ½ teaspoon cayenne
◄ 1 teaspoon garam masala
◄ ¼ cup chopped fresh cilantro

1. In the inner cooking pot of your Instant Pot, add the chicken, coconut milk, onion, garlic, ginger, mushrooms, spinach, salt, turmeric, cayenne, garam masala, and cilantro. 2. Lock the lid into place. Select Manual and adjust the pressure to High. Cook for 10 minutes. When the cooking is complete, let the pressure release naturally. Unlock the lid. 3. Use tongs to transfer the chicken to a bowl. Shred the chicken, then stir it back into the soup. 4. Eat and rejoice.

Per Serving:

calories: 378 | fat: 26g | protein: 26g | carbs: 6g | net carbs: 2g | fiber: 4g

Vegan Pho

Prep time: 10 minutes | Cook time: 20 minutes | serves 8

◄ 8 cups vegetable broth
◄ 1-inch knob fresh ginger, peeled and chopped
◄ 2 tablespoons tamari
◄ 3 cups shredded fresh spinach
◄ 2 cups chopped broccoli
◄ 1 cup sliced mushrooms
◄ ½ cup chopped carrots
◄ ⅓ cup chopped scallions
◄ 1 (8-ounce) package
shirataki noodles
◄ 2 cups shredded cabbage
◄ 2 cups mung bean sprouts
◄ Fresh Thai basil leaves, for garnish
◄ Fresh cilantro leaves, for garnish
◄ Fresh mint leaves, for garnish
◄ 1 lime, cut into 8 wedges, for garnish

1. In a large stockpot over medium-high heat, bring the vegetable broth to a simmer with the ginger and tamari. 2. Once the broth is hot, add the spinach, broccoli, mushrooms, carrots, and scallions, and simmer for a few minutes, just until the vegetables start to become tender. 3. Stir in the shirataki noodles, then remove the pot from the heat and divide the soup among serving bowls. 4. Top each bowl with cabbage, sprouts, basil, cilantro, mint, and a lime wedge.

Per Serving:

calories: 47 | fat: 0g | protein: 3g | carbs: 10g | net carbs: 7g | fiber: 3g

Shrimp Chowder

Prep time: 10 minutes | Cook time: 40 minutes | Serves 6

- ◁ ¼ cup (60 ml) refined avocado oil or melted ghee (if tolerated)
- ◁ 1⅔ cups (140 g) diced mushrooms
- ◁ ⅓ cup (55 g) diced yellow onions
- ◁ 10½ ounces (300 g) small raw shrimp, shelled and deveined
- ◁ 1 can (13½ ounces/400 ml) full-fat coconut milk
- ◁ ⅓ cup (80 ml) chicken bone broth
- ◁ 2 tablespoons apple cider

- ◁ vinegar
- ◁ 1 teaspoon onion powder
- ◁ 1 teaspoon paprika
- ◁ 1 bay leaf
- ◁ ¾ teaspoon finely ground gray sea salt
- ◁ ½ teaspoon dried oregano leaves
- ◁ ¼ teaspoon ground black pepper
- ◁ 12 radishes (about 6 ounces/170 g), cubed
- ◁ 1 medium zucchini (about 7 ounces/200 g), cubed

1. Heat the avocado oil in a large saucepan on medium for a couple of minutes, then add the mushrooms and onions. Sauté for 8 to 10 minutes, until the onions are translucent and mushrooms are beginning to brown. 2. Add the remaining ingredients, except the radishes and zucchini. Cover and bring to a boil, then reduce the heat to low and simmer for 20 minutes. 3. After 20 minutes, add the radishes and zucchini. Continue to cook for 10 minutes, until the vegetables are fork-tender. 4. Remove the bay leaf, divide among 6 small soup bowls, and enjoy.

Per Serving:

calories: 301 | fat: 23g | protein: 14g | carbs: 7g | net carbs: 5g | fiber: 2g

Spaghetti Squash Ramen Soup

Prep time: 15 minutes | Cook time: 1 hour | Serves 4

Spaghetti Squash:
- ◁ 1 medium (2-pound / 907-g) spaghetti squash
Soup:
- ◁ 1 tablespoon avocado oil
- ◁ 4 cloves garlic, minced
- ◁ 1 tablespoon minced fresh ginger
- ◁ 2 cups (5 ounces / 142 g) shiitake mushrooms, sliced
Garnishes:
- ◁ ¼ cup (0.9 ounce / 26 g) chopped green onions

- ◁ 2 tablespoons avocado oil
- ◁ Sea salt, to taste

- ◁ 8 cups chicken broth
- ◁ ⅓ cup coconut aminos
- ◁ 1 tablespoon fish sauce (optional)
- ◁ 1½ teaspoons sea salt, or to taste

- ◁ 4 large eggs, soft-boiled, peeled, and cut in half

1. Preheat the oven to 425ºF (220ºC). Line a baking sheet with foil and grease lightly. 2. Prepare the spaghetti squash: Use a sharp chef's knife to slice the spaghetti squash in half. To make it easier, use the knife to score where you'll be cutting first, then slice. Cut crosswise to yield longer noodles, or lengthwise for shorter ones. Scoop out the seeds. 3. Drizzle the inside of the halves with the avocado oil. Sprinkle lightly with sea salt. 4. Place the spaghetti squash halves on the lined baking sheet cut side down. Roast for 25 to 35 minutes, until the skin pierces easily with a knife. The knife should be able to go in pretty deep with very slight resistance. 5. Remove from the oven and let the squash rest on the pan (cut side down, without moving) for 10 minutes. Then use a fork to release the strands inside the shells and set aside. 6. Meanwhile, make the soup: In a large soup pot, heat the oil over medium heat. Add the garlic and ginger and sauté for about 1 minute, until fragrant. 7. Add the shiitake mushrooms and sauté for about 5 minutes, or until the mushrooms are soft. 8. Add the chicken broth, coconut aminos, and fish sauce (if using). Add salt to taste (start with 1 teaspoon salt and add more if needed, but I recommend 1½ teaspoons). Bring to a boil, then reduce the heat and simmer for 10 minutes. 9. Add the spaghetti squash noodles to the pot and simmer for 10 to 15 minutes, until hot and flavors develop to your liking. 10. Pour into bowls. Garnish with the green onions and soft-boiled eggs.

Per Serving:

calories: 238 | fat: 16g | protein: 10g | carbs: 10g | net carbs: 10g | fiber: 0g

Cream of Cauliflower Gazpacho

Prep time: 15 minutes | Cook time: 25 minutes | Serves 4 to 6

- ◁ 1 cup raw almonds
- ◁ ½ teaspoon salt
- ◁ ½ cup extra-virgin olive oil, plus 1 tablespoon, divided
- ◁ 1 small white onion, minced
- ◁ 1 small head cauliflower, stalk removed and broken into florets (about 3 cups)
- ◁ 2 garlic cloves, finely

- ◁ minced
- ◁ 2 cups chicken or vegetable stock or broth, plus more if needed
- ◁ 1 tablespoon red wine vinegar
- ◁ ¼ teaspoon freshly ground black pepper

1. Bring a small pot of water to a boil. Add the almonds to the water and boil for 1 minute, being careful to not boil longer or the almonds will become soggy. Drain in a colander and run under cold water. Pat dry and, using your fingers, squeeze the meat of each almond out of its skin. Discard the skins. 2. In a food processor or blender, blend together the almonds and salt. With the processor running, drizzle in ½ cup extra-virgin olive oil, scraping down the sides as needed. Set the almond paste aside. 3. In a large stockpot, heat the remaining 1 tablespoon olive oil over medium-high heat. Add the onion and sauté until golden, 3 to 4 minutes. Add the cauliflower florets and sauté for another 3 to 4 minutes. Add the garlic and sauté for 1 minute more. 4. Add 2 cups stock and bring to a boil. Cover, reduce the heat to medium-low, and simmer the vegetables until tender, 8 to 10 minutes. Remove from the heat and allow to cool slightly. 5. Add the vinegar and pepper. Using an immersion blender, blend until smooth. Alternatively, you can blend in a stand blender, but you may need to divide the mixture into two or three batches. With the blender running, add the almond paste and blend until smooth, adding extra stock if the soup is too thick. 6. Serve warm, or chill in refrigerator at least 4 to 6 hours to serve a cold gazpacho.

Per Serving:

calories: 562 | fat: 51g | protein: 13g | carbs: 19g | net carbs: 13g | fiber: 6g

Appendix 1:

MEASUREMENT CONVERSION CHART

VOLUME EQUIVALENTS(DRY)

US STANDARD	METRIC (APPROXIMATE)
1/8 teaspoon	0.5 mL
1/4 teaspoon	1 mL
1/2 teaspoon	2 mL
3/4 teaspoon	4 mL
1 teaspoon	5 mL
1 tablespoon	15 mL
1/4 cup	59 mL
1/2 cup	118 mL
3/4 cup	177 mL
1 cup	235 mL
2 cups	475 mL
3 cups	700 mL
4 cups	1 L

VOLUME EQUIVALENTS(LIQUID)

US STANDARD	US STANDARD (OUNCES)	METRIC (APPROXIMATE)
2 tablespoons	1 fl.oz.	30 mL
1/4 cup	2 fl.oz.	60 mL
1/2 cup	4 fl.oz.	120 mL
1 cup	8 fl.oz.	240 mL
1 1/2 cup	12 fl.oz.	355 mL
2 cups or 1 pint	16 fl.oz.	475 mL
4 cups or 1 quart	32 fl.oz.	1 L
1 gallon	128 fl.oz.	4 L

TEMPERATURES EQUIVALENTS

FAHRENHEIT(F)	CELSIUS(C) (APPROXIMATE)
225 °F	107 °C
250 °F	120 °C
275 °F	135 °C
300 °F	150 °C
325 °F	160 °C
350 °F	180 °C
375 °F	190 °C
400 °F	205 °C
425 °F	220 °C
450 °F	235 °C
475 °F	245 °C
500 °F	260 °C

WEIGHT EQUIVALENTS

US STANDARD	METRIC (APPROXIMATE)
1 ounce	28 g
2 ounces	57 g
5 ounces	142 g
10 ounces	284 g
15 ounces	425 g
16 ounces (1 pound)	455 g
1.5 pounds	680 g
2 pounds	907 g

Appendix 2:

The Dirty Dozen and Clean Fifteen

The Environmental Working Group (EWG) is a nonprofit, nonpartisan organization dedicated to protecting human health and the environment Its mission is to empower people to live healthier lives in a healthier environment. This organization publishes an annual list of the twelve kinds of produce, in sequence, that have the highest amount of pesticide residue-the Dirty Dozen-as well as a list of the fifteen kinds ofproduce that have the least amount of pesticide residue-the Clean Fifteen.

THE DIRTY DOZEN	THE CLEAN FIFTEEN
• The 2016 Dirty Dozen includes the following produce. These are considered among the year's most important produce to buy organic:	• The least critical to buy organically are the Clean Fifteen list. The following are on the 2016 list:

THE DIRTY DOZEN

Strawberries	Spinach
Apples	Tomatoes
Nectarines	Bell peppers
Peaches	Cherry tomatoes
Celery	Cucumbers
Grapes	Kale/collard greens
Cherries	Hot peppers

• *The Dirty Dozen list contains two additional itemskale/collard greens and hot peppers-because they tend to contain trace levels of highly hazardous pesticides.*

THE CLEAN FIFTEEN

Avocados	Papayas
Corn	Kiw
Pineapples	Eggplant
Cabbage	Honeydew
Sweet peas	Grapefruit
Onions	Cantaloupe
Asparagus	Cauliflower
Mangos	

• *Some of the sweet corn sold in the United States are made from genetically engineered (GE) seedstock. Buy organic varieties of these crops to avoid GE produce.*

Appendix 3: Recipes Index

Made in the USA
Las Vegas, NV
13 April 2024

88652957R00057